From Nazareth to Northumbria

How Christianity Came to Britain……
and Stayed.

Ven Moira Astin

From Nazareth to Northumbria

Copyright © Moira Astin 2021

A CIP catalogue record for the book is available from the British Library

ISBN: 9798735612711

Contents

Preface 1
1. Israel, the 1st Century A.D. 2
2. The Route from Israel to Britain 41
3. Christianity in Roman Britain... 48
4. Christianity after the Romans in Western Britain.. 65
5. Irish Christianity 4th to 7th Centuries 77
6. British Christianity in 'Anglo Saxon' Areas of Eastern Britain.............................107
7. Where did the British Church go?..129
Bibliography and Further Reading 131

Acknowledgements

Much of the work for this book has been done in between the day job of being a Vicar in Scunthorpe and then Archdeacon of Reigate. I'd like to thank my colleagues in both places for putting up with my repeated discussion of what to many people is an obscure period of history.

I also thank the Diocese of Southwark for a sabbatical in 2019 which enabled me to travel to many of the places in this book and to take the photographs.

Thanks to Linda Harris and Edmund Astin for proof reading the text.

Finally my thanks go to Revd Dr Timothy Astin for sharing much of the journey with me, in particular our joint discoveries and ideas about 'Celtic Hanging Bowls'. The ideas in that part of this book are as much his as mine.

All photographs are by the author unless otherwise noted in the text.

Israel in the 1st century

Preface

This journey began at Eccles in Kent. Or to be precise at Aylesford Priory near Eccles. A group of us had gathered for a consultation between people keen on new ways of doing and being church and people who want the different sorts of church we already have to work together better. As part of the introduction to this consultation a speaker had just pointed out that people in the U.K. no longer assume they are Christians just because they live here. 'Christendom', the idea that the whole country is Christian, including its government and its people, is over. But as I listened, I thought about Eccles, which I had passed on the way, and how the name Eccles is from the Latin for church. Perhaps it had gained its name way back when Latin was the official language – in Roman Britain. During the 4th century the Roman Empire became officially Christian, and then in the 5th century Rome was unable to organise the defence of its most distance provinces of Britannia. Eventually with the coming of the Angles, Saxons, Jutes and so on, the east of Britain was no longer ruled by Christian rulers – Christendom was over for the first time.

Despite this Eccles seemed to have hung onto its name – so perhaps despite the change in rulers, some Christians survived in what was to become England. If so, could we learn anything from them as to how to cope with the second end of Christendom?

So began a series of journeys to trace the route of Christianity to Britain, to discover what I could of its nature, and to see how Christianity developed in the parts of Britain around England. These took me to Israel where it all began, to Turkey where the strand of Christianity which looked to the apostle John thrived in the first century. I chose to follow this strand of Christianity, of the many that existed in the early centuries, because the Celtic Christians who debated with the Romanising Christians in 664 at the Synod of Whitby looked to John as their key apostle. Their religious men wore the tonsure of St John, rather than the tonsure of St Peter of the Roman church of the 7th century.

In the UK, there were trips to places where we know that there were Christians in the 2nd to 4th centuries, and from there on to Scotland and to Ireland where the British Christians took their Christianity and persuaded their neighbours on these islands of its value. Here, we know it as Celtic Christianity, so it is likely that the Christianity of Roman Britain would be a recognisable forebear of this rich flowering of faith in Ireland. Finally, the journey came back to England to see places where there is evidence of this Christianity even in the 'Dark Ages' when the Anglo-Saxon Kingdoms were forming, arriving at last in the places that feature in the history of that Synod of Whitby. So, this book is about places as well as relating what happened in the past. It is about places where people lived out their Christian faith and left a mark on the landscape as a witness. There may be many other places where they lived and believed but left no mark, but in these places we can know they were here, we can stand on the ground they stood on and in many of them touch what our forebears in the faith made to mark out the land as holy.

As well as the evidence on the ground in this book we will look at what the archaeologists' trowels have revealed, and what the historians of the subsequent centuries have written. In sections where is a key writer who mentions the place and what happened there, what they wrote is quoted first. In this way all the evidence will be brought together to suggest the route that Christianity took to come to Britain and to show how it stayed.

6th century stone cross at Killabuonia, Kerry Ireland

From Nazareth to Northumbria

1. Israel, the 1st Century A.D.

When the dispute as to the timing of Easter became too much for Oswy, King of Northumbria to ignore, Bede tells us of the meeting at Streonshalh, now called Whitby, in 664 to resolve it. At this the 'Scots', or Irish as we now know them argued that their traditions were those of John. Bede wrote *'Colman said, "The Easter which I keep, I received from my elders, who sent me hither as bishop; all our forefathers, men beloved of God, are known to have celebrated it after the same manner; and that it may not seem to any contemptible and worthy to be rejected, it is the same which the blessed John the Evangelist, the disciple specially beloved of our Lord, with all the churches over which he presided, is recorded to have celebrated."'* Bede, The Ecclesiastical History of the English People Book 3.25 (from here on the abbreviation EH will be used for this book)(for more on the Easter dispute see p127)

Thus, Bede tells us that the British church had a memory of being part of the Johannine churches. This being so, to understand the Celtic church, we need to look at John's Gospel to find its roots.

So, this history of the British church starts far away from Britain and Ireland, in the place where the church began, Israel/Palestine. Here we will look at places John mentions and remember what happened there, and what really mattered to him as he wrote his gospel, to see what sort of tradition came to these islands.

The Prologue

'¹In the beginning was the Word, and the Word was with God, and the Word was God... ¹⁴and the Word became flesh and lived among us, and we have seen his glory, the glory as of a father's only son, full of grace and truth.' John 1:1,14

John's gospel begins beyond time and place – in the beginning, before all things were made the Word was with God and was God. Yet what John has to write about is how the Word became flesh – became a human in time and space, and went to places we can still touch today, and spoke words which John has recorded for us to hear. God beyond all things and before all things, came close and touched what we can touch, walked where we can walk.

So, the journey begins in Nazareth. You may have expected it to start in Bethlehem where Jesus was born, but the Word became flesh before Jesus' birth. For almost nine months Mary carried God-made-flesh in her womb, and for

The Magnificat in Irish in the courtyard of the Church of the Annunciation, Nazareth

most of that time she was in Nazareth.

Today the Church of the Annunciation (Roman Catholic) is a 20th Century Church, set in a courtyard decorated with pictures of Mary and Jesus from all over the world. The church was built in 1969, on the site of other churches from the 18th, 17th and 15th centuries. Beneath these remains are those of the Crusader period and below them of a church built by the Eastern Roman Empire, often known as the Byzantine Period. All were built in or over a cave, where Mary is believed to have met with the Angel Gabriel.

As often in the Holy Land the Orthodox Church is down the road, in this case near Mary's

The cave chapel at the Church of the Annunciation, Nazareth

Israel in the 1st century

Spring. The explanation according to local tradition is that Mary first met the angel as she was drawing water and ran home in fright where the Archangel met her again. Either way, it was in this town that she lived, and as a teenager met with a stranger who told her he was a messenger from God. As she accepted her role, she became the God-bearer, the one who bore in her own body the Word become flesh. At this well she continued to draw water, in this house she continued to live as the child grew within her.

In Nazareth you can join the many pilgrims praying that as Mary accepted her call from God so in our day we will accept ours.

The Baptism, Qasr al Yahud

'*29 The next day he saw Jesus coming toward him and declared, "Here is the Lamb of God who takes away the sin of the world! 30 This is he of whom I said, 'After me comes a man who ranks ahead of me because he was before me.' 31 I myself did not know him; but I came baptizing with water for this reason, that he might be revealed to Israel." 32 And John testified, "I saw the Spirit descending from heaven like a dove, and it remained on him. 33 I myself did not know him, but the one who sent me to baptize with water said to me, 'He on whom you see the Spirit descend and remain is the one who baptizes with the Holy Spirit.' 34 And I myself have seen and have testified that this is the Son of God.'* John 1:29-34

Mary's well, the Orthodox Church of the Annunciation, Nazareth

For the apostle John this is where it really begins. John had come south to see John the Baptist, to hear what he had to say, and had been attracted by his call to turn back to God. John was also intrigued about the person the Baptist spoke of when he said that someone greater than he was about to come. So, John stayed there to see what would happen. He tells us that '*35the next day John again was standing with two of his disciples, 36 and as he watched Jesus walk by, he exclaimed, "Look, here is the Lamb of God!" 37 The two disciples heard him say this, and they followed Jesus. 38 When Jesus turned and saw them following, he said to them, "What are you looking for?" They said to him, "Rabbi" (which translated means Teacher), "where are you staying?" 39 He said to them, "Come and see."'* John 1:35-39

It is here in the Judean wilderness, where the presence of the Jordan and springs bring life, that John first sees Jesus as the one who is sent by God to give life to his people. He moves on from learning from John the Baptist to following Jesus and is encouraged to do so by the Baptist.

John tells us that the Baptiser was at Bethany across the Jordan. Today this is thought to be Al-Maghtas in Jordan, set back from the river itself by about a kilometre. It is the site of ancient churches and baptism pools dating back to the Byzantine Period. But before they were built, before John the Baptist came here, it was known to the Judeans as a place which the road from Jericho comes past as it nears the Jordan before going on to join the ancient trade route known as the King's Highway, which ran from Egypt across Sinai to Aqaba (now Eliat) and then

View across the River Jordan at Qasr al Yahud, looking towards the east bank in Jordan

From Nazareth to Northumbria

north up the east side of the Jordan valley to Damascus and beyond. This was celebrated as the place where the tribes of Israel under Joshua crossed the Jordan into their Promised Land. So, John's baptism wasn't just the washing that many Judeans used to prepare themselves for worship, but a call to start again as the people of God by re-entering the land, by crossing the Jordan afresh.

On the Israel/Palestine bank is Qasr-al-Yahud, which gives ready access to the Jordan. From here you can see to the Jordanian side, which could well be where John did his baptising. And looking across the floats in the river that mark the border what struck me was how narrow the Jordan is. If it wasn't for the soldier with his gun on the Jordanian side, it would be so easy to cross, and be on the ground John the Baptist stood on. But I can only gaze across, looking past the people from many nations who have come to the Jordan as part of their trip to the Holy Land. Here they are donning white robes and immersing themselves in the water, to renew their baptism at the site that Jesus received his, praying for a fresh experience of God's spirit to guide them as they seek to live their life as Christians.

People renewing their baptismal vows in the Jordan

The First Disciples

'43 The next day Jesus decided to go to Galilee. He found Philip and said to him, "Follow me." 44 Now Philip was from Bethsaida, the city of Andrew and Peter. 45 Philip found Nathanael and said to him, "We have found him about whom Moses in the law and also the prophets wrote, Jesus son of Joseph from Nazareth."' John 1:43-44

If you have been counting the 'next days' in John's account, you will see that we are now on the fourth day. After describing three days in Judea by the Jordan, John tells us that Jesus went to Galilee and called more disciples. But to get from Qasr al Yahud to the southern tip of Galilee would be more than a day's walk. Today it is an hour and a half's drive – so long as you don't get stopped for too long at the checkpoint as you pass from the Occupied Territory of the West Bank into Galilee. It's a bit over 70 miles, easily a 2- or 3-day walk. This points to the days meaning more than just time for John.

John then doesn't tell us where in Galilee Jesus comes to, but since he has told us that Philip is from Bethsaida, which is the city of Andrew and Peter, that is as good a place as any to go next. Bethsaida is commonly thought to be on the site of Et-Tell, which lies in the Jordan River Park. It is now 2 km north from the Sea of Galilee, with a fertile plain to the south as the Jordan flows through its silted-up delta into the Sea. 2000 years of silting mean that this fishing village

The Roman era Gate at El-Tell (possibly Bethsaida)

Israel in the 1st century

is no longer near the lake. But in the excavations carried out over various seasons from the 1980s and between 2004 and 2018 fishing equipment was found in one of the houses. (It has been suggested more recently that another site, Al-Araj is instead the site, with evidence of a Byzantine Church, which shows how tricky finding the places John mentions can be).

If El-Tell is ancient Bethsaida, then it is possible to walk its streets unperturbed by the crowds at many of the other sites around Galilee. This is not on the coach tours itinerary, so you have time to ponder alone. Here you can walk along the Roman road to the city gate, and then see the remains of several houses. Did Philip and Andrew and Peter play as boys in these streets? Did Peter learn to mend nets here? Even if the real Bethsaida is the other site, men like them did indeed grow up and learn their trade here. And since we are told in the gospels that Jesus went round all the villages and

The Fisherman's House, El-Tell

towns of Galilee, we can expect that he came along these streets, and spoke to the people who lived here, in these houses made of blocks of the local black basalt, which when eroded to sand gives the beaches of the Sea of Galilee their grey colouring.

Here too we are reminded of the more recent history of Israel/Palestine, as a gun emplacement from before the 1967 Six Day War sits on the site, made out of basalt blocks reused for this purpose. The site is just over the Jordan in the area of the Golan Heights which has been part of Israel since the 1967 war.

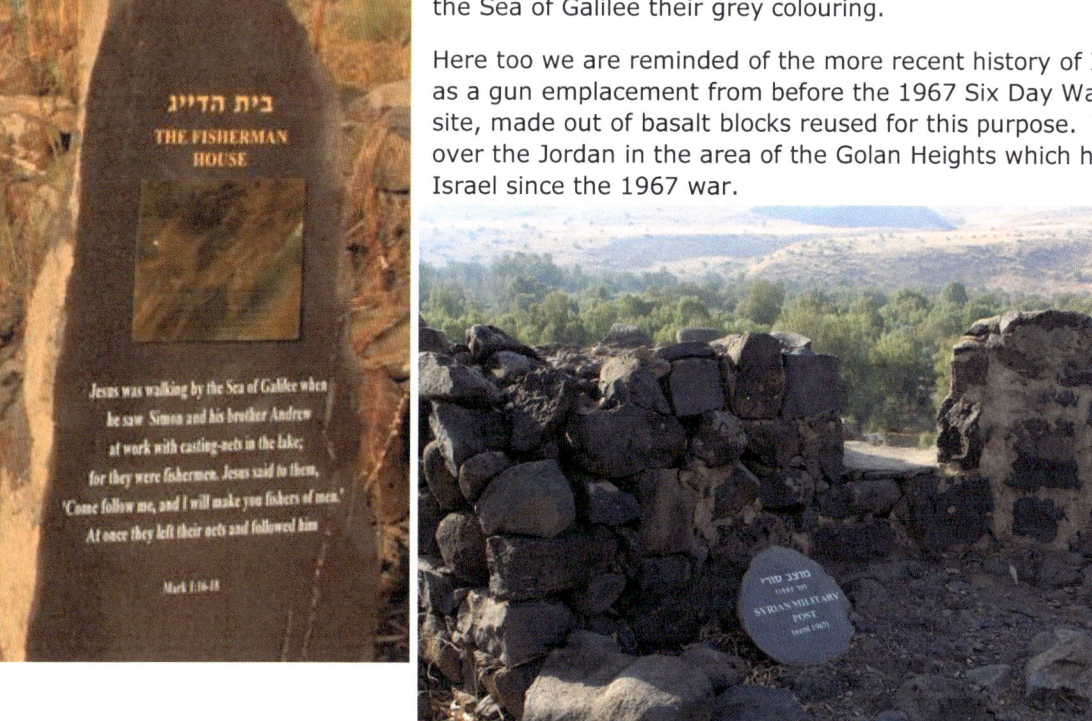

Syrian gun emplacement from the 1967 war

From Nazareth to Northumbria

Cana

'*46* *Nathanael said to him, "Can anything good come out of Nazareth?" Philip said to him, "Come and see."* John 1:46

1On the third day there was a wedding in Cana of Galilee, and the mother of Jesus was there…. 10"Everyone serves the good wine first, and then the inferior wine after the guests have become drunk. But you have kept the good wine until now." 11 Jesus did this, the first of his signs, in Cana of Galilee, and revealed his glory; and his disciples believed in him.' John 2:1, 10-11

St Bartholomew's Church Kafr Kanna

As you walk up Churches Street in Cana, to get to the Franciscan Wedding Church, built to celebrate the miracle at the wedding at Cana, you pass the church of Nathanael Bartholomew. It is usually closed and is not a very distinguished church, founded in 1885, but it does remind us that Nathanael was from Cana in Galilee, as John tells us in John 21:2.

Nathanael's comments on where Jesus was from may have been made in Bethsaida, or Capernaum - John 1 is not entirely clear on where Philip brings Nathanael to Jesus. The church dedicated to Nathanael in Kafr Kanna, as the village is known today, reminds us that Nathanael was from the hill country of Galilee, not from near the lake, as indeed Jesus was himself. Kafr Kanna is about 5 or 6 miles from Nazareth, across a valley so the people in each probably thought of the other as the lesser place, in much the same way as Manchester and Liverpool in England do today. No wonder Nathanael, good Canaanite that he is, is bemused by the idea of someone from Nazareth being a candidate for being the Messiah. To which his friend Philip just says 'Come and see'. This is a moment to experience, to find out, not to speculate.

So, as he tags along, Nathanael goes home, in company with Jesus and his other followers, to a wedding in his home town. Further up the road from the church named for Nathanael is the Franciscan Wedding Church. To get to it you pass souvenir sellers touting their wares including 'wedding wine'. I half hoped that those who bought this would open the bottle and find in it a very fine water!

Stone jar, in the basement of the Wedding Church

The Wedding Church, built in 1881, may not be the right place at all. Indeed, there are other candidates for Cana in this region and one in Lebanon. But underneath the Church is an excavation of a 4th/5th century Synagogue, and on display is an ancient stone jar. No claim is made that it is one of the ones used by Jesus, but it does give a feel for the magnitude of the jars he used. John tells us that they could each hold about 100 litres, so 6 of them held about 600 litres or 800 bottles of wine, that is rather a lot of wine for each person at the party, whatever your estimate of the size of the attendance. From this we can tell that God loves a party. The first sign of who Jesus is was at a celebration of love, and he ensured everyone could enjoy it.

When did this all happen? – 'on the third day' – the phrase would have echoed in the heads of John's hearers reminding them that Jesus rose on the third day. The third day was the celebration of new life, and what better way to celebrate than at a wedding? But if you have been counting that days since John started mentioning them, you find that with three days by the Jordan in Judea, the day Jesus went to Galilee, and now this is the third day, so we are also now on the seventh day. So, we are celebrating the day God rested in the story of creation, a sign of a completeness of a new creation. One final thought, the wine came from water, and as we will see as we journey on with John, John believed that water was very important in Jesus' understanding of the world and himself.

Israel in the 1ˢᵗ century

The Temple

'¹³The Passover of the Jews was near, and Jesus went up to Jerusalem. ¹⁴ In the temple he found people selling cattle, sheep, and doves, and the money changers seated at their tables. ¹⁵ Making a whip of cords, he drove all of them out of the temple, both the sheep and the cattle. He also poured out the coins of the money changers and overturned their tables. ¹⁶ He told those who were selling the doves, "Take these things out of here! Stop making my Father's house a marketplace!" ¹⁷ His disciples remembered that it was written, "Zeal for your house will consume me." ¹⁸ The Jews then said to him, "What sign can you show us for doing this?" ¹⁹ Jesus answered them, "Destroy this temple, and in three days I will raise it up." ²⁰ The Jews then said, "This temple has been under construction for forty-six years, and will you raise it up in three days?" ²¹ But he was speaking of the temple of his body. ²² After he was raised from the dead, his disciples remembered that he had said this; and they believed the scripture and the word that Jesus had spoken.' John 2:13-22

The Temple Mount from the Mount of Olives

Walking into Jerusalem from the Mount of Olives you see the Temple Mount, with the Dome of the Rock, the sun gleaming off its golden roof. It is the iconic view of Jerusalem and quite different from what Jesus would have seen. Instead, he would have seen the Jerusalem Temple, with the sun reflected from its large limestone walls, a glorious white affair. This edifice is known to Judaism as the Second temple, since the first one which Solomon built had been destroyed by the Babylonians when they sacked Jerusalem in 586 B.C. and took many Jews into exile. The core of the building in Jesus' day was the one that the some of the exiles started to rebuild when they returned under the repatriation policies of Cyrus (Ezra 1) and it was completed in 516 B.C., but Herod the Great had the platform on top of Mount Moriah, where the temple stood extended greatly, so the whole top of the mountain was a platform, on which the renovated Temple stood

Today all that remains of the Second Temple is this retaining wall of the platform. In 70 A.D. the Roman General Titus and his legions destroyed the Temple as part of putting down the Jewish Revolt that had started in 66 A.D. The platform remained unoccupied, until the mosque was built in 692 A.D. It is the third holiest site in Islam, being located over the 'rock', which is believed to be the foundation stone, where God created Adam, and where Abraham offered to sacrifice his son. From here the Prophet Mohammed began his Night Journey to heaven, having been brought here from Arabia on a 'Buraq', a winged white mule. It was at this place because it is the touching place between heaven and earth – the focus of God's presence on earth.

But for Jews the Mount itself today is off limits, signs near the Western Wall, the remains of Herod's platform which is closest to where the Temple was originally, say that the top of the Mount is too holy for them. So instead, to get close to where Jesus taught and walked, a visit to the Western Wall, where his fellow Jews still pray, is needed.

From Nazareth to Northumbria

Even with pictures it is hard to convey how huge the blocks of limestone that make up this retaining wall are. Most are about a metre high, a couple of metres wide and up to 12 metres long – they are huge. The Temple on top must have been an awe-inspiring building, pointing to the presence of God with his people.

The Western Wall, Jerusalem

When Jesus comes into the outer court – the Court of the Nations, he is furious. This largest court is there so that all nations can come close to God, even if you have to be a Jew to go into either of the next courts, a man to go into the inner court and a priest to go into the Holiest of Holies. But in the Temple, there was to be room for all to come to pray – and yet the current way of doing things had used up this space. The money changers had an important role. When coming to the festivals Jews would bring their Temple dues, which ensured there was enough money for the Temple worship to be paid for, and so continue when they were not there. It had come to be accepted that the Temple Tax had to be paid in Tyrian Shekels which had a greater silver content than the then current Roman currency. So, the money changers swapped the Roman coins for the Tyrian Shekels which enabled their bearers to pay their dues, and made the money changers a healthy prophet.

The women's side of the Western Wall

The animals also had their part – it was Passover, and every household that came to the festival needed a lamb to sacrifice. But carrying or herding a lamb from Galilee or further afield was impractical. So, sheep were kept in fields near Jerusalem, and then sold to the visiting pilgrims. Both animals being sold and money being changed were vital to the ongoing life of the Temple. Yet Jesus comes and drives them all out, because they were getting in the way of what really mattered – the Temple being a place for people, all people, for all nations to come to worship God. So, he stopped it all. By driving out the animals, by turning over the money changers tables, he put a spoke in the wheel of the Temple system, that day the sacrifices were stopped for a while as the animals were rounded up and the coins collected together. To Jesus they were not that important.

So, what sign could he give of his authority to stop the sacrifices like this, the Jews around him ask. He tells them that if the Temple were to be destroyed, he would raise it up in three days. Which taken in physical terms is obvious nonsense – he couldn't lift one of those stones on his own, let alone all of them. But John makes it clear that he is speaking of himself, his own body as the Temple, which he will raise on the third day. The Jerusalem Temple with its sacrifices would be over, and the new Temple would take its place.

Sychar/Nablus Jacob's well

"³He left Judea and started back to Galilee. ⁴ But he had to go through Samaria. ⁵ So he came to a Samaritan city called Sychar, near the plot of ground that Jacob had given to his son Joseph. ⁶ Jacob's well was there, and Jesus, tired out by his journey, was sitting by the well. It was about noon.
⁷ A Samaritan woman came to draw water, and Jesus said to her, "Give me a drink."' John 4: 3-7

From the events at the Temple, Jesus goes to stay somewhere, and Nicodemus comes to visit him, at night. We don't know where or when this happened – John is deliberate in saying that this was a private night-time meeting. Nicodemus, the Pharisee was careful of his reputation. So in a book on places where Jesus was

Israel in the 1st century

Icon of the woman at the well, in the Jacob's well Church, Nablus

seen through John's eyes we pass over this, with Jesus teaching on being born from above, of water and the spirit, (water again!), just noting that this is the first of a series of individual people who Jesus meets.

In contrast, when Jesus and his disciples go back north, having got wind that the Pharisees were not very happy about it all, he meets, in full daylight, a Samaritan woman.
To get to Jacob's well today, you need to get to Nablus in the Palestinian Territories. The options are to take a bus to Ramallah and a taxi from there, or to join a tour going to Nablus and Mount Gerizim to meet the Samaritan community living in a small village just outside Nablus on the slopes of the Mountain which they have always held as sacred.

Jacob's well, Nablus

So, in a small shared taxi with a driver, a Palestinian guide, and four fellow travellers, I came to the Greek Orthodox Jacob's Well Monastery in Nablus. Going into the crypt, there is the well, still available as a source of drinking water.
This is where Jesus came in the heat of the midday sun and asked a Samaritan woman for a drink. As John makes clear this was an odd thing for a Jew to do – Jews do not share things with Samaritans. I've always taken this to mean that the Jews look down on the Samaritans as following a lesser version of the worship of God, adulterated by aspects of worship brought in by those who were moved to the land of Israel by the Assyrians when they were keen on moving populations around. But having met with modern day Samaritans it may be that this is not the whole story. Nablus is built in the valley between Mount Gerizim and Mount Ebal, and near to Jacob's Well is Tel Balata, which may be the site of Shechem, the first capital of the Northern Kingdom of Israel, after the break with Judea under Jeroboam's rebellion(1 Kings 12:1). When the Assyrians destroyed the northern kingdom of Israel in 722 B.C. and deported much of the population, not all were moved. A group of the tribes of Ephraim, Manasseh and Levi were left behind, and see themselves as the keepers or guardians of the Law of Moses, the Torah. They have their own alphabet and version of Hebrew, which they believe to be an older form than that used by the Jews. While the Jews were deported from

Samaritan Torah scroll, the Samaritan Museum on Mt Gerizim

their kingdom of Judea by the Babylonians in 589 B.C., and some came back after the exile, they have remained in the land. In the 1990's the small Samaritan community of Nablus were given permission to move out of the city, to live on the slopes of their holy mountain. Today there are about 820 Samaritans living between Mount Gerizim and Holon, near Tel Aviv.

Although they live well alongside Jews and Muslims, their self-identity is as the ones who worship God in a way that is more faithful to the Torah and the ancient traditions. For them, Mount Gerizim was the location of the tabernacle during the early centuries in the land of Israel, and is the mountain where Abraham offered to sacrifice Isaac to God. So, the claims the Jews make for the Temple Mount in Jerusalem are made by the Samaritans for Mount Gerizim. Since Mount Gerizim was the holy place far earlier than the Jerusalem temple, they argue that it is the Jews who have fallen away from the original worship of God, not them. So, they refuse to eat with Jews, and have as little to do with them as they can.

So, this Samaritan woman addressed by a Jew has to decide if she will talk to him at all, for the reluctance to deal with Jews was as great for the Samaritans as was the rejection of the Samaritans by the Jews. Perhaps it was only because she was an outcast in her own community – fetching water in the heat of the day when others wouldn't be there – that she is willing to talk to him at all.

But she does talk to Jesus, and the well and its water are the focus of this discussion. For when she is bemused that he is even asking her for a drink, he replies that if she really knew the gift of God and who he is she would be asking for water from him. The water he has to give

The David Falls En Gedi

is not to be pulled up from a deep well but comes gushing out, like a spring. Even in the wilderness of Judea, where the white rocks show through and there is little vegetation, there are the occasional springs where life runs riot, such as at En Gedi. Here you don't have to labour to dig a well, or pull the water up, it just gushes out as a gift from God.

Capernaum

'*12 After this he went down to Capernaum with his mother, his brothers, and his disciples; and they remained there a few days'.* John 2:12

'*43 When the two days were over, he went from that place to Galilee…*
46 Then he came again to Cana in Galilee where he had changed the water into wine. Now there was a royal official whose son lay ill in Capernaum.
The official said to him, "Sir, come down before my little boy dies." 50 Jesus said to him, "Go; your son will live." The man believed the word that Jesus spoke to him and started on his way. 51 As he was going down, his slaves met him and told him that his child was alive.' John 4:43;46

Returning from the Passover in Jerusalem, Jesus resumes his teaching in Galilee. He is in Cana when a Royal Official from Capernaum finds him. Clearly Jesus is known in Capernaum from his time spent there. This official has been keen to find Jesus, for Cana is 24 miles walk from Capernaum, a good day's walk, and if he has been asking around as to where Jesus is it will have taken more than this to find him. Who is the official? John only tells us he is a royal official, but since this is in Galilee, we can assume he is part of the entourage of Herod Antipas, who ruled this area as a client king of the Romans. Herod Antipas built a new capital for himself, Tiberias, named after the Roman Emperor of the time. So, this official was part of the ruling system, which some Jews would have resented.

Israel in the 1st century

Yet the man is keen to find Jesus, because he has met him and knows that he is a man of God. As well as John telling us that Jesus spent some days in Capernaum with his whole family, all four gospels feature Capernaum as a place where Jesus spent time.

In Luke 4 Jesus heals Peter's mother-in-law, and so when you come to Capernaum today the focus is on Peter's house. The Space Age Church, built in 1990, was built in such a way as it sits above, but not on the remains of a 5th century A.D. Byzantine octagonal church. This was clearly built to mark an important site, and in the excavation in Capernaum, before the church was built, the remains of a 1 century B.C. house were found below the Byzantine Church. This had been altered at some point in the 1st century A.D., so that the main room was plastered over from floor to ceiling and the pottery remains from this period are of oil storage jars and lamps only – no household goods are in use. This is a church, and this is confirmed by the graffiti which are etched into the plaster which includes phrases such as 'Lord help your servant', and signs such as crosses and boats. This was the church which was then upgraded in the 5th century, when Christianity was the official religion of the Roman Empire but lost to sight when Capernaum was destroyed by an earthquake in the 8th century. Although the village itself recovered, it was now an Arab village, and the church was not rebuilt.

20th C Church over Peter's house in Capernaum

So, this is where Jesus visited and probably stayed when he was in the lakeside area. Here the royal official heard him and was impressed enough to go himself in search of Jesus, perhaps for days until he found him. When he finds Jesus, he asks to him to come back to Cana with him to heal the child, but Jesus tells him to go by himself, for his son will be well. He just goes. Having spent all this time and energy finding Jesus, when he does and Jesus speaks, he finds he doesn't need to make Jesus come back to Cana, for he trusts Jesus. Jesus speaks and it is done. And John tells us it was, what Jesus said would happen did, so Jesus could be relied on to be telling the truth, and his words have power in themselves. For John this is the second sign of who Jesus is, and his glory.

Remains of the Byzantine Church over Peter's house

From Nazareth to Northumbria

Bethesda, Jerusalem, John 5

'¹After this there was a festival of the Jews, and Jesus went up to Jerusalem.² Now in Jerusalem by the Sheep Gate there is a pool, called in Hebrew Beth-zatha, which has five porticoes. ³ In these lay many invalids—blind, lame, and paralyzed. ⁵ One man was there who had been ill for thirty-eight years. ⁶ When Jesus saw him lying there and knew that he had been there a long time, he said to him, "Do you want to be made well?" ⁷ The sick man answered him, "Sir, I have no one to put me into the pool when the water is stirred up; and while I am making my way, someone else steps down ahead of me." ⁸ Jesus said to him, "Stand up, take your mat and walk." ⁹ At once the man was made well, and he took up his mat and began to walk. Now that day was a sabbath.' John 5:1-3,5-9

The north, upper pool at Bethesda

Another festival, another trip to Jerusalem. Jesus was clearly an observant Jew, and for all he said that the Temple would be destroyed, for all he told the woman at Sychar that "the hour is coming when you will worship the Father neither on this mountain nor in Jerusalem", but in Spirit and in truth, while the temple is there, Jesus goes to the festivals.

Here we are by the water again. This time, however, the setting is not the Jewish ritual jars for a feast, or the well that Jacob dug for his descendants, albeit now used by his Samaritan descendants rather than his Jewish ones. No now we have come to water which is used by those willing to bring the ways of other gods to just outside the walls of Jerusalem.

In the courtyard of St Anne's Catholic Church, just inside the Lion Gate in the Muslim Quarter of Jerusalem, is the archaeological site of the Pool of Bethesda. It is actually two pools. The upper pool was built in the 8th century B.C. across a

The south or lower pool of Bethesda, with the Crusader church on the dam between the two pools

shallow valley to form a reservoir to capture rainwater. Water from this flowed through a channel to add to the water supply of the City of David, half a mile south of here. In the 2nd Century B.C., the high priest Simon added a second pool, south of the first. Over the next century, under the influence of those who were adapting to Greek culture, some caves to the east of the pool were adapted to serve as small baths. They were dedicated to the god Ascelpius, who was the Greek god of healing, for healing and medicine were seen as part of religion by the Greeks, health was a gift of the gods. The founders of this centre of healing may have been the soldiers at the nearby Antonia fortress. So, the reservoirs for the city become also a non-Jewish healing centre. The Hebrew name for the place Beth-zatha either means 'house of mercy' or 'house of shame'. Either would fit. This is where Jesus is walking when he sees a man who he knows has been there a long time. For 38 years he has lain there, hoping for a gift from the Greek god of healing. But with no one to

Israel in the 1st century

help him get into the pools to receive the gift, he is stuck. Until Jesus comes along, and, again, with a word heals him. He gets up and, as Jesus tells him, takes up his mat and walks.

Until the site was discovered in the 19th century people wondered if John knew what he was talking about when he talked of a pool near the Sheep Gate with 5 porticoes. In the 1960s, further archaeology showed up the Byzantine Church beneath the Crusader Church, above the dam between the two pools. The North Pool was allowed to fill up with debris during the 1st century B.C., which is why it is so much shallower.

The Byzantine Church, with the ruins of the Roman Temple to the west, furthest from the camera

The temple was to the east of the dam, and the large Byzantine church covered this as well. Votive offerings made to the healing god were found near here, which is why we can be sure it was a Roman religious site.

Some of the Jews who then saw the man who had been healed are appalled – he is carrying his mat on the sabbath. But Jesus who has not had a problem healing someone who is waiting at a Roman temple for healing, is not bothered by the fact that it is the Sabbath day. This man needed healing and was willing to trust that Jesus words would heal him, the day or place was not important to Jesus compared with the power of God's healing love.

Further Reading (O'Connor 1980)

Showing the depth of the south pool

Taghba

"*¹Sometime after this, Jesus crossed to the far shore of the Sea of Galilee (that is, the Sea of Tiberias), ² and a great crowd of people followed him because they saw the signs he had performed by healing the sick. ³ Then Jesus went up on a mountainside and sat down with his disciples. ⁴ The Jewish Passover Festival was near.*
⁵ When Jesus looked up and saw a great crowd coming toward him, he said to Philip, "Where shall we buy bread for these people to eat?" ⁶ He asked this only to test him, for he already had in mind what he was going to do.
⁷ Philip answered him, "It would take more than half a year's wages to buy enough bread for each one to have a bite!"
⁸ Another of his disciples, Andrew, Simon Peter's brother, spoke up, ⁹ "Here is a boy with five small barley loaves and two small fish, but how far will they go among so many?"
¹⁰ Jesus said, "Have the people sit down." There was plenty of grass in that place, and they sat down (about five thousand men were there). ¹¹ Jesus then took the loaves, gave thanks, and distributed to those who were seated as much as they wanted. He did the same with the fish.
¹² When they had all had enough to eat, he said to his disciples, "Gather the pieces that are left over. Let nothing be wasted." ¹³ So they gathered them and filled twelve baskets with the pieces of the five barley loaves left over by those who had eaten.

From Nazareth to Northumbria

30 So they asked him, "What sign then will you give that we may see it and believe you? What will you do? 31 Our ancestors ate the manna in the wilderness; as it is written: 'He gave them bread from heaven to eat.'"
32 Jesus said to them, "Very truly I tell you, it is not Moses who has given you the bread from heaven, but it is my Father who gives you the true bread from heaven. 33 For the bread of God is the bread that comes down from heaven and gives life to the world."
34 "Sir," they said, "always give us this bread."
35 Then Jesus declared, "I am the bread of life. Whoever comes to me will never go hungry, and whoever believes in me will never be thirsty.'

John 6:1-13; 30-35

The altar in the church at Tabgha with the ancient mosaic of the loaves and fishes

Ein Eyov waterfall

John is frustratingly vague about where this feeding of the 5000 happened – it is on the other side of the lake, but in John 5 Jesus was in Jerusalem! So, while we cannot be sure exactly where this happened, it is simplest to go to Tabgha, where there is a Church to memorialise this event. Tabgha is an Arabic adaptation of the Greek name for the area Heptapegon, which means Seven Springs. One of these is still readily visited just beyond the site at Ein Eyov waterfall.

The first church on the site was built in the 4th century and replaced by a larger church in the late 5th century. This had beautiful mosaic floors which are part of the floor of the current 1982 church. The site was excavated in the 1930's and the new church was built on the foundations of the 5th century church, to the same plan. The churches were built around an outcrop of limestone, which may be where Jesus stood when he blessed the bread and fish. In the previous chapters of John, Jesus has been speaking to individuals or to small groups of people. He met

Nicodemus by night, the Samaritan woman, the man by the sheep pool, the Jews who berated him for healing on the Sabbath. Now, he is there for thousands of people. They are attracted by his signs, by the fact he can heal the sick, and stay to hear his teaching. In the end he takes bread and breaks it and gives it to them.

Byzantine mosaics in the church at Tabgha

Israel in the 1st century

John does not record the giving of communion in his gospel – he focuses on Jesus washing the disciples feet and his teaching. So some scholars believe that this feeding of the great crowd, with Jesus teaching on giving himself as the Bread of Life is John's equivalent. If so it is clear that Jesus is not fussy about who will eat, whoever was there, whoever wanted to be included was included in this meal.

The Sea of Galilee

'*16 When evening came, his disciples went down to the lake, 17 where they got into a boat and set off across the lake for Capernaum. By now it was dark, and Jesus had not yet joined them. 18 A strong wind was blowing, and the waters grew rough. 19 When they had rowed about three or four miles,[b] they saw Jesus approaching the boat, walking on the water; and they were frightened. 20 But he said to them, "It is I; don't be afraid." 21 Then they were willing to take him into the boat, and immediately the boat reached the shore where they were heading.*

22 The next day the crowd that had stayed on the opposite shore of the lake realized that only one boat had been there, and that Jesus had not entered it with his disciples, but that they had gone away alone. 23 Then some boats from Tiberias landed near the place where the people had eaten the bread after the Lord had given thanks. 24 Once the crowd realized that neither Jesus nor his disciples were there, they got into the boats and went to Capernaum in search of Jesus.'
John 6:16-24

The disciples set off in a boat across the lake to Capernaum. This rather suggests that this feeding of the crowd was not actually at Tabgha, since that is only a mile or so along the lake shore from Capernaum.   Still we can be sure that in *this* narrative the disciples were in a boat on the Lake itself.

It is possible to see a boat of the type that Jesus disciples may have used at Yigal Allon Galilee

1st C fishing boat found in the Sea of Galilee, Yigal Allon Galilee Boat Museum in Kibbutz Ginosar

Boat Museum in Kibbutz Ginosar, about 3 miles south west of Tabgha around the lake shore. In 1986 two brothers from Kibbutz Ginosar, Moshe and Yuval Lufan, who were fishermen and amateur archaeologists found the boat when water levels in the Lake were low after a drought. They called in the experts who carefully salvaged and preserved the boat. It has been radiocarbon dated to 40 B.C. (+/-80 years) and so it very much of the time of Jesus. It is made mostly of cedar, with other woods being used to patch and mend it. Fitted with rowing points for four rowers and a mast, the boat is 8.3m long and 2.3 m wide.

The other key feature of this story is the lake, the Sea of Galilee itself. What struck me when I first saw it was that you can see the other side of the lake from where ever you are. It is 33 miles around the shore, and you can drive round in about 75 minutes. It is about twice the size of Loch Lomond, but only half the size of Loch Neagh in Northern Ireland. This lake was 'the office' to several of Jesus' disciples. They knew it's depths and it's shores, and how the winds blew, and how it's moods varied.

From Nazareth to Northumbria

The lake is the second lowest lake in the world, only the Dead Sea being lower, and the lowest freshwater lake. Like the Dead Sea it sits in a rift valley, which is part of a system of rifts which goes through the Red Sea, and on to form the East African Rift Valley. The rift valleys are caused by the Arabian Plate and the African Plate moving apart. This geological activity leads to earthquakes, and is the reason for the warm springs that occur at places around the lake.

Being in a rift valley, the lake has hills all around it, and on occasion the wind coming from the east over the Golan Heights gets funneled by the east west valleys onto the lake, causing storms with waves up to 3 metres high. Tricky for a boat which is only 2 metres wide. In the middle of one of these storms some of Jesus disciples see him walking towards them on the lake. When they let him into the boat they immediately reach the shore. It is an impressive sign in its own right, but to his disciples, versed as they were in the Hebrew Scriptures, it would have brought to mind Psalm 77:16-19

'When the waters saw you, O God,
    when the waters saw you, they were afraid;
    the very deep trembled.
The clouds poured out water;
    the skies thundered;
    your arrows flashed on every side.
The crash of your thunder was in the whirlwind;
    your lightnings lit up the world;
    the earth trembled and shook. Your way was through the sea,
    your path, through the mighty waters;
    yet your footprints were unseen.'

The Sea of Galilee as seen from the International Space Station

or Job 9:8

'who alone stretched out the heavens and trampled the waves of the Sea.'

In both places the scripture is describing God as the one who walks throught the sea, or on the waves. So seeing Jesus do this, they have witnessed him coming to them as God.

Sunset over Galilee

Israel in the 1st century

Jerusalem, the Gihon Spring

³⁷On the last day of the festival, the great day, while Jesus was standing there, he cried out, 'Let anyone who is thirsty come to me, ³⁸ and let the one who believes in me drink. As the scripture has said, "Out of the believer's heart shall flow rivers of living water."' John 7:37-38

Jesus has gone up to Jerusalem for the Festival of Booths, or Sukkot in Hebrew. It was one of the three festivals in the year when those who could get to the Jerusalem Temple were expected to go there (the others were Passover and Pentecost). It happens in September or October, depending on how the lunar year, which the Jewish festivals follow, falls compared with the solar year which is the basis of the Roman calendar which we still follow. Sukkot is also known as the festival of ingathering, the harvest festival.

Jesus has gone up to the feast quietly, although he has already started teaching during the festival and many people have been amazed by the depth of his ideas. He was not a student of one of the acknowledge rabbis, yet he taught as one who really knew what he was speaking about. His answer was that his teaching came directly from his Father, God.

The Gihon Spring in Hezekiah's tunnel, the water flows into the Pool of Siloam

Then on the last day of the feast he gets up and speaks about water. In the context of what has been going on in the festival this makes sense. As well as making and living in temporary booths during the festival, as a reminder of the tents their forebears lived in in the wilderness before they entered the Land of Israel, the festival is also the end of the agricultural year. Here God is thanked not only for the fruit of the harvest but also for the gifts that have made it possible, including rain.

Each morning during the festival the priests would go to the Pool of Siloam and draw water from it. The water would be brought into the temple with jubilation, music and dancing, and then poured into a bowl on the altar, matching the one that the daily offering of wine was poured into. Both would then be poured out as an offering of thanks to God. According to the Talmud (Rosh HaShana 16a) the offering was also a prayer that God would bless the rains of the coming year.

The pool of Siloam was used as the source of the water and is the pool into which flows water from the Gihon Spring, the only spring in the old City of David. This spring was the water source for the original Jebusite city which David captured. It was outside the walls, and so had been surrounded by a wall, and a tunnel had been dug from within the city to allow the inhabitants to collect water when they were under siege. This is how David got into the Jebusite city to capture it. Hezekiah later had a tunnel dug to reroute the water supply to a pool within the city walls, the Pool of Siloam.

A trip to see the ancient City of David includes the chance to walk through either the dry Canaanite Tunnel, or the wet Hezekiah's tunnel (up to 70cm deep in places) which is still taking the water from the spring to the Byzantine Pool of Siloam.

As the water supply for the city it was a vital resource, but it took on a spiritual role as well. Certainly before the Temple was built this was the location of Solomon's anointing and proclamation as king: 'So the priest Zadok, the prophet Nathan, and Benaiah son of Jehoiada, and the Cherethites and the Pelethites, went down and had Solomon ride on King David's mule, and led him to Gihon. 39 There the priest Zadok took the horn of oil from the tent and anointed Solomon. Then they blew the trumpet, and all the people said, 'Long live King Solomon!"1 Kings 1 38-39

Without this spring there would be no Jerusalem, so it became a symbol of the blessings of God.

Water from Jerusalem was also the sign of God's blessing used by several prophets:

'With joy you will draw water from the wells of salvation.' Isaiah 12:3.

'Then he brought me back to the entrance of the temple; there, water was flowing from below the threshold of the temple towards the east (for the temple faced east); and the water was flowing down from below the south end of the threshold of the temple, south of the altar.' Ezekiel 47:1-2.

'On that day living waters shall flow out from Jerusalem, half of them to the eastern sea and half of them to the western sea; it shall continue in summer as in winter.' Zechariah 14:8

These were read during the festival. So, when Jesus stood up and spoke of water, everyone listening knew that he was talking of God's blessing, of God's salvation. But just as earlier he had suggested that he could rebuild the Temple in three days, that he himself was the new temple, so here he is claiming to be the well-spring of this new water. For all who are spiritually thirsty, he is the answer. And they in turn will become wells, with spiritual blessings flowing from them to bring life to others.

Everything that those around him were celebrating in the festival Jesus claimed to be himself. He was either an egomaniac or really was God as a human, the Word become flesh and dwelling among us.

The 'Pool of Siloam' as dug out in Byzantine times, the pillars are the base of a church over the pool

In the Temple, the woman caught in adultery, the Light of the world

'²Early in the morning he came again to the temple. All the people came to him and he sat down and began to teach them. ³ The scribes and the Pharisees brought a woman who had been caught in adultery; and making her stand before all of them, ⁴ they said to him, "Teacher, this woman was caught in the very act of committing adultery. ⁵ Now in the law Moses commanded us to stone such women. Now what do you say?" ⁶ They said this to test him, so that they might have some charge to bring against him. Jesus bent down and wrote with his finger on the ground. ⁷ When they kept on questioning him, he straightened up and said to them, "Let anyone among you who is without sin be the first to throw a stone at her." ⁸ And once again he bent down and wrote on the ground. ⁹ When they heard it, they went away, one by one, beginning with the elders; and Jesus was left alone with the woman standing before him. ¹⁰ Jesus straightened up and said to her, "Woman, where are they? Has no one condemned you?" ¹¹ She said, "No one, sir." And Jesus said, "Neither do I condemn you. Go your way, and from now on do not sin again.

¹² Again Jesus spoke to them, saying, "I am the light of the world. Whoever follows me will never walk in darkness but will have the light of life."' John 8:2-12

The story of the woman caught in adultery may not have been written down by John, since it is not in the earliest manuscripts, but it does fit what we know of Jesus.

He is again in the Temple, now on the day after the Festival of Booths, which was is a festival in its own right. It is a day of celebration when the annual cycle of reading of the Torah ends, and begins again, (Torah is the group name for the first five books of our Bible, the books of Moses, in which the law was given to the people of Israel).

Israel in the 1st century

The Golden Menorah in Jerusalem

In this context the scribes and Pharisees are testing Jesus to see how faithful he is to the Law of Moses. Faced with their accusations he wrote on the ground. I've always wondered what he wrote, or perhaps drew. Maybe he drew a bird in a cage, longing to be set free, but trapped. We can't know. But we do know that when pushed he responded, "Let anyone among you who is without sin be the first to throw a stone at her." He did not deny the Law of Moses but showed them a way of love to deal with it. When no one condemned the woman, aware as they were of their own sin, Jesus does not condemn the woman but does invite her to live a different way.

When we return to the original text of John, Jesus is teaching in the temple still. Having spoken of water, he now speaks of light.

The Babylonian Talmud complied in about 500 A.D. captures centuries of reflection on Jewish teaching. In the section on the Festival of Booths, Sukkah the lighting of great lamps in the temple is described:

'At the conclusion of the first Festival day the priests and the Levites descended from the Israelites' courtyard to the Women's Courtyard, where they would introduce a significant repair, as the Gemara will explain. There were golden candelabra atop poles there in the courtyard. And there were four basins made of gold at the top of each candelabrum. And there were four ladders for each and every pole and there were four children from the priesthood trainees, and in their hands were pitchers with a capacity of 120 log of oil that they would pour into each and every basin. From the worn trousers of the priests and their belts they would loosen and tear strips to use as wicks, and with them they would light the candelabra. And the light from the candelabra was so bright that there was not a courtyard in Jerusalem that was not illuminated from the light of the Place of the Drawing of the Water.' Sukkah 51a.16

This celebrated the presence of God with his people in wilderness as the glowing pillar of fire. To His people God was their light. As Psalm 27:1 says

'The Lord is my light and my salvation; whom shall, I fear?'

So, Jesus second 'I am' saying is to be heard in this context. He is claiming to be the light of God's people, he is claiming to be God. No wonder the onlookers challenge him on his right to make such claims. No wonder he predicts his death, he knows they don't accept him for who he is, and so they will reject him.

'37 I know that you are descendants of Abraham; yet you look for an opportunity to kill me, because there is no place in you for my word. 38 I declare what I have seen in the Father's presence; as for you, you should do what you have heard from the Father.' John 8 37-38

Jesus tells them that even though they may be physically descended from Abraham, they are not really his children, because they don't accept him, even though he is God the Father's Word in the world. They have the light of the Torah, but they don't see it fulfilled in him, the true Light from God, God with them. After further debate over Abraham

From Nazareth to Northumbria

'⁵⁸Jesus said to them, "Very truly, I tell you, before Abraham was, I am." ⁵⁹ So, they picked up stones to throw at him, but Jesus hid himself and went out of the temple.' John 8:58-59

This 'I am' saying is blunt – Jesus is calling himself the 'I am', the name of God which was revealed to Moses in Exodus 6:14-15

'¹⁴God said to Moses, "I AM WHO I AM." He said further, "Thus you shall say to the Israelites, 'I AM has sent me to you.'" ¹⁵ God also said to Moses, "Thus you shall say to the Israelites, 'The LORD, the God of your ancestors, the God of Abraham, the God of Isaac, and the God of Jacob, has sent me to you':
This is my name forever,
and this my title for all generations.'

Pool of Siloam

'¹As he walked along, he saw a man blind from birth. ² His disciples asked him, "Rabbi, who sinned, this man or his parents, that he was born blind?" ³ Jesus answered, "Neither this man nor his parents sinned; he was born blind so that God's works might be revealed in him. ⁴ We must work the works of him who sent me while it is day; night is coming when no one can work. ⁵ As long as I am in the world, I am the light of the world." ⁶ When he had said this, he spat on the ground and made mud with the saliva and spread the mud on the man's eyes, ⁷ saying to him, "Go, wash in the pool of Siloam" (which means Sent). Then he went and washed and came back able to see.' John 9:1-7

Hezekiah's tunnel in the City of David

The blind man was probably begging near a gate to the temple, when he could expect people to give him money. As they had gone in to worship God, they would be reminded of the call to love others. What better than to sit nearby so that you were 'the other' they saw? It is likely that Jesus came out of the temple complex near the old City of David, at the far end of which is the Pool of Siloam.

Today, the pool is well outside the walls of Jerusalem in an Arab village called Silwan, and to get to the pool from the Western Wall of the temple is a 10 to 15 minute walk down steeply sloping streets. Most people who visit it, however, come through Hezekiah's tunnel, and come out at a small pool. This pool was built in the 5th century, at the end of the rock cut part of the tunnel, by the Byzantines trying to replace the Pool of Siloam, which they could not find. They then built a church on pillars over it, and the bases of the pillars are still in this pool. However, in 2004, when sewerage works were being done, the Pool of the second Temple period was found. It was partly excavated in 2004/5, but much remains covered in the mud that accumulated over the years after Jerusalem was destroyed by Titus' army in 70 A.D.

The Pool of Siloam, rediscovered in 2004

As Jesus came out of the temple area, he saw this blind man, presumably begging, and his disciples asked a theological question. ' Whose sin caused this?' Which is not an unreasonable question. If life is fair, if God is just, then surely if bad things happen to you it must be your own fault, or that of someone close to you.

Jesus reply must have surprised them, when he told them the man was born blind so that Jesus could show through healing that he,

Israel in the 1st century

Jesus, is the light of the world. This wasn't a universal answer to the universal question of suffering, although Jesus does say that it isn't as simple as a direct punishment for a particular wrongdoing. But for Jesus this man and his blindness would enable those around to see who Jesus was. His healing would be a sign to underline Jesus teaching authority, and Jesus claims to be God in human form.

So, Jesus makes a salve out of the dust nearby and his own saliva, and spread this on the man's eyes then sent him to the Pool of Siloam to wash himself and be healed. He obediently

Artist's impression of the original Pool

did this, perhaps guided by the disciples, or perhaps just aware that the pool was down this road. When he got to the pool, he walked down the fifteen steps, in three groups of five, into the water, to wash his eyes. The water in this pool, this large reservoir, was the water that had come out from the Gihon Spring. As we saw when thinking about that, the water had taken on an extra spiritual dimension. As well as being the original water supply for the Old City, it had been used in the coronation of kings and was still used for the water drawing ceremony at the festival of Booths. This pool was the 'Well of Salvation' of Isaiah 12:3, since by digging the tunnel and diverting the Gihon waters into this pool, the people of Jerusalem were saved during the siege of the Assyrians in Hezekiah's time.

And then the man could see the pool, the people, and that Jesus was who he claimed to be. For the rest of the chapter there is a debate on the spiritual blindness of the Jews who do not accept Jesus as God among them.

The Walls of Jerusalem

Before we look at the final days of Jesus time on earth, it is worth a quick look at the walls of Jerusalem. The locations of the walls have changed over time, as they have been destroyed by conquering armies, or extended to take in areas of the city that had grown up outside the previous walls. This rebuilding has meant that the old city as we see it today is not in the same place as the area bounded by walls in Jesus day. So, today's walls can distract from an idea of the geography that Jesus and his contemporaries knew. This becomes important when we look at where the final hours before Jesus crucifixion are likely to have occurred.

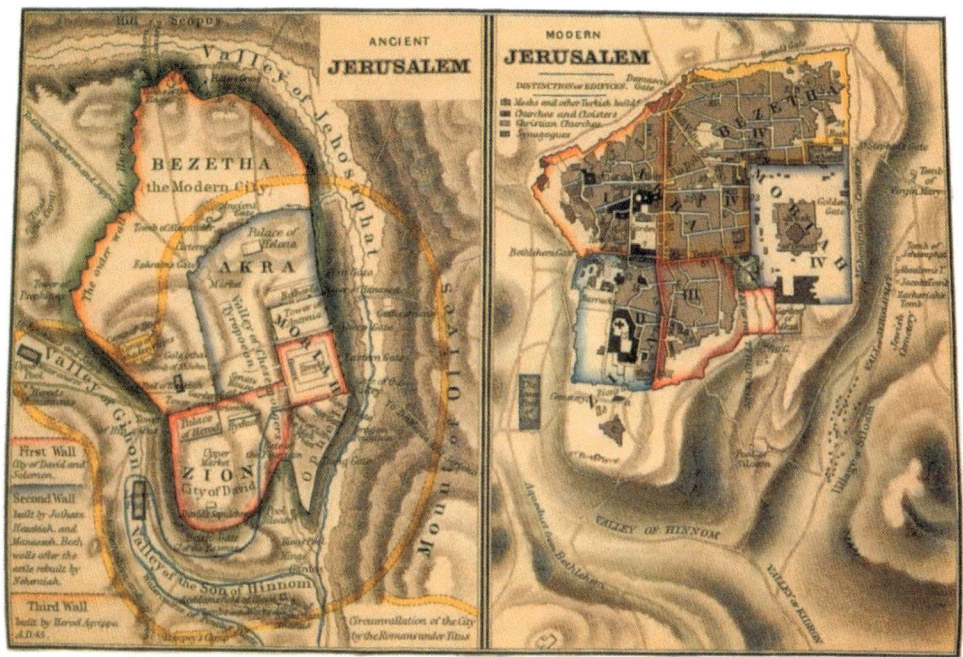
Ancient Jerusalem and Modern Jerusalem. ANCIENT JERUSALEM / MODERN JERUSALEM Lyman Coleman, in Text Book and Atlas of Biblical Geography, Philadelphia, 1854 Osher Collection, University of Southern Maine "Modern Jerusalem" is the old walled city as it existed in the mid-nineteenth century.

From Nazareth to Northumbria

The current walls were built on the orders of Sultan Sulieman I, between 1531 and 1537 when Jerusalem was part of the Ottoman Empire. The walls were in ruins at that point, and over four years just over 4 kilometres of walls were built, with 34 watch towers around the city.

The previous walls were built by the Fatimids repairing them after an earthquake in 1033. It was at this point that the southern parts of the city, the Old City of David and Mount Zion, were left outside the walls.

The previous line of the walls had been set when the city of Aelia Capitolina was built on the site of the former Jerusalem. The city was founded by Hadrian in 130 A.D., but only walled in the time of Diocletian c 289 A.D.

The sheep gate

'*[1] Very truly I tell you Pharisees, anyone who does not enter the sheep pen by the gate, but climbs in by some other way, is a thief and a robber. [2] The one who enters by the gate is the shepherd of the sheep.*'

'*[7] Jesus said again, "Very truly I tell you, I am the gate for the sheep. [8] All who have come before me are thieves and robbers, but the sheep have not listened to them. [9] I am the gate; whoever enters through me will be saved.*

'*[14] "I am the good shepherd; I know my sheep and my sheep know me"*'

'*[22] Then came the Festival of Dedication at Jerusalem. It was winter, [23] and Jesus was in the temple courts walking in Solomon's Colonnade. [24] The Jews who were there gathered around him, saying, "How long will you keep us in suspense? If you are the Messiah, tell us plainly."*'

'*[31] Again his Jewish opponents picked up stones to stone him, [32] but Jesus said to them, "I have shown you many good works from the Father. For which of these do you stone me?"*
[33] "We are not stoning you for any good work," they replied, "but for blasphemy, because you, a mere man, claim to be God."'
John 10:1-2, 7-8, 10, 22-24, 31-33

John 7-9 are set around the time of the Festival of Booths in September/October in the area of the Jerusalem temple.

John tells us in chapter 10 that the Festival of Dedication, a couple of months, later is the context for Jesus' next conflict with the Pharisees and the other Jewish leaders.

The term John uses for the festival is *ta enkainia*, which means the renewals. Today this festival is called Hanukkah. It is usually held in December, although because of the lunar calendar that sets the timing for it, it is occasionally held in late November.

The Festival was instituted in 165 B.C. by Judas Maccabeus and the elders of the nation, to celebrate the re-consecration of the Temple and especially the altar of the burnt offerings, after they had be desecrated by Antiochus Epiphanes in 168 B.C. which led to the Maccabean uprising. Antiochus Epiphanes was the ruler of the Seleucid or Greek/Syrian empire, that succeeded the empire Alexander the Great founded, in the northern part of the territories he conquered. By being part of this empire Judah and Galilee became influenced by Greek culture.

The Talmud, in Shabbat 21b, tells of the reasons for the festival

'On the twenty-fifth of Kislev, the days of Hanukkah are eight. One may not eulogize on them and one may not fast on them. What is the reason? When the Greeks entered the Sanctuary, they defiled all the oils that were in the Sanctuary by touching them. And when the Hasmonean monarchy overcame them and emerged victorious over them, they searched and found only one cruse of oil that was placed with the seal of the High Priest, undisturbed by the Greeks. And there was sufficient oil there to light the candelabrum for only one day. A miracle occurred and they lit the candelabrum from it each day for eight days. The next year the Sages instituted those days and made them holidays with recitation of *hallel* and special thanksgiving in prayer and blessings.'

So, for eight days the Temple was filled with light, just as it was during the Festival of Booths. At home an extra candle would be lit on the menorah each night as well.

In this context Jesus teaches about sheep and shepherds. At first sight that seems a bit odd – since the festival is one of light in the darkness. However, it is also a memorial of throwing off the rule of the Seleucids and having the priestly Maccabean family as the kings. But they in turn became involved in power politics. As

Israel in the 1st century

the celebrations of the restoration of kingship to Israel are occurring, Jesus speaks about himself as the true leader of God's people.

In the days of the Davidic kings, prophets had spoken out against the abuse of power of the rulers, using the imagery of shepherds.

'²Therefore, thus says the LORD, the God of Israel, concerning the shepherds who shepherd my people: It is you who have scattered my flock, and have driven them away, and you have not attended to them. So, I will attend to you for your evil doings, says the LORD.' Jeremiah 23:2

'prophesy, and say to them—to the shepherds: Thus, says the Lord GOD: Ah, you shepherds of Israel who have been feeding yourselves! Should not shepherds feed the sheep?' Ezekiel 34:2

'My anger is hot against the shepherds, and I will punish the leaders' Zechariah 10:3

Jesus has been criticised by the leaders, but he responds by talking about himself as the protection for the sheep – the gate to the fold and as the Good Shepherd. This echoes the prophecies of old. For having berated the current leaders as inadequate shepherds they speak of God coming to be Israel's shepherd.

'He who scattered Israel will gather him and will keep him as a shepherd a flock.' Jeremiah 31:10

'I myself will be the shepherd of my sheep, and I will make them lie down, says the Lord GOD'. Ezekiel 34:15

As well as this there is also a prediction of one who will be set up by God as a shepherd:

'I will set up over them one shepherd, my servant David, and he shall feed them: he shall feed them and be their shepherd'. Ezekiel 34:23

'He will feed his flock like a shepherd; he will gather the lambs in his arms, and carry them in his bosom, and gently lead the mother sheep.' Isaiah 40:11

This is why the leaders are ready to stone him. Not only does he denigrate their leadership, he also says 'I am the Good Shepherd'. They know that God is the Good Shepherd for Judah, so Jesus is claiming to be God. But they are only right that this is blasphemy if Jesus really is 'a mere man'.

Bethany

'²Now a certain man was ill, Lazarus of Bethany, the village of Mary and her sister Martha…. ³ So the sisters sent a message to Jesus, 'Lord, he whom you love is ill.' ⁴ But when Jesus heard it, he said, 'This illness does not lead to death; rather it is for God's glory, so that the Son of God may be glorified through it.' ⁵ Accordingly, though Jesus loved Martha and her sister and Lazarus, ⁶ after having heard that Lazarus was ill, he stayed two days longer in the place where he was.'

'¹⁹ When Jesus arrived, he found that Lazarus had already been in the tomb for four days… ²⁰ When Martha heard that Jesus was coming, she went and met him, while Mary stayed at home. ²¹ Martha said to Jesus, "Lord, if you had been here, my brother would not have died. ²² But even now I know that God will give you whatever you ask of him." ²³ Jesus said to her, "Your brother will rise again." ²⁴ Martha said to him, "I know that he will rise again in the resurrection on the last day." ²⁵ Jesus said to her, "I am the resurrection and the life. Those who believe in me, even though they die, will live, ²⁶ and everyone who lives and believes in me will never die. Do you believe this?" ²⁷ She said to him, "Yes, Lord, I believe that 'you are the Messiah, the Son of God, the one coming into the world.'"

'³⁸ Then Jesus, again greatly disturbed, came to the tomb. It was a cave, and a stone was lying against it. ³⁹ Jesus said, "Take away the stone." Martha, the sister of the dead man, said to him, "Lord, already there is a stench because he has been dead for four days." ⁴⁰ Jesus said to her, "Did I not tell you that if you believed, you would see the glory of God?" ⁴¹ So they took away the stone. And Jesus looked upwards and said, "Father, I thank you for having heard me. ⁴² I knew that you always hear me, but I have said this for the sake of the crowd standing here, so that they may believe that you sent me." ⁴³ When he had said this, he cried with a loud voice, "Lazarus, come out!" ⁴⁴ The dead man came out, his hands and feet bound with strips of cloth, and his face wrapped in a cloth. Jesus said to them, "Unbind him, and let him go."' John 11;2-6; 19-27;38-44

Today Bethany is called Al-Elzariya and is an Arab village, a couple of miles from the Temple Mount in Jerusalem. It should be a 35 to 40-minute walk from the Temple Mount, just 15 minutes walk beyond Bethphage. But between Jerusalem and Al-Elzariya is the Separation Wall.

From Nazareth to Northumbria

So instead of a 40 minute walk the trip to Al-Elzariya takes over an hour, including 30 minutes on the 263 bus from the Arab Bus station, Sultan Suleiman Station, near the Damascus Gate. The bus goes the long way round, since it has to go through the Check Point. Going back into Jerusalem this way we all have our papers checked by the Israeli Defence Force. The Palestinians get off the bus to wait in line, while the foreigners stay on, not realising what is happening, so the soldiers come onboard to us.

The separation wall where it runs through Al-Elzariya

But in Jesus' day Bethany was a handy place to stay close to Jerusalem. Here his friends Mary and Martha and their brother Lazarus lived. Here Lazarus took ill and died. Word was sent to Jesus that Lazarus was ill, yet he stayed in Galilee another couple of days. By the time he got to Bethany Lazarus had been dead for four days. Yes, he was well and truly dead, no question about it.

When Martha runs to meet Jesus, she is full of pain, and yet has a deep trust in Jesus and who he is:

The tomb of Lazarus - much of what you can see is from the Crusader period

Martha said to Jesus, 'Lord, if you had been here, my brother would not have died. ²² But even now I know that God will give you whatever you ask of him.' John 11:21-22.

When asked of her belief in the resurrection Martha says she believes in the resurrection at the end of time. But '²⁵Jesus said to her, "I am the resurrection and the life. Those who believe in me, even though they die, will live, ²⁶ and everyone who lives and believes in me will never die. Do you believe this?" ²⁷ She said to him, "Yes, Lord, I believe that you are the Messiah, the Son of God, the one coming into the world."' John 11:25-27

Jesus declares again who he is – the Lord of life itself. Again, this is clearly a claim to be God, albeit in human form.

But Jesus is not God on his own, for as he stands before Lazarus' tomb he prays to his Father, God, thanking him for having heard him, for although Jesus is the one who speaks to Lazarus, he is reliant on God the Father. We see a glimpse into the relationship within God, Jesus is God, but reliant on God, only acting in accordance with the will of God the Father. Then Jesus calls out to Lazarus, and Lazarus comes out of the tomb.

Three steps down into the tomb of Lazarus from the antechamber

The Tomb of the Prophets, on the Mount of Olives – 1st century tombs

Israel in the 1st century

The tomb of Lazarus was identified as such in the 4th century and is in an area where archaeologists have found other first century tombs. Above the site churches were built and rebuilt, until a mosque took over. The site is sacred to Muslims as well as Christians, which is why the village is named for Lazarus today.

In the 16th century a new entrance was cut for Christians to enter the tomb and at some point the original entrance from the mosque was sealed up. There are 24 steps down into an antechamber, and then three more steps down into the tomb itself. It may well be that Jesus was in the antechamber when he called to Lazarus. The tomb was reinforced by the crusaders – the masonry covers most of the walls leaving small gaps to see through to the original niches in one of which Lazarus' body would have lain. A better idea of what the

1st century ossuaries, Israel Museum, Jerusalem

tomb would have looked like can gained from the 1 century B.C. tomb on the Mount of Olives called the Tomb of the Prophets. It is so called because in the middle ages a tradition grew up that this was the tomb of the last three prophets Haggai, Zephaniah and Malachi, and their followers.

So, Lazarus body would have lain here, wrapped in linen bindings. It would have been buried with spices to reduce the stench as it decayed. After about a year the expectation was to collect the bones into an ossuary, which would be marked with the name of the person.

But Lazarus did not need an ossuary at this time, for when he was called he came out, a sign of the power of God over death through Jesus.

Mary Anoints Jesus

"*1Six days before the Passover Jesus came to Bethany, the home of Lazarus, whom he had raised from the dead. 2 There they gave a dinner for him. Martha served, and Lazarus was one of those at the table with him. 3 Mary took a pound of costly perfume made of pure nard, anointed Jesus' feet, and wiped them with her hair. The house was filled with the fragrance of the perfume. 4 But Judas Iscariot, one of his disciples (the one who was about to betray him), said, 5 "Why was this perfume not sold for three hundred denarii and the money given to the poor?" 6 (He said this not because he cared about the poor, but because he was a thief; he kept the common purse and used to steal what was put into it.) 7 Jesus said, "Leave her alone. She bought it so that she might keep it for the day of my burial. 8 You always have the poor with you, but you do not always have me.'" John 12:1-8*

It can't have been many weeks later that Jesus came back to Bethany. Lazarus was healed sometime between December and March; Passover is around March to April. Jesus has returned for the festival, even though the opposition to him is growing in strength and desperation. Back in his friend's house he is having dinner when Mary brings the most expensive thing she has, a pound of pure nard and pours it on his feet.

Nard, or spikenard, comes from the crushed rhizomes, the underground stems, of the spikenard plant *Nardostachys jatamansi*. This grows in the Himalayas of Nepal, India and China. And would have been imported to Judea

The Spikenard plant

along the great trade routes that came south through the country towards Egypt. It was used in anointing oils, as an antiseptic, and to perfume bodies for burial. While today 10 ml costs about £20, so a pound would cost about £1000. In Jesus day it was more expensive, we read that it cost 300 denarii, and since a denarius was a day's wages, the cost then was the equivalent of about £20,000 in today's money.

From Nazareth to Northumbria

When her brother Lazarus died Mary didn't use this precious nard, yet here was Jesus still alive and she used it, all of it on him. It was a crazy gesture, yet Jesus is glad to accept it. It is good to care for the poor, but it is also good to offer gifts of beauty and love.

Triumphal entry

'¹²The next day the great crowd that had come to the festival heard that Jesus was coming to Jerusalem. ¹³ So they took branches of palm trees and went out to meet him, shouting,

"Hosanna!
Blessed is the one who comes in the name of the Lord—
　the King of Israel!"
¹⁴ Jesus found a young donkey and sat on it; as it is written:
¹⁵ "Do not be afraid, daughter of Zion.
Look, your king is coming,
　sitting on a donkey's colt!"
The Pharisees then said to one another, "You see, you can do nothing. Look, the world has gone after him!"'
John 12:12-15

Jerusalem seen from the Mount of Olives

John doesn't tell us the route of this procession, but the other gospel writers tell us that Jesus sent his disciples into the next village, Bethphage to get the donkey for him. In Bethphage today there is a church, with a stone in it, which is traditionally the stone Jesus stood on to mount the donkey.

The road from Bethphage to Jerusalem goes up and over the Mount of Olives and is quite steep in places. From the Mount of Olives, you can see Jerusalem before you, across the Kidron Valley, with the Temple Mount closest to you, which draws your eyes. But to get to it you go down the Mount of Olives, through the graveyards that are there. They are there because In Zechariah 14 there is a prediction '³Then the LORD will go forth and fight against those nations as when he fights on a day of battle. ⁴ On that day his feet shall stand on the Mount of Olives, which lies before Jerusalem on the east…. Then the LORD my God will come, and all the holy ones with him.' Zechariah 14:3-4, 5b

Since this is where God will come in the great Day of the Lord, they want to be there for the resurrection, to be where God is.

So, on his donkey surrounded by the crowd Jesus went, deliberately fulfilling another part of Zechariah:
'⁹Rejoice greatly, O daughter Zion!
　Shout aloud, O daughter Jerusalem!
Lo, your king comes to you;
　triumphant and victorious is he,
humble and riding on a donkey,
　on a colt, the foal of a donkey.
¹⁰ He will cut off the chariot from Ephraim
　and the war-horse from Jerusalem;
and the battle bow shall be cut off,
　and he shall command peace to the nations;
his dominion shall be from sea to sea,
　and from the River to the ends of the earth.'
Zechariah 9:9-10

He is still claiming to be the answer to their prayers, the One God would send, in fact God himself in flesh coming to the temple, to judgement.

Mounting block in the church in Bethphage

Israel in the 1st century

Once in the temple Jesus teaches those who are there' including some who John calls Greeks.

'27 "Now my soul is troubled. And what should I say— 'Father, save me from this hour'? No, it is for this reason that I have come to this hour. 28 Father, glorify your name." Then a voice came from heaven, "I have glorified it, and I will glorify it again." 29 The crowd standing there heard it and said that it was thunder. Others said, "An angel has spoken to him." 30 Jesus answered, "This voice has come for your sake, not for mine. 31 Now is the judgment of this world; now the ruler of this world will be driven out. 32 And I, when I am lifted up from the earth, will draw all people to myself." 33 He said this to indicate the kind of death he was to die.'   John 12:27-33

He speaks of judgement – but a judgement to be accomplished through his own death, which is not what people were expecting at all when they looked to God to act.

Then John gives us a summary of Jesus teaching, so as we follow Jesus on his path to his death, we know what he wanted us to know:

'44 Then Jesus cried aloud: "Whoever believes in me believes not in me but in him who sent me. 45 And whoever sees me sees him who sent me. 46 I have come as light into the world, so that everyone who believes in me should not remain in the darkness. 47 I do not judge anyone who hears my words and does not keep them, for I came not to judge the world, but to save the world. 48 The one who rejects me and does not receive my word has a judge; on the last day the word that I have spoken will serve as judge, 49 for I have not spoken on my own, but the Father who sent me has himself given me a commandment about what to say and what to speak. 50 And I know that his commandment is eternal life. What I speak, therefore, I speak just as the Father has told me."' John 12:44-50

The upper room

'1Now before the festival of the Passover, Jesus knew that his hour had come to depart from this world and go to the Father. Having loved his own who were in the world, he loved them to the end. 2 The devil had already put it into the heart of Judas son of Simon Iscariot to betray him. And during supper 3 Jesus, knowing that the Father had given all things into his hands, and that he had come from God and was going to God, 4 got up from the table, took off his outer robe, and tied a towel around himself. 5 Then he poured water into a basin and began to wash the disciples' feet and to wipe them with the towel that was tied around him.' John 13:1-5

The 'Room of the Last Supper'

This surely isn't where Jesus had his final meal before his crucifixion. It is a large medieval hall like space, above the 'tomb of King David' in the Mount Zion area of Jerusalem. But the tradition that this is David's tomb only goes back to the 12th century – old, but not nearly old enough. The rooms, upper and lower are crusader built. However, here is as a good a place as any to remember what the Son of David did as he prepared for his death.

First, he took water. Water has been key in his teaching about himself so far, and here, as a sign of who he is and what he is about to do for them, he takes water and washes them. A simple sign of his humility, becoming a servant, is also a sign of his power to wash and heal and revive, not just physically but spiritually.

Then during the meal Jesus speaks to his disciples:

'21After saying this Jesus was troubled in spirit, and declared, "Very truly, I tell you, one of you will betray me."' '30 So, after receiving the piece of bread, he [Judas] immediately went out. And it was night.' John 13:21;30

Sign outside 'The Room of the Last Supper'

From Nazareth to Northumbria

It is night, when the light of the sun is not shining, and so we are reminded that Jesus is the Light of the World, but by walking away from him, to betray him, Judas is turning his back on the light, and choosing the darkness of night.

He also misses Jesus teaching, where we hear Jesus tell us who he is in his final 'I am' sayings. In the face of death, he comforts his disciples:

'¹"Do not let your hearts be troubled. Believe in God, believe also in me. ² In my Father's house there are many dwelling places. If it were not so, would I have told you that I go to prepare a place for you? ³ And if I go and prepare a place for you, I will come again and will take you to myself, so that where I am, there you may be also. ⁴ And you know the way to the place where I am going." ⁵ Thomas said to him, "Lord, we do not know where you are going. How can we know the way?" ⁶ Jesus said to him, "I am the way, and the truth, and the life. No one comes to the Father except through me. ⁷ If you know me, you will know my Father also. From now on you do know him and have seen him."' John 14:1-7

Even though he will be killed he is still the Life that he told them of when he raised Lazarus.

He gives his new commandment to love, and promises:

'¹⁵"If you love me, you will keep my commandments. ¹⁶ And I will ask the Father, and he will give you another Advocate, to be with you forever.'

The 'Tomb of David', below the 'Upper Room'

'²⁶ But the Advocate, the Holy Spirit, whom the Father will send in my name, will teach you everything, and remind you of all that I have said to you. ²⁷ Peace I leave with you; my peace I give to you. I do not give to you as the world gives. Do not let your hearts be troubled, and do not let them be afraid.' John

'²⁶"When the Advocate comes, whom I will send to you from the Father, the Spirit of truth who comes from the Father, he will testify on my behalf. ²⁷ You also are to testify because you have been with me from the beginning.' John 14:15-16;26-27; 15:26-27

Here is the closest to a statement about the Trinity that there is in John's gospel. The Holy Spirit, whom the Father will send in Jesus name, when Jesus has returned to the Father. As the promise of the Holy Spirit to be with them comes, Jesus also gives his peace, perhaps he gives peace through the presence of the Holy Spirit, God himself with us each day. Through the power of the Holy Spirit his disciples are to testify, to tell others of who Jesus is.

In John 15 we come to the final 'I am'

'¹"I am the true vine, and my Father is the vine grower. ² He removes every branch in me that bears no fruit. Every branch that bears fruit he prunes to make it bear more fruit.' John 15: -1-2

This is steeped in the traditions of the prophets.

'You brought a vine out of Egypt; you drove out the nations and planted it.' Psalm 80:8

'For the vineyard of the LORD of hosts is the house of Israel, and the people of Judah are his pleasant planting; he expected justice, but saw bloodshed; righteousness, but heard a cry!' Isaiah 5:7

'Yet I planted you as a choice vine, from the purest stock. How then did you turn degenerate and become a wild vine?' Jeremiah 2:21

Israel is God's vine or vineyard, which he had tended, but so often the fruit they bear is bitter. Jesus is God's true vine, his people as he always longed for them to be, and the fruit he is about to bear will be as God longs for it to be. His disciples are branches of this true vine, as are all who are part of his people, his church today.

At last after his final teaching:

Israel in the 1st century

'¹After Jesus had spoken these words, he looked up to heaven and said, "Father, the hour has come; glorify your Son so that the Son may glorify you, ² since you have given him authority over all people, to give eternal life to all whom you have given him.' John 17:1-2

Jesus prays for his branches, his disciples as they take on the task, he has begun of being the new Israel.

After prayer for them and for us he is ready to face the night himself, to face it and by his self-giving love bring light into it.

The Kidron Valley and Gethsemane

'¹After Jesus had spoken these words, he went out with his disciples across the Kidron valley to a place where there was a garden, which he and his disciples entered. ² Now Judas, who betrayed him, also knew the place, because Jesus often met there with his disciples'. John 18:1-2

The Kidron Valley cuts east between the Temple Mount and the Mount of Olives ridge. On the south side is a Muslim cemetery and the north side, on the Mount of Olives is a Jewish cemetery. Here also are the 'Tomb of Zechariah' and the 'Tomb of Absalom', which are probably the tombs of neither. The 'Tomb of Zechariah' (seen

The Kidron Valley, with the Mount of Olives on the left

in the mid distance on the left in the above picture) does not even have a burial chamber in it, but seems to be a 1st century B.C. funeral monument.

The Franciscan 'Garden of Gethsemane'

The valley cuts down south east through the Jerusalem limestones, and extends as far as the Dead Sea, entering that valley just south of the Qumran caves. Mostly it is a dry valley, but when the rains come, the wadi fills with water which runs down to the rift valley of the Dead Sea. Near Jerusalem it is also called the Valley of Jehoshaphat.

On the slopes of the Mount of Olives opposite the Temple Mount is a small olive grove. This has been identified with the Garden of Gethsemane since 1681 when Croatian knights of the Holy Order of Jerusalem, Paul, Antun and James bought the Gethsemane Garden and donated it to the Franciscan community, and the Roman Catholic Church is built over a rock which could be the rock

Inside the Catholic Church, perhaps the rock where Jesus prayed

where Jesus prayed. The nearby Greek Orthodox and Russian Orthodox churches also claim that they have the real Garden of Gethsemane. Whichever garden is the real site of Jesus' prayers and arrest, the Franciscan Garden is the easiest to access and to get a feel of the place.

The ancient olive trees here are at least 900 years old and may be on an older root set. They have probably been grown from the seeds of the seeds of the trees that Jesus knelt among.

Jesus was praying with his disciples in a small olive garden just five minutes from the Temple Mount.

Here in the night, Judas brings the soldiers of the chief priests and a group of Pharisees. These two groups, the Priests and the Pharisees, were usually opponents but are brought together by a common desire to be rid of Jesus.

Via Dolorosa, Flagellation, Prison

'¹²*So, the soldiers, their officer, and the Jewish police arrested Jesus and bound him.* ¹³ *First they took him to Annas, who was the father-in-law of Caiaphas, the high priest that year.* ¹⁴ *Caiaphas was the one who had advised the Jews that it was better to have one person die for the people*.' John 18:12-14

From Gethsemane it is a five minute walk back across the Kidron Valley to the Lions Gate of Jerusalem. This was built in the 16th century and is the start of the Via Dolorosa, the Way of Sorrow.

The route which Jesus took from Gethsemane to his trials and death was hotly debated over the centuries. Today's route may be right, or may be wrong, but it was settled on in the 14th century.

There are various stops, or stations on the route, drawn from the events escribed in different gospels. The events at the High Priest's House are not part of this route. The High Priest's House was on Mount Zion, across the current old city and out the other side.

Model of Jerusalem in the 1st century at the Jerusalem Museum

Israel in the 1st century

What is more, Herod's palace was over that side too, where Pilate may have stayed when he was in Jerusalem (his residence was in Caesarea Maritima) so it may well be that the Via Dolorosa is in completely the wrong place.

The Orthodox Prison of Christ on the Via Dolorosa

'15 Simon Peter and another disciple followed Jesus. Since that disciple was known to the high priest, he went with Jesus into the courtyard of the high priest, 16 but Peter was standing outside at the gate. So, the other disciple, who was known to the high priest, went out, spoke to the woman who guarded the gate, and brought Peter in.' John 18:15-16

'25 Now Simon Peter was standing and warming himself. They asked him, "You are not also one of his disciples, are you?" He denied it and said, "I am not." 26 One of the slaves of the high priest, a relative of the man whose ear Peter had cut off, asked, "Did I not see you in the garden with him?" 27 Again Peter denied it, and at that moment the cock crowed.' John 18:25-27

Simon Peter's denial of Jesus is commemorated at the Church of St Peter Gallicantu, on the eastern slope of Mount Zion, just outside the current walls of Jerusalem. The first church on the site was built in 457 A.D., and the current building enables you to see down into the caves which were part of the original church. If this is indeed Caiaphas' House Jesus may have been imprisoned for a time in one of these.

'Then they took Jesus from Caiaphas to Pilate's headquarters. It was early in the morning. They themselves did not enter the headquarters, so as to avoid ritual defilement and to be able to eat the Passover.' John 18:28

St Peter Gallicantu Church, Mount Zion, above, the caves below the church, the other site where Jesus may have been held, below

The Jewish leaders are not the ultimate leader of the nation – they have to look to the Romans to deliver 'justice'. So, they take Jesus to where Pilate is, but they keep themselves outside. This so that they are kept clean to be able to be involved in the Passover sacrifices later that day. For John, the Last Supper is not a Passover meal as such, at least it certainly wasn't eaten on the day of Passover itself. Instead, the true Passover lamb, Jesus is sacrificed at the time of the slaughtering of the Passover lambs.

'33 Then Pilate entered the headquarters again, summoned Jesus, and asked him, "Are you the King of the Jews?" 34 Jesus answered, "Do you ask this on your own, or did others tell you about me?" 35 Pilate replied, "I am not a Jew, am I? Your own nation and the chief priests have handed you over to me. What have you done?" ³⁶ Jesus answered, "My kingdom is not from this world. If my kingdom were from this world, my followers would be fighting to keep me from being handed over to the Jews. But as it is, my kingdom is not from here." ³⁷ Pilate asked him, "So you are a king?" Jesus answered, "You say that I am a king. For this I was born, and for this I came into the world, to testify to the truth. Everyone who belongs to the truth listens to my voice." ³⁸ Pilate asked him, "What is truth?"' John 18:33-38

'¹Then Pilate took Jesus and had him flogged. ² And the soldiers wove a crown of thorns and put it on his head, and they dressed him in a purple robe.' John 19:1-2

'¹³Pilate brought Jesus outside and sat on the judge's bench at a place called The Stone Pavement, or in Hebrew Gabbatha. ¹⁴ Now it was the day of Preparation for the Passover; and it was about noon. He said to the Jews, "Here is your King!" ¹⁵ They cried out, "Away with him! Away with him! Crucify him!" Pilate asked them, "Shall I crucify your King?" The chief priests answered, "We have no king but the emperor." ¹⁶ Then he handed him over to them to be crucified.' John 19:13-16

If Pilate was not at Herod's Palace, but had his own residence, then after being interrogated at Caiaphas' House, Jesus was brought back across the city to near the Antonia Fort, which was right against the north west of the Temple Mount. It had been built under the Maccabean Kings to guard the Temple and act as a vestry for it, but under the Romans was occupied by soldiers instead of clergy.

On the site of the Fort are the Church of Ecce Homo, named for Pilate's speech to the Jews, 'behold the man', the Church of the Condemnation and the Church of the Flagellation. Under these an extensive Roman Pavement can be seen, which could be the Stone Pavement John mentions.

1st century pavement just off the Via Dolorosa at the Ecco Homo church

The Crucifixion

'*So they took Jesus; ¹⁷ and carrying the cross by himself, he went out to what is called The Place of the Skull, which in Hebrew is called Golgotha. ¹⁸ There they crucified him, and with him two others, one on either side, with Jesus between them.*' John 19: 16b-18

So along past the souvenir sellers on the Via Dolorosa. The Greek Orthodox believe that they have the site where Jesus and the other prisoners were kept.

Along past the Austrian Hospice, with a roof terrace with a glorious view across the top of the Temple Mount, then a left turn and then a right turn, and on towards the Church of the Holy Sepulchre.

In 326 A.D. a church was built over the site that Helena, Constantine's mother, had identified as the place where Jesus was buried and raised. She was helped by the Bishop of Caesarea of the time, Eusebius, and the Bishop of Jerusalem, Macarius, to identify a temple of Jupiter and Venus as the site. Constantine ordered this to be removed, and below was a rock cut tomb. Nearby, Helena identified the site of the crucifixion, and each

Israel in the 1st century

was marked by a church, with a courtyard between them. This was rebuilt in 630 after it had been destroyed by the Persian invasion, and under Muslim rule was protected until 1009, when the Caliph decided to destroy Christian sites in Palestine and Egypt. The Byzantines were allowed to rebuild it in the 11th century, and in 1099 A.D. it was taken by the Crusaders.

The Crusader period saw the area enclosed in a large basilica, with various chapels covering the important sites. During the 16th century the Franciscans covered the site of Jesus tomb with marble to protect it from souvenir hunting pilgrims.

Pilgrims wait to touch the cleft in the rock where Jesus' cross was raised

Today, the church is split between the Armenians, the Copts, the Greek Orthodox and the Roman Catholics, in the form of the Franciscans.

It is the Greek Orthodox who care for the area believed to be Calvary.

To the right of the doorway into the Crusader Church is a staircase. At the top are the Franciscan chapel of the nailing, where Jesus was nailed to the cross, and to the left of this is the Orthodox chapel of the Crucifixion, with the altar above the limestone peak where Jesus was crucified. The rock itself is covered by a copper plate, but there is a hole in this to allow the pilgrim to reach down and touch the rock crevice where Jesus cross was wedged. The rock is visible in the area below the chapel.

The rock of Calvary in the Church of the Holy Sepulchre

In the Israel Museum is a gruesome exhibit. It is a copy of a heel bone and nail which were found in a 1st century ossuary of a man named Yehohanan. He had been crucified, and his heel still bears the mark. It is the only direct evidence we have of crucifixion in the period and shows that in his case at least the heels were nailed to the sides of the cross.

'25Meanwhile, standing near the cross of Jesus were his mother, and his mother's sister, Mary the wife of Clopas, and Mary Magdalene. 26 When Jesus saw his mother and the disciple whom he loved standing beside her, he said to his mother, "Woman, here is your son." 27 Then he said to the disciple, "Here is your mother." And from that hour the disciple took her into his own home.

28 After this, when Jesus knew that all was now finished, he said (in order to fulfil the scripture), "I am thirsty." 29 A jar full of sour wine was standing there. So, they put a sponge full of the wine on a branch of hyssop and

1st century heel bone with nail in the Jerusalem Museum

held it to his mouth. ³⁰ When Jesus had received the wine, he said, "It is finished." Then he bowed his head and gave up his spirit.' John 19:25-30

Back down the stairs there is a great slab of rock, which since the time of the Crusaders has been believed to be where Jesus body was prepared for burial.

Today there are throngs of people around these sites, from all over the world, who come to see where it all happened, to pray and to reaffirm their faith in Jesus.

When Jesus died there were throngs of people too. A few we there for him, but most came to mock, or just gawk, letting the macabre spectacle give them a little thrill.

Today's crowds are a fulfiment of the words Jesus spoke as he came towards his final days:

'And I, when I am lifted up from the earth, will draw all people to myself.' John 12:32

Burial

'³⁸ After these things, Joseph of Arimathea, who was a disciple of Jesus, though a secret one because of his fear of the Jews, asked Pilate to let him take away the body of Jesus. Pilate gave him permission; so, he came and removed his body. ³⁹ Nicodemus, who had at first come to Jesus by night, also came, bringing a mixture of myrrh and aloes, weighing about a hundred pounds. ⁴⁰ They took the body of Jesus and wrapped it with the spices in linen cloths, according to the burial custom of the Jews. ⁴¹ Now there was a garden in the place where he was crucified, and in the garden, there was a new tomb in which no one had ever been laid. ⁴² And so, because it was the Jewish day of Preparation, and the tomb was nearby, they laid Jesus there.'

John 19:38-42

The rock of the anointing in the Church of the Holy Sepulchre

The Aedicula in the Church of the Holy Sepulchre

The queue to see inside the Aedicula, the chapel of the sepulchre, in the Church of the Holy Sepulchre is one of the poorest managed queues in the world! A gap between two

Israel in the 1st century

barriers lets the pilgrims into a space to the right of the small building. The queue spreads out to about ten people wide, only to have to narrow to get round the Aedicula and form a single person wide queue on the left side to come into the chapel. This narrowing is unmanaged, and so every time there is movement the whole queue presses forward, to avoid being left behind. So, you queue for two hours in a crush very much like being on an underground train in the rush hour.

Inside the chapel are two areas. The antechamber which is also known as the chapel of the angel with a fragment of the stone which sealed the tomb, and the chapel of the tomb. What you see today is a marble covering from the 14th century, but when works were done to the Aedicule in 2016 this was removed. Under some fill was found another marble layer, over a limestone layer. The mortar between was dated to 345 AD. So, the real tomb is well below what you can see or touch today.

To get a better feel for what Jesus' tomb was like you don't have to go far. For behind the Aedicule is the Syriac Orthodox Chapel with the tomb of

Antechamber to the tomb of Joseph of Arimathea

Joseph of Arimathea. This is entered through a low doorway. Inside you can still see two of the original six places where bodies could be laid. These have attracted the tradition that they were the tombs of Joseph of Arimathea and Nicodemus. We don't really know, but they are certainly tombs of the right period.

When these were still new, or possibly before they had been cut, Jesus was laid nearly in a limestone tomb, and the door was sealed by a stone. His body was briskly prepared with spices and wrapped in a linen shroud. The Jewish leaders had kept out of the place of judgement so as to be able to eat the Passover, but out of love Nicodemus and Joseph accepted ritual uncleanness.

Inside the tomb of Joseph of Arimathea

The Resurrection

'¹*Early on the first day of the week, while it was still dark, Mary Magdalene came to the tomb and saw that the stone had been removed from the tomb.* ² *So she ran and went to Simon Peter and the other disciple, the one whom Jesus loved, and said to them, "They have taken the Lord out of the tomb, and we do not know where they have laid him."* ³ *Then Peter and the other disciple set out and went toward the tomb.* ⁴ *The two were running together, but the other disciple outran Peter and reached the tomb first.* ⁵ *He bent down to look in and saw the linen wrappings lying there, but he did not go in.* ⁶ *Then Simon Peter came, following him, and went into the tomb. He saw the linen wrappings lying there,* ⁷ *and the cloth that had been on Jesus' head, not lying with the linen wrappings but rolled up in a place by itself.* ⁸ *Then the other disciple, who reached the tomb first, also went in, and he saw and believed;* ⁹ *for as yet they did not understand the scripture, that he must rise from the dead.* ¹⁰ *Then the disciples returned to their homes.'* John 20 :1-10

The inside of the Garden Tomb

From Nazareth to Northumbria

It is hard to get a feel of what it was like on that first Easter Sunday in the interior of the Church of the Holy Sepulchre. So, although it is the site that has been recognised for longest as the place where Jesus was buried and rose, another location is worth a visit. This is the Garden Tomb, which was proposed by Protestant scholars of the 19th century as a possible location for Jesus passion. Near to the tomb, the rock face looks a little like a Skull, and Golgotha means place of the Skull. More recent archaeological opinion dates the tomb to about 700 B.C., so it cannot itself be the new tomb that Joseph of Arimathea had cut. But the garden around it, bought in 1894 by The Garden Tomb (Jerusalem) Association, is a place for contemplation in the middle of the bustling city of Jerusalem.

Here you can picture Mary and the other women (who are mentioned in the other gospels) coming to the tomb, then running for support in the form of Simon Peter and the disciple whom Jesus loved, who we think is John himself.

Here you can remember the dawning realisation that this was not a stolen body, but a resurrection. Not just calling back to life in the way Lazarus had come back to life still needing others to help him out of the linen wrappings, but a triumph over death.

'12But Mary stood weeping outside the tomb. As she wept, she bent over to look into the tomb; **12** and she saw two angels in white, sitting where the body of Jesus had been lying, one at the head and

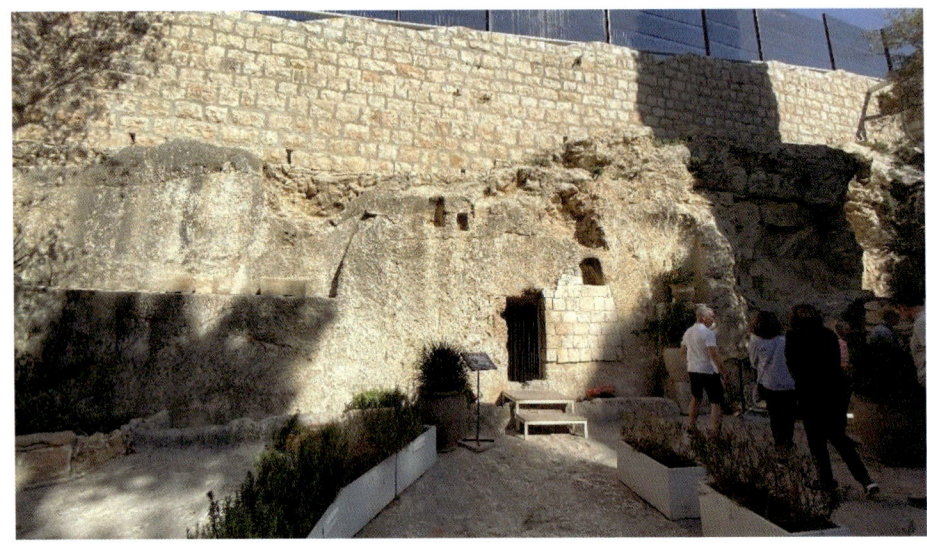

The Garden Tomb

the other at the feet. 13 They said to her, "Woman, why are you weeping?" She said to them, "They have taken away my Lord, and I do not know where they have laid him." 14 When she had said this, she turned around and saw Jesus standing there, but she did not know that it was Jesus. 15 Jesus said to her, "Woman, why are you weeping? Whom are you looking for?" Supposing him to be the gardener, she said to him, "Sir, if you have carried him away, tell me where you have laid him, and I will take him away." 16 Jesus said to her, "Mary!" She turned and said to him in Hebrew, "Rabbouni!" (which means Teacher). 17 Jesus said to her, "Do not hold on to me, because I have not yet ascended to the Father. But go to my brothers and say to them, 'I am ascending to my Father and your Father, to my God and your God.'" 18 Mary Magdalene went and announced to the disciples, "I have seen the Lord"; and she told them that he had said these things to her.' John 20:11-18

'Supposing him to be the gardener', is a phrase that captures the bewilderment of Mary's situation. While John and Peter have come and gone, Mary stays on, gripped by the location where she last saw Jesus' body. She cannot see what is before her, perhaps because of grief, or perhaps because she is kept from seeing.

But when he says her name, who he is becomes clear. However impossible it may seem, he is alive. Having lost him once, she grasps him, but is told not to hold on to him. Instead she is sent to the disciples, as the apostle to the apostles, called by Jesus his brothers, to tell them 'I am ascending to my Father and your Father, to my God and your God.'

Why does Jesus want them to know of his ascension at this point? Perhaps it is because his death, resurrection and ascension are all theologically part of the same act, the offering of himself in his humanity to God the Father. As his humanity is accepted by the Father, he will send the Holy Spirit so that his divinity can continue in the world, in his brothers, those who are part of his body on earth the Church.

Appearances in Jerusalem

'19 When it was evening on that day, the first day of the week, and the doors of the house where the disciples had met were locked for fear of the Jews, Jesus came and stood among them and said, "Peace be with you." 20 After he said this, he showed them his hands and his side. Then the disciples rejoiced when they saw

Israel in the 1st century

the Lord. ²¹ *Jesus said to them again, "Peace be with you. As the Father has sent me, so I send you."* ²² *When he had said this, he breathed on them and said to them, "Receive the Holy Spirit.* ²³ *If you forgive the sins of any, they are forgiven them; if you retain the sins of any, they are retained."'*

John 20 19-23

Back in the upper room in Jerusalem, Mary has delivered her message, and the disciples are gathered. They are still fearful, having seen how the Jewish leaders acted just a few days before. Yet into this locked room, and into their fear comes Jesus with his gift of peace.

To say 'Peace be with you' in some ways is not a surprising greeting. It is used in modern Hebrew as a common way of saying 'hallo' or 'goodbye', and it may well have been used so in Jesus day. Yet John records it and emphasises its use. It is more than just a casual phrase for him; for him Jesus came to them bringing the peace he had gained for the world through his death, resurrection and ascension.

For Jesus has now gone to the Father. He told Mary he was ascending, and he now comes to them having gone away. As he said in John 16:7 'it is to your advantage that I go away, for if I do not go away, the Advocate will not come to you; but if I go, I will send him to you.'

As Jesus comes to them having gone up to the Father, he now gives them the Holy Spirit. In fact, he breathes on them the gift of the Holy Spirit, since in Greek the word for breath and the word for Spirit are the same. So, he says 'Receive Holy Breath'. *They* are now where his Spirit on earth is, they are now *his* physical body.

'²⁶*A week later his disciples were again in the house, and Thomas was with them. Although the doors were shut, Jesus came and stood among them and said, "Peace be with you."* ²⁷ *Then he said to Thomas, "Put your finger here and see my hands. Reach out your hand and put it in my side. Do not doubt but believe."* ²⁸ *Thomas answered him, "My Lord and my God!"* ²⁹ *Jesus said to him, "Have you believed because you have seen me? Blessed are those who have not seen and yet have come to believe."'* John 20:26-29

A week later Jesus comes to his disciples again. I wonder what that week had been like for them? They have a growing sense that there is more for them to do, but they don't really yet know what that will look like. Thomas is with them again, having missed out the week before, and not at all sure that his friends aren't just a little bit bonkers.

Then Jesus comes and brings his peace to them again. Thomas, sees and believes, not just that Jesus is no longer dead, but that he is what he said he was all along – God with them. It is Thomas who puts into straightforward words what they have all come to see, Jesus is God, just as his Father is God.

Back in Galilee

'¹*After these things Jesus showed himself again to the disciples by the Sea of Tiberias; and he showed himself in this way.* ² *Gathered there together were Simon Peter, Thomas called the Twin, Nathanael of Cana in Galilee, the sons of Zebedee, and two others of his disciples.* ³ *Simon Peter said to them, "I am going fishing." They said to him, "We will go with you." They went out and got into the boat, but that night they caught nothing.*

⁴ *Just after daybreak, Jesus stood on the beach; but the disciples did not know that it was Jesus.* ⁵ *Jesus said to them, "Children, you have no fish, have you?" They answered him, "No."* ⁶ *He said to them, "Cast the net to the right side of the boat, and you will find some." So, they cast it, and now they were not able to haul it in because there were so many fish.* ⁷ *That disciple whom Jesus loved said to Peter, "It is the Lord!" When Simon Peter heard that it was the Lord, he put on some clothes, for he was naked, and jumped into the sea.* ⁸ *But the other disciples came in the boat, dragging the net full of fish, for they were not far from the land, only about a hundred yards off.*

⁹ *When they had gone ashore, they saw a charcoal fire there, with fish on it, and bread.* ¹⁰ *Jesus said to them, "Bring some of the fish that you have just caught."* ¹¹ *So Simon Peter went aboard and hauled the net ashore, full of large fish, a hundred fifty-three of them; and though there were so many, the net was not torn.* ¹² *Jesus said to them, "Come and have breakfast." Now none of the disciples dared to ask him, "Who are you?" because they knew it was the Lord.* ¹³ *Jesus came and took the bread and gave it to them and did the same with the fish.* ¹⁴ *This was now the third time that Jesus appeared to the disciples after he was raised from the dead.'* John 21:1-14

The beach near Tabgha, the traditional site of the appearance of Jesus after the resurrection

John doesn't tell us how long after the events at Passover this takes place. All we know is that the disciples have gone home, back to Galilee. Here, Simon Peter, in the lead as ever, decides he may as well go fishing. So, seven of them get in the boat and go out into the night, and achieve precisely nothing.

As they are heading back to the shore, they see someone on the beach, who gives them advice on fishing. This is the only time in John's gospel that the disciples are depicted as fishing. In John 6 they have had a boat available to get them across the Sea of Galilee, and we know from the other gospels that they were active fishermen when Jesus called them. But John told us of Peter and John meeting Jesus when they were in Judea following John the Baptist.

Still, here they are, now that John the Baptist is dead and Jesus crucified, risen and ascended, gone back to the way of life they knew. Except, for all their experience they have a fruitless trip until the man on the shore tells them where to fish. Then they catch 153 fish, which while an enormous number, still don't tear the net. 153 is a triangular number, it is the sum of 1,2,3,4,5,6,7,8,9,10,11,12,13,14,15,16 and 17. It may have been the number of nations there were thought to be at the time, or it may simply have been the number of fish they actually caught, but somehow I don't see anyone really stopping to count at that point. Either way, to John it is an amazing catch, only made possible by Jesus.

The beach at Tabgha is the site traditionally thought to be the location of this meeting. Even though it is well visited, it still retains a sense of calm. Ironically there are signs forbidding barbeques today, even though that is what Jesus had on the beach when he called to the disciples. He already had fish on the charcoal fire but invited the disciples to bring some of theirs to add to the meal. Then he took bread and broke it and did the same with the fish – as he had done some years before nearby when he fed the 5000.

Jesus then took Peter aside and gently restored their relationship: '"Simon son of John, do you love me more than these?" He said to him, "Yes, Lord; you know that I love you." Jesus said to him, "Feed my lambs."' John 21:15

Some of this conversation is lost in translation to English. For in Greek Jesus asks Peter if he has agape love for Jesus and Peter replies that he has phila, friendship, love for him. The final time Jesus alters his question to Peter, to use the same word for love that Peter uses. Peter can't quite own that he has the perfect sort of love that 'agape' is, but he knows he is really devoted to Jesus in his own way. For Jesus this is enough, and Jesus gives him the role as shepherd of his sheep.

Israel in the 1st century

Nearby there is a church dedicated to the Primacy of Peter. The 1933 church includes some foundations of the 4th century church on this spot. It also surrounds a rock called the Mensa Christi, or rock of Christ, which is believed to be where Jesus laid out the food he had cooked to give to the disciples.

'20 Peter turned and saw the disciple whom Jesus loved following them; he was the one who had reclined next to Jesus at the supper and had said, "Lord, who is it that is going to betray you?" 21 When Peter saw him, he said to Jesus, "Lord, what about him?" 22 Jesus said to him, "If it is my will that he remain until I come, what is that to you? Follow me!" 23 So the rumour spread in the community that this disciple would not die. Yet Jesus did not say to him that he would not die, but, "If it is my will that he remain until I come, what is that to you?"
24 This is the disciple who is testifying to these things and has written them, and we know that his testimony is true. 25 But there are also many other things that Jesus did; if every one of them were written down, I suppose that the world itself could not contain the books that would be written.'   John 21:20-25

Mensa Christi, the table of Christ where Jesus laid the food he gave the disciples

John ends his gospel aware that there was much more he could have said, yet believing he has said enough to show who Jesus was. Perhaps it is in his name for himself throughout his gospel that he says what he knows of Jesus most clearly. To John what matters most is that he was loved by Jesus. This love is the agape love that Peter had felt he was not yet able to say he had for Jesus. This perfect, Godly, self giving love was what John had known from Jesus and by the Holy Spirit continued to know.

On the razor wire boundary of the beach at Tabgha

From Nazareth to Northumbria

Pointers to Johannine churches

From following the places where John mentions around Galilee we have found that there are aspects of John's gospel which are distinctive and may help us to spot places where his strand of teaching has had a particular influence.

1. **The value of the physical**

   'The Word became flesh and lived among us, and we have seen his glory' John 1:14

   While John gives us plenty of Jesus teaching, he makes it all grounded in particular places. For John, Jesus is the eternal Word of God made human, visible, physical in a particular time and place. So, a Johannine church will not shy away from the physical, but be happy to mark holy places with something physical.

2. **Water**

   Water appears so often in John's gospel – from the pools where John is baptising to the well at Sychar and the water poured out at the Temple celebrations. If Celtic Christianity comes from John's teaching it can be expected to value water.

3. **Teaching**

   John's gospel is structured around seven signs which are the springboard for teaching. He also records Jesus' use of 'I am' sayings, again as the heart of teaching. Any church springing from this strand of Christianity would be expected to value teaching.

These are what we will be looking for to see if it makes sense to say that the British Church came from the tradition of John.

Water bringing life in the desert at En Gedi

2. The Route from Israel to Britain

We hear little of John's life after the end of his gospel. The Acts of the Apostles focuses on Peter and Paul, so we have to look to later authors for clues as to what became of the other apostles.

Ephesus

'There are also those who heard from him that John, the disciple of the Lord, going to bathe at Ephesus, and perceiving Cerinthus within, rushed out of the bath-house without bathing, exclaiming, Let us fly, lest even the bath-house fall down, because Cerinthus, the enemy of the truth, is within.

Then, again, the Church in Ephesus, founded by Paul, and having John remaining among them permanently until the times of Trajan, is a true witness of the tradition of the apostles.'

Irenaeus Against the Heresies III.3.4

Irenaeus was the Greek born bishop of Lyon in the late 2nd century, wrote his work to defend Christianity against the ideas of those who argued that they had better hidden knowledge about Jesus and how to reach God. One of his arguments was that he could trace the knowledge he had back to John himself who knew Jesus, while these other teachers, with their 'secret' knowledge had no such link.

John presumably lived on in Galilee, teaching others about what he had known of Jesus, until the persecutions which Luke describes in Acts forced him to flee. Irenaeus, who was taught his faith by Polycarp, tells us that Polycarp had learnt from John. It was Polycarp who told Irenaeus of John's flight from the bathhouse when his opponent Cerinthus was there.

The remains of Ephesus are impressive, and even if you discount the Library of Celsus which was built in the 110s A.D., there is still plenty which would have been around in John's day. In 27 B.C. it was made the capital of the region of 'proconsular Asia', which covered what it now western Turkey. Although it is today 3 miles inland, before the harbour silted up, Ephesus was a major port. It flourished and many civic buildings were erected, including those around the two agorae, the marketplaces, and the two amphitheatres. The smaller amphitheatre, near the upper entrance to the site, was probably the site of the riot which is recorded in Acts 19, since this was where the city council met.

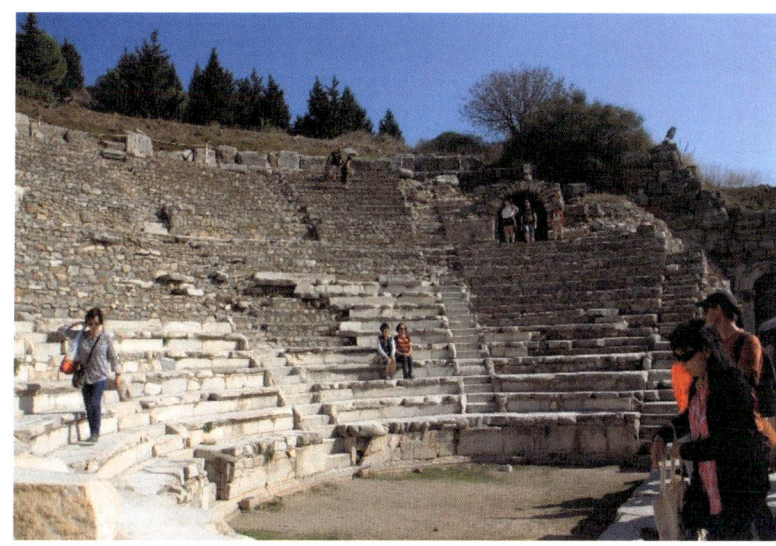

The upper amphitheatre at Ephesus

The great temple of Artemis, one of the seven wonders of the ancient world, also stood, 2 miles from the current ruins. All that remains today is one reconstructed column. Much of the material was robbed in the 6th century to make the Byzantine Basilica of St John.

A Chi Rho carved into the stone at Ephesus

The temple of Artemis

Ephesus' glory days came to an end in 262 A.D. when it was attacked by Goths. It was rebuilt but declined as the harbour silted up. From the time when Apollos worked in the city, and then Paul visited, the church grew. John the Apostle settled here and was known as the Elder of the Church in Asia. Signs of these days are to be found in graffiti etched into the stones of the city.

When John died, he was buried on the Ayasoluk Hill, which dominates modern Selcuk and is about 2 miles from the Ephesus Archaeological Park. The name of the hill, and the name of the town until 1914, is a corruption of Agios Theologios,

The early Byzantine Church on Ayasoluk Hill

the Holy Theologian, which was the name of the church dedicated to St John by emperor Justinian I. An early Byzantine church (5th century) was built near the top of the hill, perhaps on the site of John's house in the suburbs of ancient Ephesus where he wrote his gospel. Only the apse of this remains; it was converted into a cistern when the top of the hill became a fort in the 13th -14th century when the Seljuk Turks settled in the area. The grander basilica which is built around St John's tomb dates from the 6th century, and was built at the direction of Justinian I. The tomb of St John is between the four pillars in front of the apse.

John taught here in Ephesus, and some of his students became bishops for other cities in Asia Minor among them Polycarp who was the Bishop of Smyrna.

Smyrna

'I can speak even of the place in which the blessed Polycarp sat and

The tomb of St John in the Byzantine church

disputed, how he came in and went out, the character of his life, the appearance of his body, the discourses which he made to people, how he reported his intercourse with John and with the others who had seen the Lord, how he remembered their words, and what were the things concerning the Lord which he had heard from them, and about their miracles, and about their teaching, and how Polycarp had received them from the eyewitnesses of the word of life' Fragment of a Letter of Irenaeus to Florinus, preserved in Eusebius Ecclesiastical History V.XX

'For this is the manner in which the apostolic churches transmit their registers: as the church of Smyrna, which records that Polycarp was placed therein by John; as also the church of Rome, which makes Clement to have been ordained in like manner by Peter.' Tertullian Prescription Against Heretics 32

Tertullian lived in Carthage, in what is now Tunisia in north Africa between 155 and about 240 A.D. Like Irenaeus he tells us of Polycarp as part of the reason that the mainstream churches were to be taken teaching the truth about Jesus is that they can show the line of people who passed the teaching on.

The remains of ancient Smyrna are to be seen in the Archaeological Park in Izmir, in Western Turkey. Today to get from Selcuk where the ruins of Ephesus are to Izmir with its remains of Smyrna is an hours train journey. In Polycarp's day it was a short hop on a boat around the Cesme Peninsula. The remains in Izmir are of the agora (the commercial centre) of Smryna. Most of what is there is from the rebuilding after an earthquake in the second century. But the marbles steps and pillars may well be the same as the ones Polycarp walked on and looked at.

The Route from Israel to Britain

We know about Polycarp both from Irenaus and Tertullian, and we also have the letter he wrote to the Philippians, and an account of his death, the Martydom of Polycarp.

In the fragments of Irenaeus' works which Eusebius preserves in his Ecclesiatical History we learn that:

'when the blessed Polycarp was sojourning in Rome in the time of Anicetus, although a slight controversy had arisen among them as to certain other points, they were at once well inclined towards each other [with regard to the matter in hand], not willing that any quarrel should arise between them upon this head. For neither could Anicetus persuade Polycarp to forego the observance [in his own way], inasmuch as these things had been always [so] observed by John the disciple of our Lord, and by other apostles with whom he had been conversant; nor, on the other hand, could Polycarp succeed in persuading Anicetus to keep [the observance in his way], for he maintained that he was bound to adhere to the usage of the presbyters who preceded him. And in this state of affairs they held fellowship with each other; and Anicetus conceded to Polycarp in the Church the celebration of the Eucharist, by way of showing him respect; so that they parted in peace one from the other, maintaining peace with the whole Church, both those who did observe [this custom] and those who did not.' Eusebius Ecclesiastical History V. XXIV, 11-18.

The Agora at Smyrna

The basement of the agora buildings in Smyrna

This is a good example of disagreeing well, but this disagreement over when to keep Easter, a key issue between the followers of John's tradition and the Roman Church, would continue for many centuries to come, not always being dealt with so generously.

Locations of the early churches in Asia Minor, today in Turkey

Kadifekale Mount in Izmir in the 1880s

From Nazareth to Northumbria

Polycarp died around 155 A.D., martyred in the stadium in Smyrna. This is not visible today, but Strabo, writing his Geography in the earliest years of the 1st century A.D. of the Ionian league tells us about Smyrna: 'The city was in ancient times round the Athenaeum, which is now outside the city near the Hypelaeus, as it is called; so that Smyrna was near the present gymnasium, behind the present city'. If this gymnasium is the stadium of Polycarp's day, then Polycarp died on the slopes of the mountain on which the oldest part of the city sits, called in Turkish Kadifekale and in Greek Pagos.

'Now, as Polycarp was entering into the stadium, there came to him a voice from heaven, saying, Be strong, and show yourself a man, O Polycarp! No one saw who it was that spoke to him; but those of our brethren who were present heard the voice. And as he was brought forward, the tumult became great when they heard that Polycarp was taken. And when he came near, the proconsul asked him whether he was Polycarp. On his confessing that he was, [the proconsul] sought to persuade him to deny [Christ], saying, Have respect to your old age, and other similar things, according to their custom, [such as], Swear by the fortune of Caesar; repent, and say, Away with the Atheists. But Polycarp, gazing with a stern countenance on all the multitude of the wicked heathen then in the stadium, and waving his hand towards them, while with groans he looked up to heaven, said, Away with the Atheists. Then, the proconsul urging him, and saying, Swear, and I will set you at liberty, reproach Christ; Polycarp declared, Eighty and six years have I served Him, and He never did me any injury: how then can I blaspheme my King and my Saviour?....

The proconsul then said to him, I have wild beasts at hand; to these will I cast you, unless you repent. But he answered, Call them then, for we are not accustomed to repent of what is good in order to adopt that which is evil; and it is well for me to be changed from what is evil to what is righteous.
But again the proconsul said to him, I will cause you to be consumed by fire, seeing you despise the wild beasts, if you will not repent.

But Polycarp said, You threaten me with fire which burns for an hour, and after a little is extinguished, but are ignorant of the fire of the coming judgment and of eternal punishment, reserved for the ungodly. But why do you tarry? Bring forth what you will.

While he spoke these and many other like things, he was filled with confidence and joy, and his countenance was full of grace, so that not merely did it not fall as if troubled by the things said to him, but, on the contrary, the proconsul was astonished, and sent his herald to proclaim in the midst of the stadium thrice, Polycarp has confessed that he is a Christian....

Then it seemed good to them to cry out with one consent, that Polycarp should be burnt alive. For thus it behooved the vision which was revealed to him in regard to his pillow to be fulfilled, when, seeing it on fire as he was praying, he turned about and said prophetically to the faithful that were with him, I must be burnt alive....

When he had pronounced this *amen*, and so finished his prayer, those who were appointed for the purpose kindled the fire. And as the flame blazed forth in great fury, we, to whom it was given to witness it, beheld a great miracle, and have been preserved that we might report to others what then took place. For the fire, shaping itself into the form of an arch, like the sail of a ship when filled with the wind, encompassed as by a circle the body of the martyr. And he appeared within not like flesh which is burnt, but as bread that is baked, or as gold and silver glowing in a furnace. Moreover, we perceived such a sweet odour [coming from the pile], as if frankincense or some such precious spices had been smoking there.

At length, when those wicked men perceived that his body could not be consumed by the fire, they commanded an executioner to go near and pierce him through with a dagger. And on his doing this, there came forth a dove, and a great quantity of blood, so that the fire was extinguished; and all the people wondered that there should be such a difference between the unbelievers and the elect, of whom this most admirable Polycarp was one, having in our own times been an apostolic and prophetic teacher, and bishop of the Catholic Church which is in Smyrna. For every word that went out of his mouth either has been or shall yet be accomplished.

These things Caius transcribed from the copy of Irenaeus (who was a disciple of Polycarp), having himself been intimate with Irenaeus. And I Socrates transcribed them at Corinth from the copy of Caius. Grace be with you all.

And I again, Pionius, wrote them from the previously written copy, having carefully searched into them, and the blessed Polycarp having manifested them to me through a revelation, even as I shall show in what follows. I have collected these things, when they had almost faded away through the lapse of time, that the Lord Jesus

The Route from Israel to Britain

Christ may also gather me along with His elect into His heavenly kingdom, to whom, with the Father and the Holy Spirit, be glory for ever and ever. Amen.'
The Martyrdom of Polycarp 9,11,12,15,16,22

So, while John died of old age in the 1st century, Polycarp was killed, in the mid-2nd century, refusing to renounce his faith. The ending of the martyrdom shows how important it was to the early writers to show where they had their information from, to underline its authenticity.

Lyons, Irenaeus

'For, after our Lord rose from the dead, [the apostles] were invested with power from on high when the Holy Spirit came down [upon them], were filled from all [His gifts], and had perfect knowledge: they departed to the ends of the earth, preaching the glad tidings of the good things [sent] from God to us, and proclaiming the peace of heaven to men, who indeed do all equally and individually possess the Gospel of God. Matthew also issued a written Gospel among the Hebrews in their own dialect, while Peter and Paul were preaching at Rome, and laying the foundations of the Church. After their departure, Mark, the disciple and interpreter of Peter, did also hand down to us in writing what had been preached by Peter. Luke also, the companion of Paul, recorded in a book the Gospel preached by him. Afterwards, John, the disciple of the Lord, who also had leaned upon His breast, did himself publish a Gospel during his residence at Ephesus in Asia.

2. These have all declared to us that there is one God, Creator of heaven and earth, announced by the law and the prophets; and one Christ the Son of God. If anyone does not agree to these truths, he despises the companions of the Lord; nay more, he despises Christ Himself the Lord; yea, he despises the Father also, and stands self-condemned, resisting and opposing his own salvation, as is the case with all heretics.' Irenaeus Against Heresies (AH) III.3.1-2

Although he was a Greek born in Smyrna in about 130 A.D. into a Christian family, Irenaeus became the second bishop of Lugdunum (Lyons) in Gaul (France). He died in Lugdunum in about 202.

Lugdunum was founded as a Roman city *Colonia Copia Felix Munati* in 43 B.C., but by the end of the first century A.D. its name reverted to Lugdunum, a latinised version of the Gaulish Lugudunon which means hill or fortress of the god Lugh, and is probably the name of a prior settlement on the site. This god Lugh appears in medieval Irish literature, and as 'Llew' in medieval Welsh tales. The name changed to Lyons over time.

The Roman Theatre in Lyons

Irenaeus' only complete surviving book is Against Heresies. The heresy in particular is Gnosticism, the term comes for the Greek word gnosis which means knowledge. This is a group of teachings which claimed that they are superior to ordinary people who are part of the Church. The Church is for people who are still only of the material part of creation. The Gnostics themselves are in tune with the spiritual part, through their knowledge. So much so that it doesn't matter what the do with their physical bodies, since they are only part of the material world which will be lost at the end of all things. What matters is the spiritual self.

To counter their views Irenaeus does several things.
First, he summarises the teachings of the Church, and says that this is the teaching wherever the church is:

'The Church, though dispersed through our the whole world, even to the ends of the earth, has received from the apostles and their disciples this faith: [She believes] in one God, the Father Almighty, Maker of heaven, and earth, and the sea, and all things that are in them; and in one Christ Jesus, the Son of God, who became incarnate for our salvation; and in the Holy Spirit, who proclaimed through the prophets the dispensations of

From Nazareth to Northumbria

God, and the advents, and the birth from a virgin, and the passion, and the resurrection from the dead, and the ascension into heaven in the flesh of the beloved Christ Jesus, our Lord, and His [future] manifestation from heaven in the glory of the Father "to gather all things in one," and to raise up anew all flesh of the whole human race, in order that to Christ Jesus, our Lord, and God, and Saviour, and King, according to the will of the invisible Father, "every knee should bow, of things in heaven, and things in earth, and things under the earth, and that every tongue should confess" to Him, and that He should execute just judgment towards all; that He may send "spiritual wickednesses," and the angels who transgressed and became apostates, together with the ungodly, and unrighteous, and wicked, and profane among men, into everlasting fire; but may, in the exercise of His grace, confer immortality on the righteous, and holy, and those who have kept His commandments, and have persevered in His love, some from the beginning [of their Christian course], and others from [the date of] their repentance, and may surround them with everlasting glory.' AH (I.10.1)

This is one of the oldest statements of faith there is. And for Irenaeus it doesn't matter whether you are very intelligent and so able to follow and grasp the Gnostics teachings or rather dim and so not able to, because we are saved by what God has done for us, not by how well we can gain knowledge of some complicated system.

Then he points out that there are a lot of different Gnostic schools, each with a different scheme for the deeper knowledge you need– so how do you know which is the real system, the real knowledge to have? Whereas all over the world there is one Church with one faith.

To back this up he shows how the apostles chose bishops for the churches, and that if there had been any extra hidden knowledge surely the apostles would have taught it to these bishops. He then gives the succession at Rome, seeing it as 'the very great, the very ancient, and universally known Church founded and organized at Rome by the two most glorious apostles, Peter and Paul; as also [by pointing out] the faith preached to men, which comes down to our time by means of the successions of the bishops. For it is a matter of necessity that every Church should agree with this Church, on account of its pre-eminent authority, that is, the faithful everywhere, inasmuch as the apostolical tradition has been preserved continuously by those [faithful men] who exist everywhere.' AH III.3.2

Irenaeus then gives his own apostolic credentials through Polycarp: 'But Polycarp also was not only instructed by apostles, and conversed with many who had seen Christ, but was also, by apostles in Asia, appointed bishop of the Church in Smyrna, whom I also saw in my early youth, for he tarried [on earth] a very long time, and, when a very old man, gloriously and most nobly suffering martyrdom, departed this life, having always taught the things which he had learned from the apostles, and which the Church has handed down, and which alone are true. To these things all the Asiatic Churches testify, as do also those men who have succeeded Polycarp down to the present time,-a man who was of much greater weight, and a more steadfast witness of truth, than Valentinus, and Marcion, and the rest of the heretics.' AH III.3.4

He confidently believes that what he has been taught is the true faith because he can trace it back to the apostles, just as the Church in Rome can trace the same faith back to Peter and Paul.

As we have seen from what he wrote about Polycarp over the timing of Easter he knows that there are different traditions of how and when things are done in the church, but not in the faith that is proclaimed.

So, we have traced the Christian faith, as witnessed by John the Apostle around Israel/Palestine, to Ephesus, Smyrna and Lugdunum. But how does it get to Ireland from there, so that the Celtic Christians can claim that their traditions go back to St John?

Here the documents fade away, but the archaeological evidence gives us some clues as to what happened next.

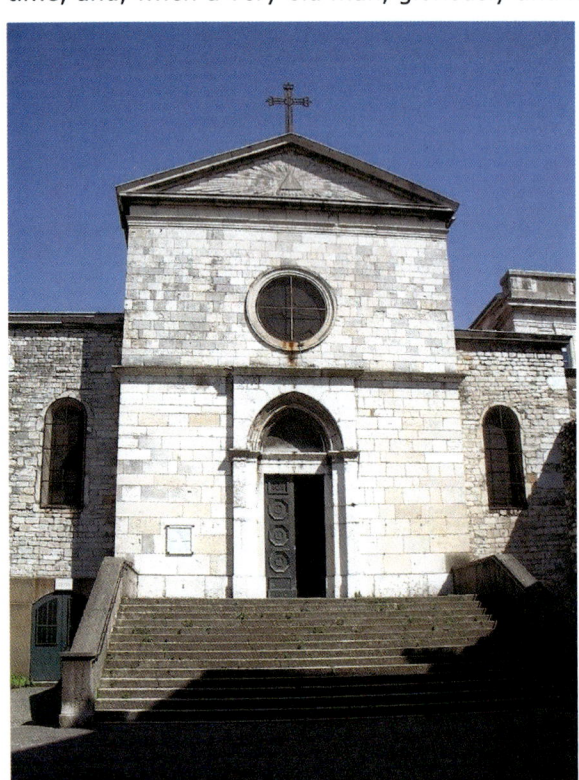

St Irenaeus Church Lyons

The Route from Israel to Britain

How Christianity reached Britain

We have traced the tradition of John from Israel/Palestine through Turkey to Lyons in France. There is evidence that there were Christians in Manchester by 182 A.D. How did Christianity reach them?

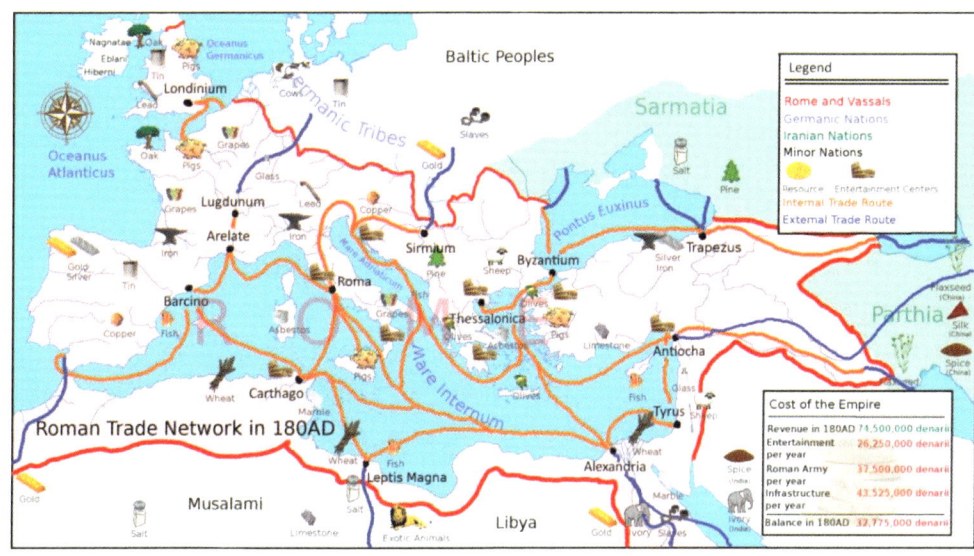

There are two routes that are suggested. The first is one which follows trade routes from the Eastern Mediterranean to Western Britain, via the Straits of Gibraltar. When road travel was on foot with pack animals the route across land was slow and dangerous. While having dangers too, the sea routes were quicker, and larger cargoes could be carried.

Roman Trade Network in 180A.D. (used under CC license from Wikipedia)

Since the Phoenicians began trading by sea in about 1200 B.C. or earlier there was a route from the southwest of Britain to bring tin to the eastern Mediterranean. Between the Phoenicians and the Greeks, colonies were founded along the western Mediterranean coasts to ease the trade in raw materials.

By the middle of the Roman Empire trade, trade networks also used overland roads and, more effectively, river networks. Although the above map does not show it there was a route across France using the River Rhone which brought goods from the south to Lugdunum(Lyon), the capital of the province, and from there a comparatively short cross country route to the River Loire, down to the Bay of Biscay and across the sea to Britain.

In this way, Britain was well integrated into the trade networks of the Roman Empire. We have evidence of this in the museums of towns which have a Roman past. For example, in the Corinium

Major rivers of France which were used to transport goods

museum in Cirencester there is a Samian Ware pottery bowl. This a type of pottery that was produced in South Gaul from the 1st century on. The British Museum has about 1000 examples of this imported pottery, so clearly trade with France was significant. It is likely that ideas flowed with trade, and so Christianity was introduced to the British who were in Gaul collecting goods, or by the Gauls visiting Britain to sell, telling their contacts of the new ideas.

Gaulish Samian Ware bowl found in Leaholme Fort in 1961, now in the Corinium Museum, Cirencester.

47

Christianity in Roman Britain

3. Christianity in Roman Britain

Cirencester

'by this time, the varied races of the Gætulians, and manifold confines of the Moors, all the limits of the Spains, and the diverse nations of the Gauls, and the haunts of the Britons — inaccessible to the Romans, but subjugated to Christ, and of the Sarmatians, and Dacians, and Germans, and Scythians, and of many remote nations, and of provinces and islands many, to us unknown, and which we can scarce enumerate?'

Tertullian An Answer to the Jews 7

The origins of Christianity in Britain are unclear. By the time he wrote his book about a debate between a Christian and someone who had chosen to become a Jew, Tertullian believed that Christianity had reached even parts of the British Isles that the Romans had not conquered. Tertullian lived from c155 – c240 A.D. in Carthage, in what is now Tunisia. Although he lived his life there, and wrote many books about Christianity, he knows that Christianity has spread far and wide. He may of course have just mentioned the places where the Britons live as a rhetorical flourish, since to someone living on the southern shores of the Mediterranean the British Isles would have seemed the end of the world. However, Carthage, as the capital of the Roman province of Africa, had a good harbour and would have had plenty of travellers come through to tell of life elsewhere.

Although this is inconclusive evidence, there are other clues about the presence of Christianity in Britain by the end of the second century A.D.

In Cirencester in Gloucestershire is the Corinium Museum. In 44 A.D., a year after the Roman invasion of Britain, a fort was established near hillfort of Bagendon, which was the tribal centre the Dobunni. In the 70s, the fort was no longer needed by the military and became a town which was the centre of the administration for local area and was named Corinium Dobunnorum. The street plan developed over next 20 years to include two agorae (marketplaces), baths, and private houses. An amphitheatre was also built.

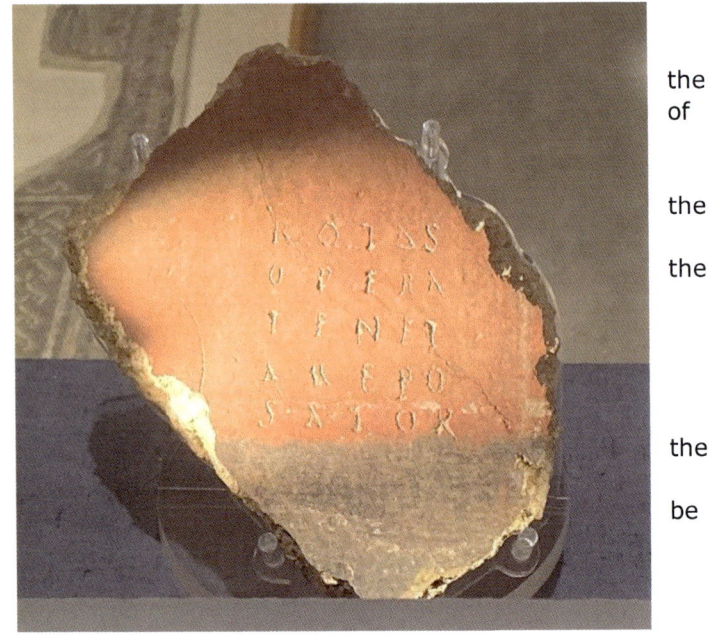

In one of the townhouses an acrostic was scratched into the wall plaster sometime during 2nd century. When the main town was abandoned in 430 the house collapsed, only to

the of

the

the

the

be

The Cirencester ROTAS square

excavated when the area of Victoria Road was dug in 1868. Today it is on display in the Corinium Museum.

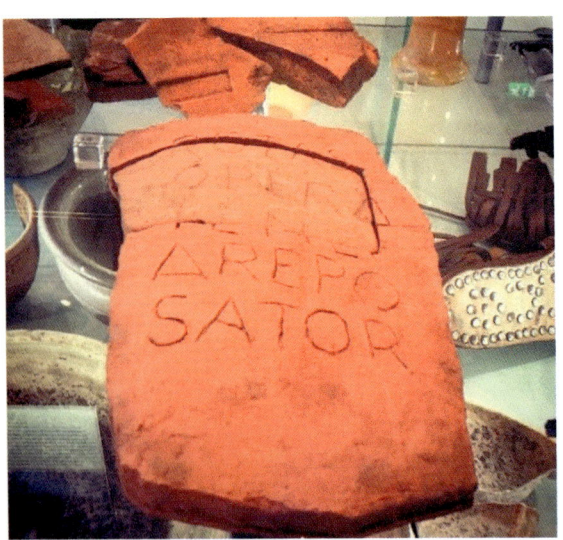

The graffiti has been recognised as a ROTAS square. A similar ROTAS square was found on a fragment of tile in Manchester in the 1970s, and from the layering of the deposits above and below, this has been dated very precisely to 182 A.D. The fragment may be older than that since it may have been made some time before it broke and was thrown away, but it cannot be younger than this. So, we know for sure that there were people using this acrostic in both Corinium and at the Mancunium Fort in what would become Manchester.

Manchester ROTAS square

From Nazareth to Northumbria

The square has been found in the ROTAS form and in the reverse form by which is it more commonly known, which begins with the word SATOR. Since it can be used in either form, clearly the people using it were not particularly bothered by its face value meaning. It translates as something like 'Arepo the sower holds the work wheels', which doesn't make a lot of sense anyway.

The oldest dateable versions were found in Pompeii and in Heraculaneum. In the latter city the square was scratched into a black sandstone pillar at the large palaestra (gymnasium) near the amphitheatre. This must be older than 79 A.D. when these cities were buried in a volcanic eruption.

These squares have been found in many different places. Four were found in the excavations at Duro-Europos in what is now Syria, which also had a house church with frescos which dated to the 3rd century. (These were removed by the excavation team from Yale University and so have escaped being destroyed in the Syria civil war.) One was found in a 4th century house underneath S Maria Maggiore in Rome.

Some think the SATOR square has a Jewish background or may find its roots in the worship of the god Mithras. However, where it has been found on a religious building, it is on a church. So, it seems to have been accepted as a Christian symbol by those who later built churches and used it as a decoration on them.

Looking at the letters it is clear that apart from the central N, the other letters are either duplicated or for O and A there are four of each in the set of letters. The reason for this becomes clear if a double anagram is solved.

The extra two As represent Alpha and the Os Omega. The other letters form Pater Noster, the Latin for Our Father.

The ROTAS square of Corinium and of the Mancunium Fort are evidence of Christianity in Britain as early as the late 2nd century.

Further Reading: (Thomas, Christianity in Roman Britain to AD500 1981)

Caerleon Julius and Aaron

The excavated barracks block at Caerleon

Christianity in Roman Britain

'God, therefore, as willing that all men should be saved, magnified his mercy unto us, and called sinners no less than those who regard themselves righteous. He of His own free gift, in the above-mentioned time of persecution, as we conclude, lest Britain should be completely enveloped in the thick darkness of black night, kindled for us bright lamps of holy martyrs. The graves where their bodies lie, and the places of their suffering, had they not, very many of them, been taken from us the citizens on account of our numerous crimes, through the disastrous division caused by the barbarians, would at the present time inspire the minds of those who gazed at them with a far from feeble glow of divine love. I speak of Saint Alban of Verulam, Aaron and Iulius, citizens of Caerleon, and the rest of both sexes in different places, who stood firm with lofty nobleness of mind in Christ's battle.' Gildas, On the Ruin and Conquest of Britain

Gildas writing in the mid-6th century of the parlous state of Britain in his day, with the Saxons, who had been invited to help the Britons against the Picts and Scots, having become an internal enemy. To remind the current princes and clergy whom he is berating of the heights from which they have fallen, he gives a brief history of Britain, from just before the Roman Conquest. Christianity having come to these shores, he notes the martyrs, whose names he knows, and suggest that there are others too. Gildas assigns their martyrdoms to the time of Diocletian, but for Aaron and Julius this is unlikely since the fort at Caerleon was no longer in use then.

The Amphitheatre at Caerleon

Aaron and Julius, citizens of Caerleon, is all we know about these two men, who Gildas tells us died for their faith. So little is known that some have questioned if they even existed. However, by the ninth century there was definitely a chapel dedicated to these two men in Caerleon, when it was mentioned in a land charter.

Caerleon itself was dominated in the 3rd century by the Roman Fort. Remains of one of the barracks blocks, the baths, and the amphitheatre are visible today. The Fort was built in 74 A.D. and was the permanent home of the Legion II Augusta until it was moved to Richborough in Kent in the late 280s. The youngest item found in the excavation of the baths in the 1970s dated to 287 A.D.

The amphitheatre built in 90 A.D. could seat over 6000, more than the number of men in the Legion, so presumably local civilians were allowed in to enjoy the entertainment.

By calling Aaron and Julius citizens Gildas may imply they were civilians in the town which grew up around the fort. But Gildas thought they died in the Diocletian persecutions, which is unlikely since the fort had been abandoned 20 years before then, and as for Alban, it is unlikely that an Eastern Emperor's decree affected the far West of the Empire. More likely is a mid-3rd century date.

The name Aaron is unusual at this time and may mean that he was a Jewish Christian. However, Julius was a very common name for soldiers, or the children of soldiers.

All we know for sure then is that Christianity had spread at least as far as the western most fort in Britain, probably by the mid-3rd century.

Since the locals could use the baths, while we don't know if Julius and Aaron were occupants of the barracks we can see today, we can be fairly sure they bathed at the baths and enjoyed themselves at the amphitheatre, until the day that they themselves became the focus of the crowd.

Part of the Baths complex at Caerleon

From Nazareth to Northumbria

St Albans

'This Alban, being yet a pagan, at the time when the cruelties of wicked princes were raging against Christians, gave entertainment in his house to a certain clergyman, flying from the persecutors. This man he observed to be engaged in continual prayer and watching day and night; when on a sudden the Divine grace shining on him, he began to imitate the example of faith and piety which was set before him, and being gradually instructed by his wholesome admonitions, he cast off the darkness of idolatry, and became a Christian in all sincerity of heart. The aforesaid clergyman having been some days entertained by him, it came to the ears of the wicked prince, that this holy confessor of Christ, whose time of martyrdom had not yet come, was concealed at Alban's house. Whereupon he sent some soldiers to make a strict search after him. When they came to the martyr's house, St. Alban immediately presented himself to the soldiers, instead of his guest and master, in the habit or long coat which he wore, and was led bound before the judge…. St. Alban, who had voluntarily declared himself a Christian to the persecutors of the faith, was not at all daunted at the prince's threats, but putting on the armour of spiritual warfare, publicly declared that he would not obey the command. Then said the judge, "Of what family or race are you?" "What does it concern you," answered Alban, "of what stock I am? If you desire to hear the truth of my religion be it known to you, that I am now a Christian, and bound by Christian duties." "I ask your name," said the judge; "tell me it immediately." "I am called Alban by my parents," replied he; "and I worship and adore the true and living God, who created all things." Then the judge, inflamed with anger, said, "If you will enjoy the happiness of eternal life, do not delay to offer sacrifice to the great gods." Alban re-joined, "These sacrifices, which by you are offered to devils, neither can avail the subjects, nor answer the wishes or desires of those that offer up their supplications to them. On the contrary, whosoever shall offer sacrifice to these images shall receive the everlasting pains of hell for his reward." Being led to execution, he came to a river, which, with a most rapid course, ran between the wall of the town and the arena where he was to be executed. He there saw a multitude. of persons of both sexes, and of several ages and conditions, who were doubtlessly assembled by Divine instinct, to attend the blessed confessor and martyr, and had so taken up the bridge on the river, that he could scarce pass over that evening. In short, almost all had gone out, so that the judge remained in the city without attendance. St Alban, therefore, urged by an ardent and devout wish to arrive quickly at martyrdom, drew near to the stream, and on lifting up his eyes to heaven, the channel was immediately dried up, and he perceived that the water had departed and made way for him to pass. Among the rest, the executioner, who was to have put him to death, observed this, and moved by Divine inspiration hastened to meet him at the place of execution, and casting down the sword which he had carried ready drawn, fell at his feet, praying that he might rather suffer with the martyr, whom was ordered to execute or, if possible, instead of him.

While he thus from a persecutor was become a companion in the faith, and the other executioners hesitated to take up the sword which was lying on the ground, the reverend confessor, accompanied by the multitude, ascended a hill, about 500 paces from the place, adorned, or, rather clothed with all kinds of flowers, having its sides neither perpendicular, nor even craggy, but sloping down into a most beautiful plain, worthy from its lovely appearance to be the scene of a martyr's sufferings. On the top of this hill, St. Alban prayed that God would give him water, and immediately a living spring broke out before his feet, the course being confined, so that all men perceived that the river also had been dried up in consequence of the martyr's presence. Nor was it likely that the martyr, who had left no water remaining in the river, should want some on the top of the hill, unless he thought it suitable to the occasion. The river having performed the holy service, returned to its natural course, leaving a testimony of its obedience. Here, therefore, the head of the most courageous martyr was struck off, and here he received the crown of life, which God has promised to those who love Him. But he who gave the wicked stroke, was not permitted to rejoice over the deceased; for his eyes dropped upon the ground together with the blessed martyr's head.' Bede Ecclesiastical History of the English People (EH) I.7

The Theatre at Verulamium

Christianity in Roman Britain

'The first of these martyrs, St. Alban, for charity's sake saved another confessor who was pursued by his persecutors, and was on the point of being seized, by hiding him in his house, and then by changing clothes with him, imitating in this example of Christ, who laid down his life for his sheep, and exposing himself in the other's clothes to be pursued in his stead. So pleasing to God was this conduct, that between his confession and martyrdom, he was honoured with the performance of wonderful miracles in presence of the impious blasphemers who were carrying the Roman standards, and like the Israelites of old, who trod dry-foot an unfrequented path whilst the ark of the covenant stood some time on the sands in the midst of Jordan; so also the martyr, with a thousand others, opened a path across the noble river Thames, whose waters stood abrupt like precipices on either side; and seeing this, the first of his executors was stricken with awe, and from a wolf became a lamb; so that he thirsted for martyrdom, and boldly underwent that for which he thirsted.' Gildas On the Ruin of Britain (6th century)

When the Romans made Britain part of their empire, they found in what is now Hertfordshire a settlement called Verlamion, which was the tribal centre for the Catuvellauni. Under the Romans it developed into the significant city of Verulamium, the ruins of which can be seen in the Verulamium Park, downhill from St Alban's Cathedral.

Here Alban lived, and met a 'confessor' who was being threatened during a bout of persecution. We know of what happened to Alban due to a 5th century account of his Martyrdom known as the Passio Alban. There are six surviving manuscripts with three slightly different versions. The oldest existing copy dates from the 8th century. A visit to the Shrine of St Alban by Germanius when he came from Gaul to help sort out Pelagianism in Britain is mentioned in the Vita Germani, which was written by Constantius of Lyon about 480 A.D. These are the sources which were embellished by Gildas and in his turn Bede as they wrote about the British Church in the Roman period.

While Gildas sees Alban as going across the Thames before his Martyrdom, his cult grew up on a hill outside Verulamium. This geography fits with the older version of the story of St Alban's death in the Passio Albani.

A walk in Verulamium Park, allows you to see some of the walls of the town that Alban would have seen, and to visit the theatre he may have visited. A visit to the Cathedral, permits a view of the shrine of the martyr, in all its medieval glory.

Alban was executed for protecting a fellow Christian, but there is debate as to when this happened. The earliest suggestion is that it was in 209 A.D. since in the Turin version of the Passio Albani the Emperor Severus is mentioned as the one who had Alban killed:

The shrine of St Alban

'Alban received a fugitive cleric and put on his garment and his cloak that he was wearing and delivered himself up to be killed instead of the priest… and was delivered immediately to the evil Caesar Severus.'

Severus was in Britain from 208 to 211 so this is possible, but it may be that the words 'evil Caesar Severus' were added later, to a version which just had the word judge. The latest that Alban could have been martyred is in the persecutions of Diocletian in the years following 303 A.D. Such a date is made unlikely by the fact that Diocletian was the Eastern Roman Emperor appointing Maximian in the West. So, the persecutions of the 3rd century are the most likely time for Alban's death.

Whenever Alban was martyred it is clear that by the mid-5th century there was a significant cult around his tomb, and his death is a witness to the presence of Christianity in Britain before the 4th century.

Silchester

A pleasant 11-mile cycle from Reading, through the villages of Grazely Green and Stratfield Mortimer, brings you to the church of St Mary Silchester. Next to the church are visible the walls and amphitheatre of Calleva Atrebatum, the town which was fortified by the Romans.

The chief of the Atrebates had already established his tribal centre here and fortified it with earthworks. Under Roman rule, the classic grid pattern was used for the town and the walls built to protect the town which

From Nazareth to Northumbria

was at a major crossroads. Unlike most Roman towns in Britain it was abandoned after the 7th century and not the site of later building. You can walk around the walls or go and sit in the amphitheatre and imagine the crowds roaring around you.

The first excavations on the site were in 1866 by Revd James Joyce, Rector of the nearby village of Stratfield Saye, who discovered 'the Silchester eagle'. The site was explored more extensively in the period between 1890 and 1909, and the layout of the town was discovered. During these excavations a building with an apse and a geometrical mosaic were discovered. Since 1980 the University of Reading has been re-exploring the site.

Roman walls at Silchester

Silchester Amphitheatre

There has been debate about whether the building first identified as a church in the 1890s really could have a been a church, partly because the style of mosaic is similar to that popular in the 2nd century. However the shape of the building is the same as that which would become common in subsequent centuries for churches ad the lack of pictures in the mosaic is unusual. If it is a church, then we have a solid sign of Christians worshipping publicly in what would become Hampshire.

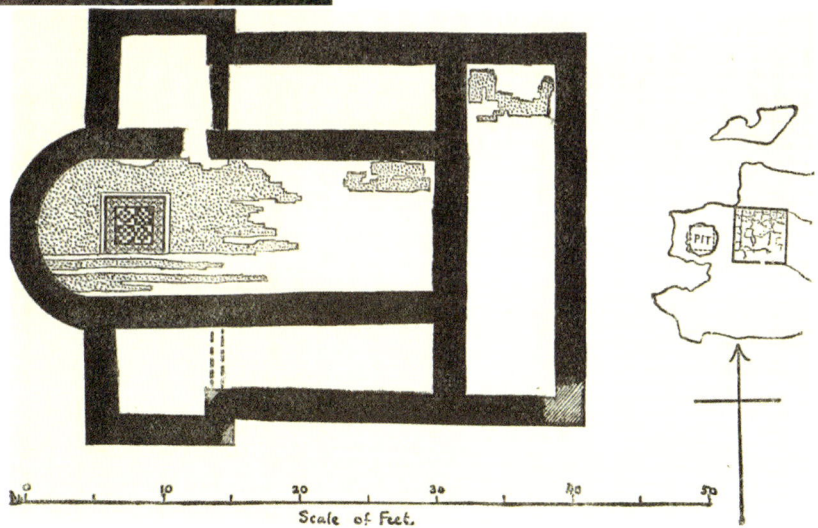

A plan of the church at Silchester from the 1893 excavations

Christianity in Roman Britain

Lincoln

'Eborius, bishop of the city of York (de civitate Eboricensi) in the province of Britain.
Restitutus, bishop of the city of London (de civitate Londenensi), in the province above mentioned.
Adelfius, bishop in the city of Lincoln (de civitate Colonia Londenensium)
Sacerdos, priest.
Arminius, deacon.'

Among the signatories at the Council of Arles (Charles Munier 1963)P14-22

In 314, the year after Christianity was made a legal religion in the Empire by the Edict of Milan, a Council was called by Constantine for the bishops of his area of the Empire. The presenting problem was the conflict in Carthage, between those who had buckled under persecution and those who believed that the church had to be made up only of the pure. The latter group followed Donatus Magnus, and were incensed at the ordination of Caecilian as bishop of Carthage by Felix of Aptungi. Felix had handed over holy books during the persecutions commanded by Diocletian in the early 300s, and so was a 'traditor'. From this Latin word, which means someone who hands something over, we get our words tradition and traitor.

Those who opposed the ordination by a traditor arranged their own ordination of a bishop, first Majorinus, and on his death in 313 A.D., Donatus Magnus.

In 312 they went to Rome to appeal to the Church there to support their cause. But they were disappointed when a meeting of Italian Bishops found in favour of Caecilian. So, they appealed to Constantine, and so set a precedent for later councils which the Emperor called.

Constantine required bishops from Gaul, Rome, Sicily and Africa to attend at Arles, then called Arelate, in southern Gaul. Among the bishops, possibly as part of the Gaullish group, were three from Britain. We know this since the bishops were called on to subscribe to the decisions of the Council, and their names and cities were reproduced on copies of the original document. Over the years an error crept into the copying and the third bishop Adelfius was said to be of Colonia Londenensium. Since there was nowhere of this name in Britain, it is likely that the scribe has been confused by having just written Londenensi. The most likely place name to have been corrupted in this way is Colonia Linsenensium, also known as Lindum Colonium, now Lincoln.

The Donatists lost the argument, since while the council agreed to depose from the clergy anyone who was a traditor, it affirmed that what they had done as clergy, even after they had handed over the books was still valid. So, despite Felix's failings, what he had done in ordaining Caecilian still stood.

The interest in this for Britain is that we had at least three bishops in this period, who must have been ordained as bishops before the Edict of Milan in 313. There were clearly also priests and deacons, since one of each accompanies the British party. The church in Britain had an organisation.

It was in the 1970s that it was decided to knock down the Victorian church of St Paul in the Bail in Lincoln. Since it was known the church stood on the remains of at least one other church, the archaeologists got to work. When they had

Open space at St Paul in the Bail, the bricks show the outline of the Roman Church

From Nazareth to Northumbria

removed the late medieval layers, they found early medieval burials, and beneath them a wooden church over the foundations of a stone church with an apse. This is probably a Roman period church and may be where the bishop who was at Arles spent much of his time.

The site was left as an open space, with the outline of the earliest church marked with bricks.

Water Newton

One of the glass cases in Room 49 of the British Museum holds the Water Newton Hoard.

In February 1975, while walking across a ploughed field a metal detectorist, Alan Holmes, spotted a large black pot. He unearthed 9 silver vessels and 19 plaques and on consulting a local archaeologist, John Peter Wild, they realised they had a major find. The site was in the north east part of the site of the Roman town Durobrivae, which was on Ermine Street where it crossed the River Nene.

The Peterbough Archaelogy website suggests that the silverwear which is clearly Christian was in use in the 3rd century.

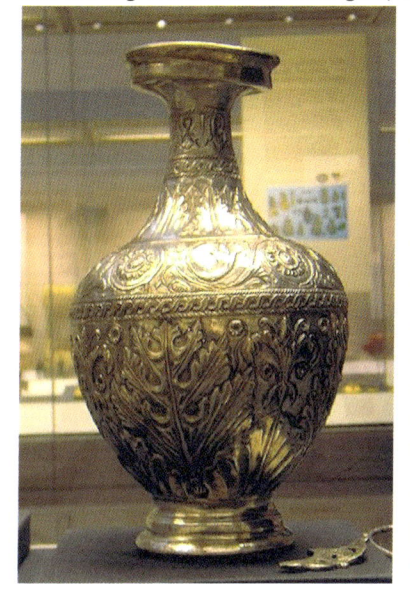

Flagon in the Water Newton hoard

Water Newton hanging bowl

The bowls include two with incriptions. One reads SANCTUM ALTARE TUUM DOMINE SUBNIXUS HONORO and has the name Publianus on the base. Put together this translates as 'O Lord, I Publianus, relying on you, honour your holy altar'. The words are between two chi rhos. Another reads 'Innocentia and Viventia offered this'.

The silver plaques have a triangular form and are very similar to those found associated with non-Christian temples. These are clearly Christian, since they bear the chi rho. One has an inscription 'Anicilla has fulfilled the vow she promised'.

Clearly all these items were gifts to the church, but the bowls were probably useful too. The third bowl does not have an inscription but is carefully decorated. The decoration continues all the way under the bowl and the bowl has rings so it can be hung. It is likely that it was designed to be hung at head height. Hanging bowls are a vital piece of evidence for Christianity in the post Roman period. This bowl is more intricately decorated than later ones. The form of decoration is similar to that in the Chaourse treasure, found near the village of that name in northern France, which is dated to the third century, and is also in the British Museum.

The oldest communion chalice anywhere

The Publianus bowl

55

Christianity in Roman Britain

If the treasure was used in the third century this is an amazing find. It shows that people were meeting for Christian worship including Holy Communion in a Roman town and using valuable silver. Where they met had an altar, and so is likely to have been a dedicated church. So, while Christianity was not yet fully recognised as a religion in the Roman Empire, in Britain it was becoming part of the urban scenery.

Offertory flags with chi rho on display in the British Museum

London

Until an excavation in the 1990s there was little evidence for Christianity in London, despite it being the capital of Roman Britain. Then in 1992 and 1993 the Museum of London Archaeological Service carried out an excavation at Colchester House, north west of Tower Hill, in the south east of the Roman City of London. Unfortunately, the building had been robbed out after it went out of use, so there wasn't much for the excavators to find. But what they found was enough to know that they had the north-east corner of a large, aisled building, 50 m wide, and about 80 to 100m long. Fragments of marble and window glass show that the building had been splendidly decorated. From the pottery found in the remains of the building it has been dated to the mid fourth century.

Nothing was found in the building to give a certain pointer to what it was used for, so it was suggested that it could have been a large granary or a cathedral. However, a large granary would be unlikely to be decorated with marble! Also, work on the coins which have been found in the building by James Gerrard of Newcastle University shows that the pattern of dates when the coins were lost matches well the pattern of known religious sites of the period.

Further Reading: (Gerrard 2010)

Lullingstone

To discover more of Christianity in Britain in the Roman period we need to look at the traces it has left.

Among the more dramatic of these is the villa at Lullingstone in Kent. Built in the Darent Valley, just south of the intersection of the M25 and the M20, this villa was in use for over 300 years. It was first constructed at the end of the 1st century, and extended and modified over subsequest centuries before going out of use in

From Nazareth to Northumbria

the 5th century. It lay under the soil until it was excavated in the 1950s. The excavators found in one area the wall plaster in thousands of pieces, which when put together showed the decorations of a house church. The row of people praying with hands rised was not unlike the frescos of the Christian catacombs of Rome, and the Chi-Rho ws unmistakeable as a christian symbol. The room they decorated was made in the 330s over a lower room that had been used for non-Christian worship, and may have continued to be used in that way.

So we have clear evidence of Christians worshipping in Kent in the mid 4th century

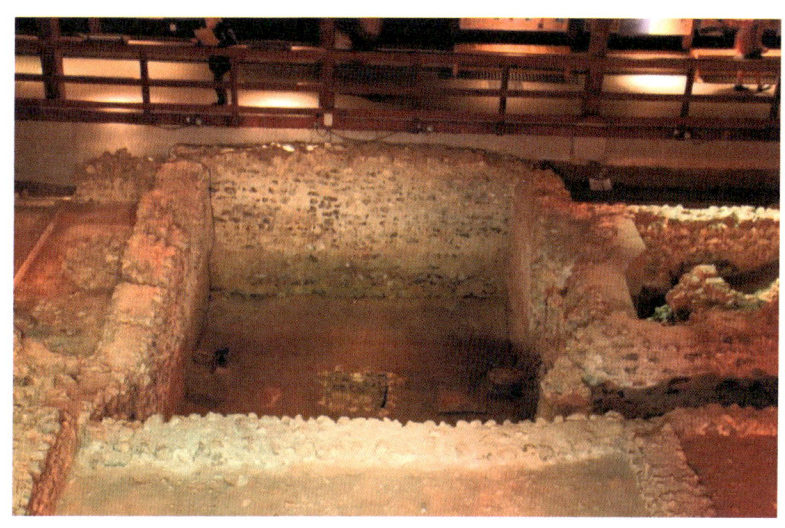

The 'house church' at Lullingstone

The people praying, now in the British Museum

The Chi Rho fresco, now in the British museum

Colchester

"Late Roman apsidal building situated next to a large Roman inhumation cemetery (MCC481) and interpreted as a church. Aligned E to W, with apse at east end, c.7.5m wide x 24.80m long; the apse was added c.AD 380. Now consolidated and on display to the public. The building was prominently placed on the slope above a small valley which runs E to W immediately outside the town walls and would have been visible from Head Gate. The building stood on what was probably the north-west corner of the Butt Road cemetery and was built in an area where burials seem absent (with one exception). No graves seem to have existed to the west of the church and the steepness of the slope to the north makes it probable that none existed to the north. The building did not suffer full-scale demolition at the end of the Roman period but survived as a ruin.

The outer walls of the church … were of stone which was probably plastered and painted inside. There were internal partitions or colonnades of timber, some of which incorporated wattle and daub. The roof was of tile. No evidence was found for solid floors of any kind. The building probably incorporated some carved stone and a veneer of Purbeck Marble and Purbeck burr. The building has been heavily damaged in post Roman times and it is conceivable that traces of flooring or window glass could have been lost. The walls were of mortared greensand and tile. A large number of coins found during the various excavations indicate that a major phase of coin loss equates with the construction of the church started sometime between AD 320 and 340 and lasted until the end of the century. Internal features included two possible burials and various post holes relating to the aisles and a possible north-south partition." https://colchesterheritage.co.uk/monument/mcc476

(An apisidal building is one which has an apse, a curved area at one end. The first churches built had such an apse, so an apsidal building may well be an early church)

Christianity in Roman Britain

The Roman Church at Colchester

Within a few years of the Edict of Milan (312 A.D.) in which Christianity became legal in the Western Roman Empire a church was built in the corner of a cemetery outside the walls of Camulodunum, the Roman town which today is Colchester. The cemetery, when fully excavated, had over 1000 graves, of which about 2/3rds were West-East aligned. The vast majority had been buried in wooden coffins, although a couple had lead coffins. The West-East graves were laid out regularly in rows, and date to a later phase than the graves which were more or less North South. They also had fewer grave goods – only 2% were accompanied by such goods, compared to 30% in the earlier graves. The move to West East burial is significant since this is the direction of burial of Christians in their churchyards down the centuries. The reason was so that at the resurrection when Jesus returned the person would be facing Jerusalem and Jesus. The reduction in grave goods is due to the change in understanding of the afterlife, since Christians did not believe they could take anything into heaven, and would not need anything from this life there.

Most of the graves were probably dug after the church was built, but others pre-date it. It was been deliberately built over one of the graves; perhaps there is another British martyr whose name is unknown to us here, or it may be that the grave is that of the founder of the church in Camulondunum.

Roman Britain evidence

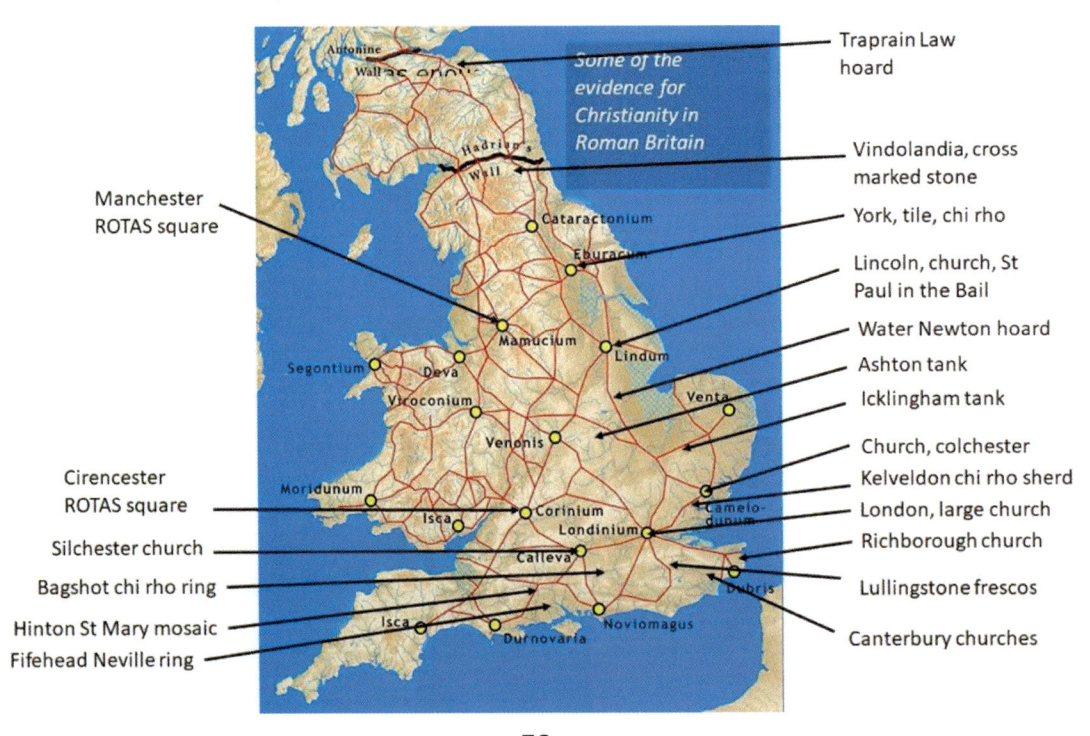

We have seen the ROTAS squares from Cirencester and Manchester, churches at Lincoln and Silchester, Colchester and London, the hoards from Water Newton and Mildenhall and the frescos from Lullingstone But there are other physical remains of Roman era Christianity in Britain. The map below shows the distribution of some of the evidence.

(Thomas, Christianity in Roman Britain to AD500 1981), mapped the finds that were then available and showed that the evidence is strongest in Kent and the southeast of England, with further areas around York and Hadrian's wall. This is unsurprising since Roman culture was most accepted in the southeast and in areas of significant troop deployment.

Hinton St Mary

In 1963 Walter White decided to explore his garden a bit more. In doing so, he uncovered a large mosaic, the centrepiece of which is on display in the British Museum. It shows a Roman figure, with the chi rho behind his head. While it is possible that the figure is meant to be Constantine, it is more likely that this is a Roman British image of Jesus Christ.

The building from which the mosaic was lifted remains unexplored, so it is not clear what the room that the mosaic occupied was used for. It could have been the dining room of a villa, or this could be evidence of a 4th century house church. Either way this splendid mosaic shows an allegiance to Christianity in what would become Dorset.

Mosaic of Christ, Hinton St Mary, now in the British Museum

Icklingham

If you go to Room 49 of the British Museum to see the Hinton St Mary Mosaic and the Lullingstone frescos, you will also find other evidence of Christianity in Roman Britain. In the corner, tucked behind the façade of a building from Meonstoke is a large lead tank. It is one of three that were found in the excavation of a cemetery and early church at Icklingham in Suffolk. It is clearly marked with a W, a chi rho and an A. If the W and A are probably meant to be omega and alpha, and this could be an early baptistry. If so, it would could have been the place that the candiate stood while water was poured over their head. This is known as baptism by affusion (from the Latin word 'affusio' meaning to pour.

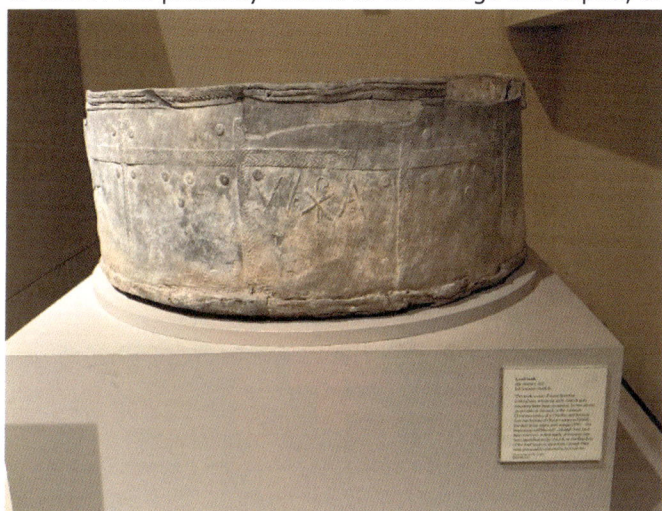

Twelve such lead tanks have been found in England, half of which have the chi rho on them. The lead tank which was found at Walesby, in Lincolnshire and is in the Collection Museum in Lincoln, bears a chi rho. It also has a frieze on it showing someone about to be baptised. It was deliberately broken up before it was abandoned, presumably at the end of its useful life.

Lead tank from Icklingham on display in the British Museum

Christianity in Roman Britain

Chedworth Roman Villa, Gloucestershire, Nymphaeum

For much of the villa's life the owners were content to worship traditional gods. They had a water shrine, or nyphaeum, built, which is fed by a spring. The shrine was decorated with statues of the water spirits, the nymphs. But in the late 4th century the then owner removed them and had a chi rho engraved on one of the coping stones. The nymphaeum was now a spring fed baptistry.

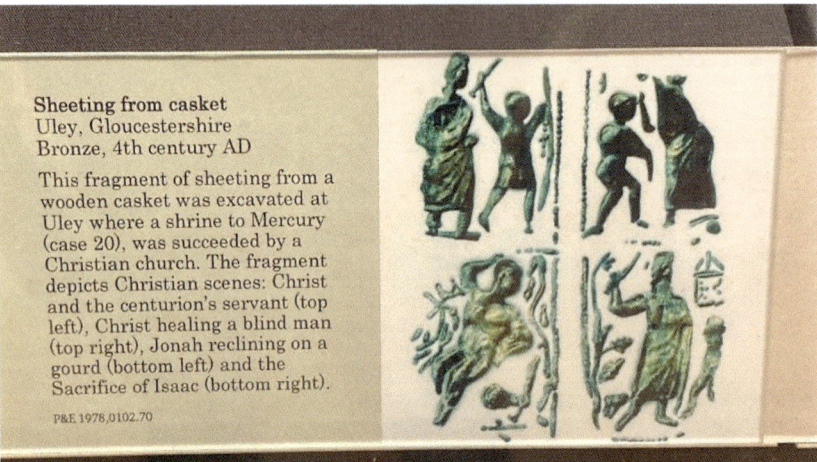

A casket was found at the Roman Villa at Uley and a sheet from it is displayed in Room 49 in the British Museum.

Biddulph spoon, 4C

Other portable finds include toothpicks, including this one found in Canterbury, made in the 4th century. Spoons are also found with the chi rho on them, including this one from Biddulph in Staffordshire.

This ring was engraved in reverse and so was intended to be used to mark wax as a seal. It was found with another similar ring in Brentwood in Essex. The bird sitting in a fruiting tree was adopted from the cult of Bacchus, into Christianity. This ring is also on display in Room 49, British Museum.

Canterbury 4C toothpick

Brentwood signet ring

60

From Nazareth to Northumbria

Near the ring is displayed a 'crossbow' brooch, with a boar's head (or possibly it is a horse's head) decoration. The boar has two glass eyes. But the more interesting part of the piece is the design on the head covering the spring. For this is a cross with a rho head as part of it.

Crossbow brooch with cross and rho decoration, 4th to 5th century Sussex

In the same room is this pewter plate from Stamford, Lincolnshire, dated to the 4th century. The close up of the decoration shows that some of the crosses have been adapted to be chi rhos.

Stamford pewter plate 4th century A.D.

An interesting group of objects which show Christian symbols are belt buckles and strap ends. Belts were an important way in which people, particularly men, showed their status.

On the buckle a peacock and tree of life is a recognised Christian symbol. The peacock was adopted by Christians early as a symbol of immortality, since the ancient greeks believed that the flesh of the peafowl did not decay. Bronze belt buckles with a peacock and the tree of life have been found at Cave's Inn Farm in Warwickshire, Penycorddyn in Clwyd, Harlow in Essex, Stanwick in North Yorkshire and Wortley in Gloucestershire. A particularly fine example was found in Tripontium, just outside modern Rugby.

The peacock and tree of life also appear on strap ends, including two at Wavedon Gate Roman settlement in Milton Keynes, Kenchester in Herefordshire, Monkton Deverill in Wiltshire, Rivenhall in Essex, Thrapston in

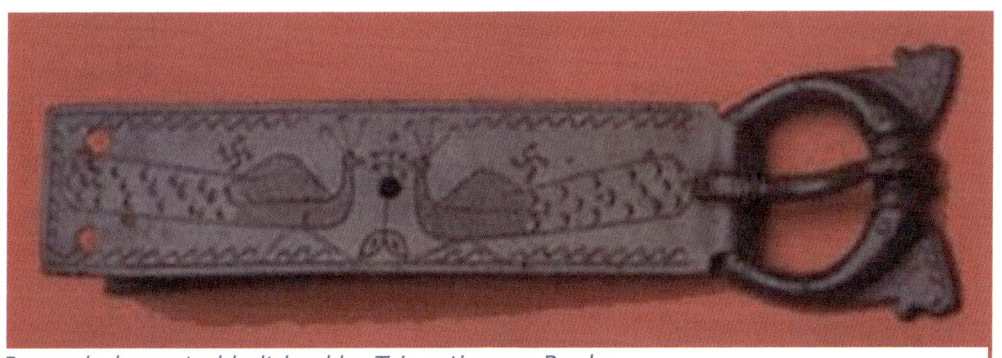

Peacock decorated belt buckle, Tripontium nr Rugby

Christianity in Roman Britain

Northamptonshire, and a peacock on it's on at Orton Longueville in Cambridgeshire and Rushall Down Wiltshire.

Richborough Saxon Shore Fort

Richborough is on the River Stour just outside Sandwish in Kent. It is about a mile inland, and was probably one of the bridgeheads when the Romans invaded Britain. The Romans called the port they built here Rutupiae and built a road from here which became Watling Street. At Durovernum (Canterbury) this road met with others from the ports of Dubris (Dover), Lemanis (Lympne), and Regulbium (Reculver). The military moved on from the port once it was well established and a town grew up where their accommodation had been. Towards the end of the 3rd century the fort was built as part of the fortifications along the English Channel, on both sides to defend against Saxon pirates.

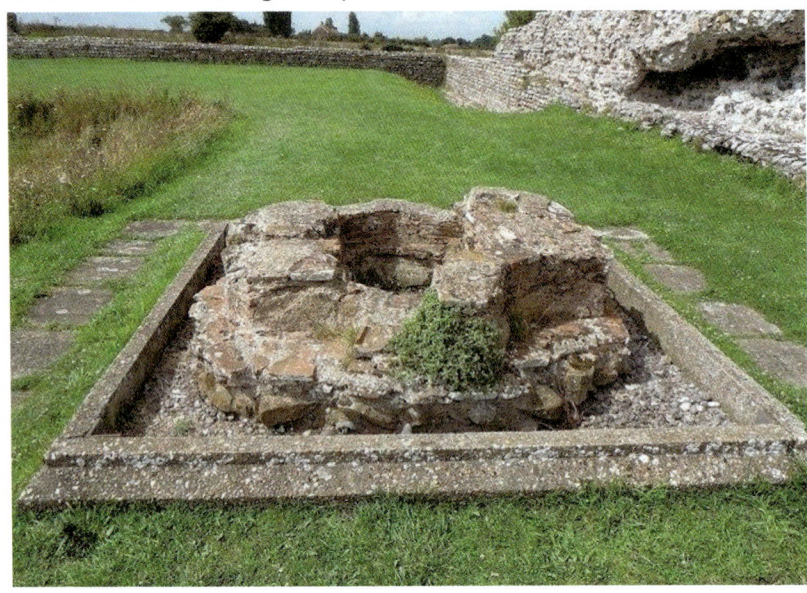

In the surface layers cleared to enable the excavation in 1931 a shard of pottery with a chi-rho was found as well as a ring with a chi rho and inscription (Kevin Greene A Christian Monogram from Richborough, Kent in Britannia Vol. 5 (1974), pp. 393-395). In 1923 an excavation of two trial trenches found a hexagonal structure, measuring 7ft 4in by 6 ft 6in, made of tile and mortar. The exterior was covered in pink plaster 2/3 in thick, the interior was 3 ft 2 in by 2 ft and covered also in pink plaster. There was a chase cut through the east side down to the floor level of the interior and the excavators felt this probably had had a lead pipe when the structure was in use. So, they decided it was a tank or a water feature, probably in a garden. However, the structure was built within a fort – where there are unlikely to be gardens!

© *Rob Farrow and licensed for reuse under CC BY-SA 2.0*

P.D.C. Brown compared it to those found near three 5th century churches in Europe and decided that it was most likely to be a font or baptistry. As was common in this period, the candidate would stand in the baptistry and have water poured over them.
(Brown 1971)

View across Richborough Fort, Image © Acabashi, Creative Commons CC-BY-SA 4.0, Wikimedia Commons

From Nazareth to Northumbria

Traprain Law

Traprain Law is a distinctive hill, near Haddington in East Lothian Scotland. It was used as a hill fort from about 1000 B.C., occupied on and off over the subsequent years. From the mid-3rd century A.D., it was the capital of the Gododdin tribe, known as the Votadini by the Romans, until the mid-5th century when the site was abandoned, possibly in favour of Din Eidyn, Castle Rock in Edinburgh.

From 1914 to 1923 it was excavated, and the remains of stone and timber houses were found under the turf. The most impressive find was made in

Traprain Law, East Lothian

1919 when the Traprain Law treasure was unearthed. There were over 250 pieces of silver objects, many of which were cut up, either so that the silver could be shared, or to get it ready for reuse. From coins found in the treasure the date at which it was buried is thought to be in the early fifth century. (Gallic coins were discovered with the hoard; one of the emperor Valens (364-378), three of Arcadius(394-408, Eastern Roman Emperor) and one of Honorius (395-423, Western Emperor)).

Among the objects are items that are clearly Christian, including a wine strainer with a pierced chi rho, and the words IESUS CHRISTUS just below the rim and a spoon with a small chi rho in the bowl. The narrow-necked flask has depictions of Adam and Eve, the adoration of the Magi, Moses striking the rock and another less obvious scene.

The hoard may be the result of the Romans paying off the Gododdin to stop them raiding south of the boarder, or may be the payment for mercenaries which were hired by the people living south of the wall to defend them from raid from the Picts who lived north of the Gododdin.

They show that there were Christians in the north of Britain. Most likely they were among those who made this payment. But possibly the Christian material is not part of the payment at all but was used by the Gododdin themselves. This is not impossible, since Christians such as Ninian and Patrick went from Roman Britain to the north and the west with the message of Christ.

Chi Rho marked items in the Traprain Law hoard

63

Uley, Gloucestershire

On a high point of the Cotswold escarpment near Stroud in south Gloucestershire is West Hill, Uley. Between 1977 and 1979 English Heritage excavated this site and the findings were published in 1993 (Leach and Woodward 1993) and make interesting reading. What was found was a sacred place that had been used from Pre-history to the 7th or 8th century.

In the Neolithic age standing stones were erected, while in the Iron Age two timber shrines were built. A 2nd century B.C. stone Roman-Celtic temple came next, which was altered in the 4th century. Other buildings were found around the central shrine, which from the votive offerings and other small finds seems to have been dedicated to Mercury. In the 5th century this was knocked down and its contents buried elsewhere in the site. On the place where the shrine had stood a timber church was built, with an octagonal baptistry alongside it. Some of the post holes which were dug to support the timber pillars of the church contained broken up parts of previous cult statues. They had been deliberately destroyed and then put to practical use supporting the new church. In time this was replaced by a smaller stone church, but the baptistry continued as before. The stone church was extended, and an apse added, probably not very long after it was built in the late 5th or early 6th century. This building had parts of a statue of Mercury broken up and used as its foundations. When this church was in turn knocked down it had fragments of 7th or 8th century red-streaked window glass. It was followed by a series of wooden framed buildings, before the site was given over to agriculture.

The timber basilica was given an enclosing bank, which formed an oval precinct, similar to the ones found in early Christian sites in Ireland and so may be a sign that this became an ecclesiastical settlement in the 5th or early the century. The replacement of the timber church by a stone one which then continued in use until the late 7th or 8th century shows that once this became a church site it stayed one for about 300 years.

From Nazareth to Northumbria

4. Christianity after the Romans in Western Britain

Carmarthen Museum

'Then all the councillors, together with that proud tyrant Gurthrigern [Vortiporius], the British king, were so blinded, that, as a protection to their country, they sealed its doom by inviting in among them like wolves into the sheep-fold), the fierce and impious Saxons, a race hateful both to God and men, to repel the invasions of the northern nations. Nothing was ever so pernicious to our country; nothing was ever so unlucky.' Gildas, On the Ruin of Britain II.23

Gildas wrote his work 'On the Ruin of Britain' in the early part of the 6th century, sometime between 510 and 540 A.D. as a tirade against the leaders of his country both religious and secular. He clearly views the Britain he knows as Christian but writing in the tradition of the Biblical prophets sees it as fallen away from the true ways of God's people.

In his work he first gives a brief narrative of British History from the coming of the Romans to his own day, including the pleas of the Britons for help from the Roman armies against their northern neighbours.

Having set the scene in the first part of his work he goes on to decry five British kings: Constantine, Aurelius Conanus, Vortiporius, Cuneglas, and Maelgwn.

Constantine was king of Dumnonia, who is also recorded in the genealogies of that people. Dumnonia covered Devon and Cornwall and some of Somerset. Aurelius Conanus is otherwise unknown, while Cuneglasus, or Cynlas Goch was a prince of Rhos in Gwynedd, Wales, known in the Welsh form in the genealogies of Gwynedd. Maelgwn is known from other records to have been a High King in Gwynedd, being seen as senior to many other rulers, including those of the Scottish Coast. He was a founder of churches but is also upbraided by Gildas. Finally, Vortiporus was a king in Dyfed, now Pembrokeshire. Little is known about him, but he appears in Irish genealogies as Guortipir, and is said to be descended from Eochaird Allmuir who lead the settlement of some of the Deisi of Ireland in Dyfed in about 270 A.D.

In the Carmarthenshire Museum, at Abergwilli near Carmarthen stands a stone that was found in 1895 near the church in Castell Dywran. It has a cross and a dedication in both Ogham and Latin.

The Latin reads *Memoria Voteporigis Protictoris*, which translates to

Monument of Voteporigis the Protector

The Ogham reads Votecorigas

The Voteporigis stone, Carmathenshire Museum

Some modern scholars doubt this is the same person as mentioned in Gildas since there the name is Vortiporius, but having seen a lot of inscribed stones I can well believe that the same name could have been written down with and without a 'r'. Spelling had not been standardised in the 6th century. If so, this is a physical reminder of the king of Dyfed, who was one of those who thought that the Saxons could be controlled as mercenaries.

Llandough

'In 1994 Cotswold Archaeology undertook an archaeological excavation adjacent to the church of St. Dochdwy at Llandough near Cardiff (NGR: ST 1681 7331). It was quickly realised that a major cemetery had been found, and excavation over an area of 0.22 ha revealed 1026 burials. The present church of St Dochdwy largely dates to the mid-19th century but has long been considered to overlie the site of one of the major early-medieval monasteries of Glamorgan. Excavations to the south of the church in 1979 had found a Roman villa which was occupied until the early 4th century AD.'
https://archaeologydataservice.ac.uk/archives/view/llandough_cadw_2004/

Christianity after the Romans in Western Britain

There are clues in the churchyard of St Dochdwy's in Llandough, near Cardiff, that this is an ancient site. The most obvious is the cross shaft in the churchyard. This has been dated to the late tenth or early 11th century. The other hint is that the churchyard boundary is curved – this is a common feature of pre-Norman churchyards.

But it took the development of the surrounding area as a housing estate for the oldest evidence to come to light – a 4th century Roman villa and an early medieval graveyard.

The remains were radiocarbon dated. The earliest dated to between 370 and 640 A.D., the latest to 885 -1035 A.D. Shards of imported amphorae (large wine containers) were found in 5 of the graves, which from their style could be dated to the late 5th or early 6th century. So, evidence had been found of the people who lived in the early medieval monastery of Llandough, which first appears in records in the mid-7th century but is likely to date from the late 5th century or early 6th century.

It is common for Early Medieval cemeteries to be found near Roman Villas in Western Europe, although few have been found in Britain.

The sex and age of the burials is interesting. 30% of the bodies are definitely male and 25% definitely female, the rest are a bit too broken up to be sure. 26% are children, so this community was not one of only celibate men which we think of when we use the word

Cross base at St Dochdwy's church, Llandough

monastery. But in Wales historical evidence shows that clergy were married, and celibacy was not expected of people committed to God's service. The cemetery at Llandough suggests that this 'monastery' was a community of men and women living together, getting married, having children, but being committed to their common life of worship of God and service to others.

Further Reading: (Holbrook and Thomas 2005)

(Knight 2005)

Margam

Close to Margam Abbey and the ruins of the Abbey buildings is a Victorian School House which is now a museum of a collection of carved stones, which date from the 6th to the 16th century. They bear witness to the richness of the Christian culture of this area of Wales.

The oldest of the stones are three with Latin inscriptions.

The red sandstone milestone was set up on the Roman Road near Port Talbot in the early 4th century. In the 6th century it was turned upside down and used as a grave marker – the later inscription reads

HIC IACIT CANTVSVS PATER PAVLINVS

translates as 'Here lies Cantusus – his father was Paulinus'

Roman milestone reused as a gravestone in the 6C, Margam Stones Museum

From Nazareth to Northumbria

At first sight there is nothing particularly Christian about this. However, the use of 'HIC IACET' 'here lies' is typical of Christian burials in Gaul at this time, so this formula is accepted as a sign of a Christian grave marker. Another pointer is the fact that it is in Latin. The further West we go in Wales the less impact the Romans had as such, but the British Church used Latin as the language of worship.

The Pumeius or Kenfig Stone is inscribed in Latin: PUMPEIVS CARANTORIVS (An expansion of this gives '[The stone of] Pumpeius, [son of] Carantorius'). These are a Roman and a Latinised British name. It was inscribed in the 6th century and erected on the road to Kenfig 2 miles south of Margam.

The stone is also marked in ogham. This is a script that developed in the 4th or 5th century among Irish speakers to enable them to record Irish. This stone has two Ogham inscriptions:
(top left) transliterates as P[AM]P[E]S (taken to be a repetition of 'Pumpeius')
(right side) ROL[ACU]N M[A]Q ILL[U]NA (translated as 'Rolacun son of Illuna', two Irish names).

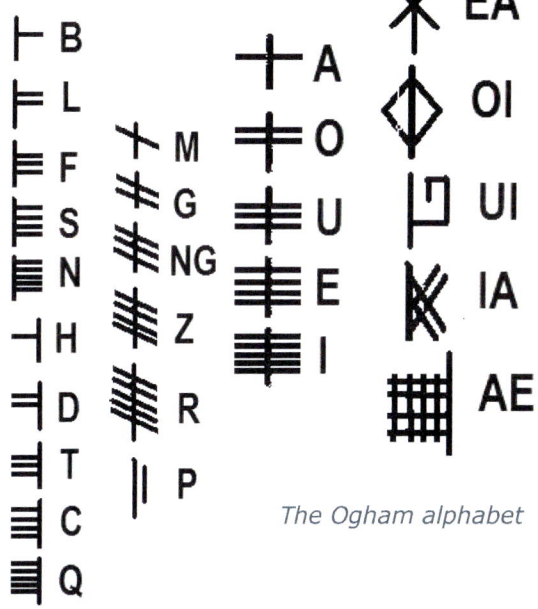

Ogham is a script that was developed for carving rather than writing. The edge of a stone or a stick forms a vertical reference line, and the lines etched to one side, or the other, or across the reference line represent letters.

The Ogham alphabet

Kenfig stone

The inscription is carved from the bottom upwards, over the top and down the other side.

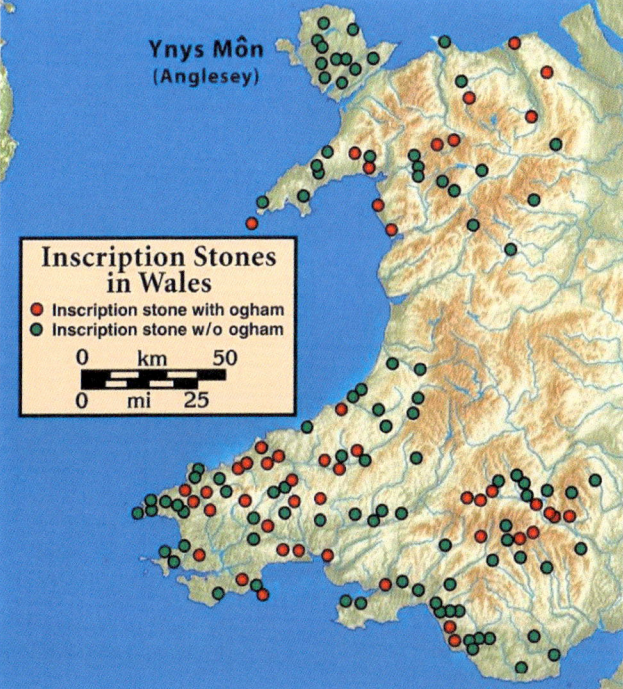

According to a medieval book called the Briatharogam the letters are named for trees. So, B is beith, the Irish for birch, L is Luis, meaning blaze, and understood to be the rowan. Inscribed stones of the 5th to 7th centuries are found in many places across the south of Wales, and a few in the north of Wales as well. This shows that people who could read Irish were living across these areas.

The third stone in the area which was inscribed in the late 6th century, or possibly the early 7th century, and records four generations of the same family. It was set up on Margham mountain on a pre-historic barrow, probably to tie the family to the ancient dwellers in the area, and so reinforce their claim to land ownership. From this stone we know the names for people who lived in the Margham area in the 6th century, and the oldest may have been alive in the 5th century. The inscription reads

BODVOCI HIC IACIT FILIUS CATOTIGIRNI PRONEPUS ETERNALI VEDOMAVI

The Bodvoc Stone

Christianity after the Romans in Western Britain

which translates as '[The Stone] of Bodvoc. Here he lies, son of Cattegern [or Cattegirn], and great-grandson of Eternalis Vedomavus'. The oldest of these men had a Latin name, Eternalis Vedomavus. The name Eternalis was probably Christian, and his great-grandson was certainly remembered with this Christian grave marker.

These three stones show that there was a Christian community in the Margam area in the 5th to 7th centuries. This community continued into later centuries and produced more memorials. At first these were simple crosses carved into stones, such as the 8th or 9th century Thomas Pillar.

In the 9th century the carvers developed a more elaborate style. The cross of Einion was carved in the late 9th century and set up at Margam, the first physical evidence of the Christian settlement here, which later developed into Margam Abbey. The inscription reads

CRUX XPI +ENNIAUN P[RO] ANIMA GUORGORET FECIT

'The Cross of Christ +Enniaun for the soul of Guorgorest had this made'
The Margam Stones Museum holds several other fine crossed which were erected in the area in the 10th and 11th centuries including the cross of Conbelin

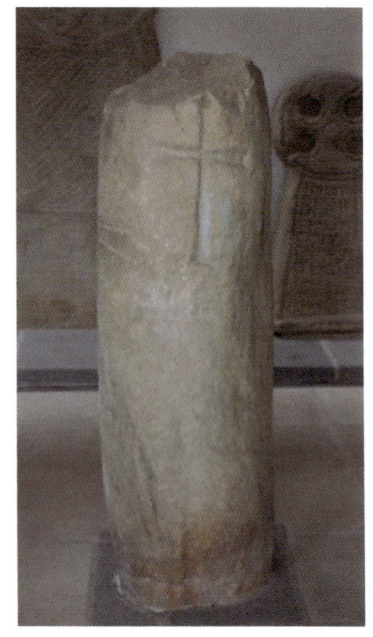

The Thomas pillar

Cross of Einion (left) and Cross of Conbelin (right)

Llantwit Major

20 miles along the South Wales coast from Cardiff is the intriguingly names Llantwit Major. Major means this is the larger place named Llantwit. Llan mean enclosure of, usually implying a church enclosure. So, who then was 'Twit' for whom the place was named? Well there was no 'twit' here, but the English, when they came, could not manage the name Illtyd, who is the founder of the Christian settlement here, and so the name was corrupted by them to Llantwit from Llanilltyd.

Illtyd, or Illtud, also spelt Eltut, was the founder-abbot of a religious community here, which was also a centre of learning. He may in fact have been the reviver of an earlier school since Emperor Theodosius I is believed to have had a college established on the site in 395 A.D., which was abandoned after being attacked by the Irish in the mid 5th century. Illtyd re-founded it c 508 A.D. and it may be Britain's earliest such centre of teaching, and here Saints David, Gildas and Samson of Dol studied, among over 1000 students. We don't know for sure the dates of Illtyd's life, but it is likely to have been about 450 to about 525 A.D.

Although the Life of Illtyd was written in the 12th century and so is not very useful for historical details about him, the Life of St Samson of Dol was written about 700 A.D., and possibly earlier. This tells of Samson being committed by his parents to the College of St Illtyd for his education. It also tells us that Illtyd was a follower of Germane, the Bishop of Auxerre in France, and was ordained by him. We don't know if Illtyd was a Briton, from Brittany or a Gaul. All we really know of Illtyd is that he was the founding abbot of the college, and that he was 'the most learned of all the Britons in the knowledge of Scripture, both the Old Testament and the New Testament, and in every branch of philosophy — poetry and rhetoric, grammar and arithmetic, and he was most sagacious and gifted with the power of foretelling future events.' First Life of St Samson of Dol.

While study was important, 'what made Llanilltud distinctive was the fact that it was a community which devoted itself to prayer alongside the concerns of daily living – family life, farming the land, education, hospitality, caring for others, recreation – all of the things which make up the very stuff of life. Prayer suffused everything that they did – like the patterns on the Celtic stones it wove into all of their activity heightening their awareness of the presence of God in and through all things'. (Llanilltud.org.uk)

Houlet Cross

The community at Llanilltyd, like that at Llandough was almost certainly a mixed one, with those committed to the religious life also being part of families and raising children.

Illtyd had a big impact on the Britons of South Wales over the subsequent centuries, and there are churches dedicated to him across the area, including on the Gower and in Brecknock, as well as in Leon, Treguier and Vannes in Brittany.

9th C Samson Pillar

The Church of St Illtyd is on the site of the Early Medieval college, and in contains some ancient carved stones. They do not date back to the college's founding but the inscription on the 9th century Cross of Samson (which lacks its head) reads:

+SAMSON POSUIT HANC CRUCEM + PRO ANIMA EIUS +, or "Samson placed his cross for his soul."

The east face reads: + ILTUTI SAMSON REGIS SAMUEL + EBISAR +, or "(For the soul of) Illtud, Samson the King, Samuel Ebisar.

The Houelt Cross commemorates the father of Houelt ap Rhys (Hywel ap Rhys), ruler of Glywysing (Glamorgan) in the 9th century. The inscription has been translated as In the name of God, the Father and the Holy Spirit, Houelt (PN) prepared this cross for the soul of Res (PN) his father.

Ninth century carved stones in the Galilee Chapel at St Illtud's Church Llantwit Major

These crosses show that Illtyd's foundation was still going strong in the 9th century.

Christianity after the Romans in Western Britain

St Davids

'[David] expounded the gospel and the law as from a trumpet. In the presence of all a snow-white pigeon, sent from heaven, settled on his shoulders, which remained as long as he preached. While he was holding forth in a voice clear to all, both to those nearest to him and equally to those who were far off, the ground beneath him swells upward and is raised into a hill. Placed on the top he is seen by all, so that standing on a high hill he might lift his voice like a trumpet. On the top of this hill a church is situated. The heresy is expelled. The faith is confirmed in sound hearts. All are in agreement. They pay thanks to God and to Saint David.' (Rhygyfarch's Life of St David, late 11th century)

Writing many years after David, Rhygyfarch was keen to show that David was as much an Archbishop as the Archbishop of Canterbury. He told of how David went to Jerusalem and was made an Archbishop by the Patriarch there, and then shows how orthodox David was by describing a miracle occuring as he spoke to the Synod at Brevi which met to debate Pelagianism. Pelagianism was the teaching of a British Christian who argued that God made it possible for humans to gain perfection by how they lived. Augustine of Hippo countered this argument, saying that if perfection were possible for us then we would have no need of God's grace.

While the miracle of another hill rising in Wales is perhaps the least needed miracle of all time, the supposed event was recounted to show God's blessing on David.

David was born around 500 A.D. We know of his existence from Irish sources as well as the colourful 'Life of David' which records the legends surrounding him. The Irish sources include the eighth-century Catalogue of the Saints of Ireland which contains the earliest reference to David. It says that the sixth-century church in Ireland received its liturgical form of celebrating mass "from holy men of Britain, to wit, from St. David and St. Gildas and St. Docus." Another version of this text names these three men as "Bishops" and "Britons." Also, from Ireland, the Martyrology of Oengus, dated around 800, lists as a church festival under March 1st, "Dauid Cille Muni," or "David, of the 'monastery' of Mynyw."

The Life of St. Paul Aurelian, written in Brittany around 884, says that David was a fellow-disciple with Paul, Samson and Gildas under their teacher, St. Illtud. It also notes that David was nicknamed "the Aquatic," a Latin translation of the Welsh Dewi Dyvrwr, "Dewi the waterman," probably alluding to his practice of drinking only water (an extreme asceticism for which St. Gildas opposed him), but also suggesting the dominance of water as a theme throughout the Life: : springs burst out of the ground around David; he could divine water for

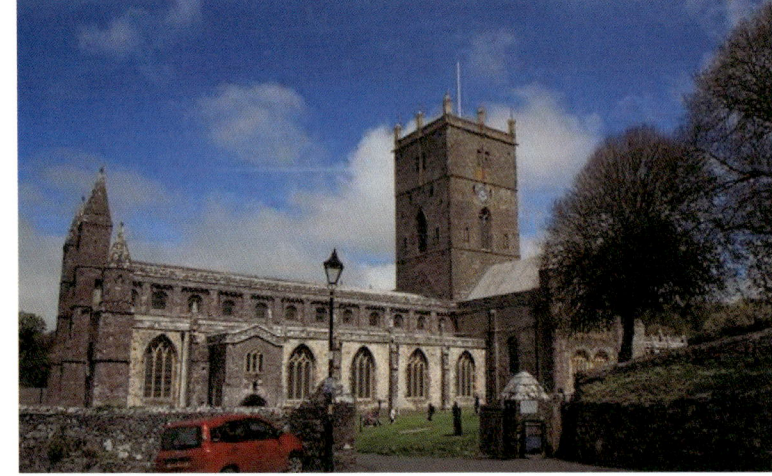

St David's Cathedral

St Non's chapel (above) and St Non's well (left)

needy farmers and thirsty monks alike; when sea winds were too slow, he sent a visiting abbot home to Ireland riding the saint's horse over the water; and everywhere

From Nazareth to Northumbria

the reader finds angels carrying objects back and forth over the Irish sea between David and his friends and former disciples.

But it is to Rhygyfarch we must turn for more details of David's life. He tells us that David's mother gave birth to him in a storm at what is now St Non's chapel. This is certainly an ancient site, with a stone of 7th to 9th century date found in the same field and now propped up in the chapel ruins.

Having trained under St Illtyd, David established religious communities at what is now St David's, in Cornwall and in Brittany. The rule for his communities was austere. The monks pulled their ploughs by hand, were vegetarian and drank only water.

St Non's cross, 7th to 9th century

David was made bishop at St David's and the later medieval writers argued for his role as an archbishop, but that may be in part to set up an alternative to Canterbury. We don't know for sure when David died, but it was probably on 1st March in 589 or 601. He was buried in St David's and his shrine is there today. In his last sermon before he died David said "Arglwydi, vrodyr, a chwioryd, Bydwch lawen a chedwch ych ffyd a'ch cret, a gwnewch y petheu bychein a glywyssawch ac a welsawch gennyf i. A mynheu a gerdaf y fford yd aeth an tadeu idi" which translates as, "Lords, brothers and sisters, Be joyful, and keep your faith and your creed, and do the little things that you have seen me do and heard about. And as for me, I will walk the path that our fathers have trod before us."

Refurbished tomb of St David in the Cathedral at St Davids

South Wales Other Places

The map of South wales is dotted with place names commemorating local saints. These are in themselves evidence of the vibrance of the Early Medieval Church in Wales. In addition to this is the evidence from inscribe stones, many of which are to be found preserved at the back of these churches. A few have been reused as building stone and so adorn the outside of a late medieval church or are gate posts in the church yard wall. Some still stand where they were erected up to 1500 years ago, while a few have been moved to museums to make them easier to access. All are a witness to the Christian faith of those who carved them and are place where the past is touchable.

In Swansea museum is what was once a Roman altar which was reused later as a grave marker. It was found in the Rectory garden at Loughor on the Gower peninsular. The ogham marks are now faint but show that this 2/3rd century altar was reused in the 5th century as a memorial to one of the Irish speaking residents of the area.

Loughor stone

In the church of St Oudoceus in Llandawke, Carmarthenshire, is this ogham and Latin stone. The Latin reads BARRIVEND FILIVS VENDVBARI HICIACIT, which means of Barrivendus son of Vendubarus, here he lies.

Christianity after the Romans in Western Britain

St Oudoceus stone

But the ogham reads …MAQIM DUMELIDONA, meaning …son of Dumelidu, so they are inscriptions to two different people. The ogham was added first in the 5th century and the Latin in the early 6th century. The church is in an oval churchyard and is likely to be an early medieval site. The grave marker pre-dates the saint for whom the church is named – Oudoceus was a bishop at Llandeilo Fawr in the 7th century.

Four early medieval inscribed stones were built into St Tysilo's church at Llandissilio, Pembrokeshire when it was constructed in the 13th century, on the site of a much older church - it sits in a large circular raised churchyard. The boulder near the east end of the church is a grave marker with a Latin inscription, which translates as of Clutorix son of Paulinus Marinilatio. It was probably carved in the 5th century. St Tysilo was a 7th century prince of Powys in north Wales and a bishop.

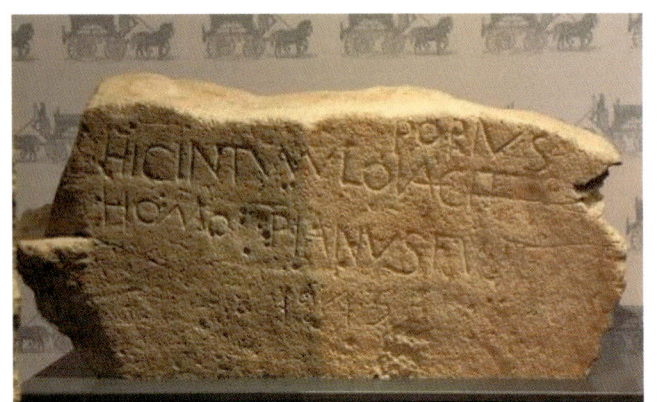

Inscribed stone in Llandissilio church wall

Visiting the National Museum of Wales at St Fagan's enables you to see a variety of Welsh buildings, dating from the Iron Age to the Victorian period, re-erected in one place. There are also galleries of items from all over Wales, including one on how the Welsh commemorated their death. Here, you find the memorial to Porius. The inscription translates as

The Porius stone

'Porius lies here in the tomb. He was a Christian man'. Porius died in the 5th century. The stone comes from Trwsfynydd in north west Wales

St Clydai's church at Clydau in Pembrokeshire sits in its curved churchyard, away from any houses. Yet it was once the centre of a community and is home now to four ancient stones.

The beautiful cross stone at the left has been reused. The first inscriptions in Ogham and in Latin commemorate Dobaticus son of Evolengus and the stone was set up in the 5th or 6th century. The stone was turned upside down and the cross carved in the 7th to 9th centuries. This stone shows how the communities continued to thrive through the early

Clydau church inscribed stones

From Nazareth to Northumbria

medieval period. Clydai was a daughter of Brychan Brycheiniog who was a legendary 5th-century king of Brycheiniog. He was Irish, but gained the kingdom of Brecon through his wife.

Another stone that has been changed over time stands where it was erected in the churchyard at St David's Brindell in Pembrokeshire. The oghams of the 5th century are for Nettasagre son of the kindred of Briaci. The cross was added in the 9th to 10th century.

A similarly tall stone is inside St Thomas Church at St Dogmael's, Pembrokeshire. The village is dominated by a ruined Benedictine abbey which was named for a 6th century saint Dogmael who was possibly a cousin of St David. The current church of St Thomas was built in 1847 using stone from the ruined abbey. It holds the Sagranus stone which is inscribed in Ogham and Latin and was used in 1848 by scholars to decipher the ogham alphabet. It is dedicated to Sagranus son of Cutonamus and was carved in the 5th – 6th century. St Dogmaels is the site of an early medieval religious settlement from the 5th century until it was destroyed by the Danes in the 10th century.

The Brindell stone

The Latin and ogham stone in the church at St Dogmaels

There are many other early inscribed stones across Wales, showing how widely Christianity spread in the area in the centuries after the Roman armies left.

Over the years the styles of carving changed, so that fewer inscriptions were made, but many crosses were carved.

A pair of these are to be found in the churchyard wall at Marthry Church in Pembrokeshire. They

7th to 9th C crosses in Marthry churchyard wall

have been dated to the 7th to 9th centuries.

In the churchyard of St David's, Llanychaer, Pembrokeshire stands a pillar that had been used in the fireplace at a nearby farm. Each of the sides bears a cross, as does the top, it was carved in the late 8th to 9th century.

Three faces of the Llanychaer churchyard stone

Christianity after the Romans in Western Britain

St Cadmarch, Llangammarch Wells in Powys is another ancient site with a raised rounded churchyard. Over the porch of the medieval church is this carving, which dates to the 9th – 10th century.

Caldey Island, just off Tenby in Pembrokeshire is worth a visit for the chance to see red squirrels, a walk to the old lighthouse and a visit the Cistercian monastery which was founded in the 20th century. There is also an ancient church of St Illtyd, known as the Old Priory Church, which houses this stone. It has 5th century oghams and an eighth or early ninth century Latin inscription and cross. The Latin reads 'With the sign of the cross I fashioned on that? I ask all walking there that they pray for the soul of Catuoconus'.

Caldey was a religious settlement from the 6th century, with Pyro as its first abbot, followed by St Samson.

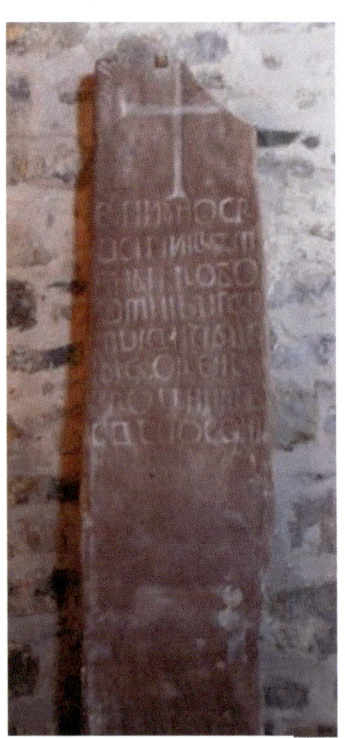

Carving in the porch wall at St Cadmarch Llangammarch Wells

The Caldy Island stone

Celtic Inscribed Stones and Christianity

The stones described so far are just a few of the over two hundred and forty inscribed stones that there are across western and northern Britain. The stones in Wales were first catalogued by V.E. Nash-Williams in The Early Christian Monuments of Wales (Cardiff, 1950). Nancy Williams, Mark Redknap and John M. Lewis between them produced the three volumes of descriptions of all the early medieval carved stones of Wales in A Corpus of Early Medieval Inscribed Stones and Stone Sculpture in Wales. Many of the later carved stones are clearly Christian since they have crosses inscribed on them or are shaped as crosses. But the stones from the 5th and 6th centuries as shown in the previous sections are often plainer, bearing only the inscription. Yet they too have been interpreted as the product of a Christian society.

They are distinctive, and different from inscribed stones in Gaul and Spain in this period. There the inscriptions are on flat stones, which lay on the ground marking the burial place of the person named. Whereas in Britain the stones are vertical, which implies they had a different function. Ken Dark (2021) says 'The use of vertical pillars for British inscribed stones, unlike the continental series, must, therefore, be explained in terms contemporary with their inscriptions, perhaps by an intention to make these monuments highly visible – either in emulation of fifth-century ogham stones or as an independent innovation.' He argues that the stones are markers where people gathered to remember Christian saints. 'Saintly tombs might be expected in ecclesiastical establishments or cemeteries, as at the Catstane near Edinburgh which seems to have had a focal role in cemetery development. By roadsides or at prominent local landmarks such as hills they could have served as places of prayer for travellers. Such monuments might also have been used, as other scholars have suggested, to assert land-ownership or to indicate territorial boundaries, whether those of church land or of monasteries' secular patrons. If inscribed stones marked saintly burials in isolated or wayside locations, then this may also explain why although many stones were found at the sites of later medieval churches many have no such association.'

His argument is based on the fact that only a couple of the stones recall the person who died in terms which speak of them having secular power. One that clearly does so on Anglesey remembers Catamanus Rex and describes him as 'sapientissimus', wisest, which is a term used of clerics. However others refer to sub-deacons, priests or bishops, and sometimes bishop's wives.

Dark concludes 'Reinterpreted in this way, the British inscribed stones can be understood as memorials to people afforded saintly status by the monastic communities which produced the inscriptions. They provide evidence both for the ecclesiastical culture of those communities and for clerical mobility within Britain and overseas. This combination of monastic communities, the cult of saints and an outward-looking perspective is widely found in the world of late antiquity. Elsewhere, it is associated with a specific role for monasteries as at

From Nazareth to Northumbria

the vanguard of converting rural populations to Christianity, evidenced from late fourth-century north-west Gaul to the sixth-century Holy Land. This may be the best explanation for the apparently rapid evangelisation of the west and north of Britain in the fifth and sixth centuries, where populations relatively untouched by the faith in the late fourth century had been comprehensively converted by the sixth.'

Whithorn and South Scotland

'For the southern Picts, who dwell on this side of those mountains, had, it is said, long before forsaken the errors of idolatry, and received the true faith by the preaching of Bishop Ninias, a most reverend and holy man of the British nation, who had been regularly instructed at Rome in the faith and mysteries of the truth; whose episcopal see, named after St. Martin the bishop, and famous for a church dedicated to him (wherein Ninias himself and many other saints rest in the body), is now in the possession of the English nation. The place belongs to the province of the Bernicians, and is commonly called the White House, because he there built a church of stone, which was not usual among the Britons.' Bede Ecclesiastical History III.IV

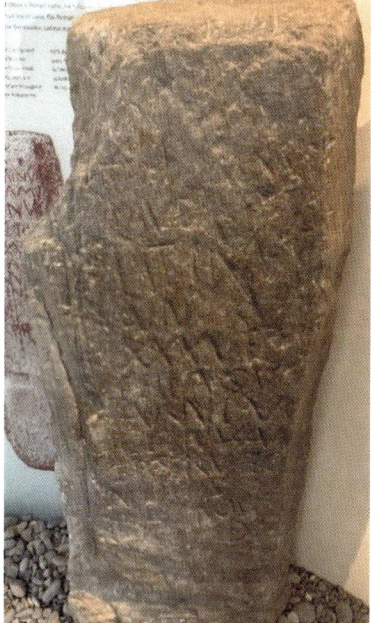

Part of the medieval Whithorn Abbey

When explaining how St Columba came to preach to the northern Picts, in passing Bede relates that Ninias, whom we usually call Ninian, came to the southern Picts. Bede is the earliest to mention Ninian and we really know very little about him. He is presumed to have preached in the Whithorn area in the early 5th century. Whithorn's name is derived from the Saxon 'Hwir AErn' which means white house, which is what Bede calls the place where Ninian built his church. Whithorn is in the far south west of Scotland, in Dumfries and Galloway. Whithorn Priory, built in the early 12th century, is thought to be on the site of Ninian's White House, of Candida Casa as it is in Latin. The bishop Bede refers to in St Martin of Tours (316-397 A.D.).

In the region are six of the thirteen early Christian Inscribed Stones of southern Scotland. Two of these are in the museum at the Priory, one is now lost and three are in the porch of the Old Kirk at Kirkmadrine on the neighbouring peninsular.

The Latinus Stone, Whithorn Museum

The Latinus Stone dates to about 450 A.D. and was found close to Whithorn Priory. The inscription translates as 'We praise thee, Lord. Latinus, of 35 years, and his daughter, of 4 years, here made a sinus. (He was) a descendant, or grandson, of Barrovadus'.

The St Peter stone is much younger, dating to the 7th century. It stood on the roadside half a mile south of Whithorn. The inscription is LOCI / PETRI APV/STOLI, which means place of Peter the Apostle. On one of the arms of the cross an extra line has been added to make a rho.

The Rho on the St Peter Stone

75

Christianity after the Romans in Western Britain

Kirkmadrine Kirk

The stones at Kirmadrine Kirk were all found in the area of the Kirk.

The stone dedicated to Florentius has a maltese cross on it, but with the vertical part of the cross made into a rho. This was probably carved early in the 6th century.

Another stone is inscribed:

HIC IACENT S(AN)C(T)I ET PRAECIPUI SACER DOTES
IDES VIVENTIUS ET MAVORIUS ('Here lie the holy and chief priests, that is Viventius and Mavorius'). So clearly there was a church, and perhaps a religious community in the area when the stones were carved. This is also likely to have been carved in the early 500s – so within 100 year of Ninian bringing Christianity to the region. The carving style is similar to that used in Gaul at the time, so it is likely that the initial links that lead St Martin of Tours to be revered in this area, continued into the next generations.

The Florentius Stone

The third stone is inscribed INITIUM/ ET FINIS, meaning 'the beginning and the end' a reference to John's vision of Christ in Revelation 1. It also has a rho added to the cross, this time with an open hook to the rho. This could date to the early 7th century.

Further reading: (Thomas, The Early Christian Inscriptions of Southern Scotland 1991)

Viventius and Mavorius Stone

Initium et Finis Stone

5. Irish Christianity 4th to 7th Centuries

It is clear from the ogham stones of South Wales that there were links between Ireland and Wales at the end of the Roman period and into the centuries. There were people who saw themselves as Irish in South Wales, celebrating their dead using ogham as well as Latin, adopting and accepting both writing and Christianity. So next we go to Ireland to see the evidence of the development of Christianity on that island.

Ireland was never conquered by the Romans Empire, never had its governance structured in the Roman way with dioceses, provinces and civitas. Instead it retained a strong sense of kinship – land was 'owned' by the whole family, and decisions on who would lead the grouping was made by the derbfine, the meeting of 3 generations of the family group, who would select the most suitable for the role. We know this because in the 7th century the Irish law codes were written down, and these have been preserved in later collections. The codes were followed until the English brought their legal system with them as they annexed Ireland.

Clans were then part of a larger grouping – the 'tuath', which was the regional government of an area of several villages, led by a minor king, selected in the same way as any other family picked their leader. These were subject to an area king, who in turn was subject to the king of one of the 5 kingdoms of Ireland – the Ulaidh in what is now Ulster, the Connacht, the Muman of Munster, the Laiglin of Leinster and the High King who ruled the Mide in what is now Meath from the royal site of Tara.

Christianity seems to have diffused into this society over a couple of centuries, with some areas accepting the new faith, and others holding to the older ways of the Celtic religions. From what we can tell of these religions, which is from fragmentary evidence, they may have readied the Irish to receive Christianity. Such evidence includes the epic sagas and poems written down by medieval scribes, in which the erstwhile gods are seen as heroic humans with some supernatural gifts. These scribes were of course Christians, and so makes it hard to be certain that what they pass on is not influenced too much by their own beliefs. That said, we know from Latin and Greek sources that there was a 'spiritual' class, known as druids. From the Irish poems it is seen that some of the gods seem to have been triple deities – so Brigid the dawn goddess, was also thought of as three sisters each called Brigid.

By 700 A.D. there were Christian sites all over Ireland, it had been thoroughly Christianised. The map above shows just a few of the hundreds of churches and Christian communities that had been founded.

We don't know who first brought Christianity to Ireland, but it is likely it came with traders. Certainly we know that there were Christians in Ireland by 431 for Prosper of Aquitaine's Chronicles tell us that in this year '*Palladius, having been ordained by Pope Celestine, is sent as first bishop to the Scotti believing in Christ*', Scotti then being the term for the Irish. So, our journey in Ireland begins where St Palladius is believed to have founded a church.

Carndonough Cross, Donegal

Christianity in Ireland in the 4th to the 7th Centuries

Kileen Cormac (Cell Fine Chormaic, church of the kindred of Corac)

The cows look bemused as you walk across their field to the circular enclosure in the centre. Surrounded by a stone wall is a mound which has been a burial place for many, many centuries. The presence of pillar stones, several of which are ogham stones, show the antiquity of the place. On one of the pillar stones there is a carved face – perhaps of Christ. On top of the mound is a dip – probably the site of the ancient church which gave the site its name.

The mound of Kileen Cormac

Close to the boundary of counties Kildare and Wicklow, on an esker near the River Greese, Killeen Cormac sits in the middle of the field, just off the road from Crookstown to Ballyhurtin. Now, it feels like the middle of nowhere, but on one of the neighbouring eskers is a large rath, or fortified farm, Rathownbeg.

In 1866 J.F Shearman presented a paper to the Royal Irish Academy on this site and suggested that this is the Cell Fine mentioned in the Vita Tripartita.

The Vita Tripartita is a 9th century account of the life of St Patrick, written in both Latin and Irish. While its focus is Patrick, it mentions Palladius early on - 'The Airchinnech that was in Rome at that time was Celestinus, the forty-second man from Peter. He sent Palladius, a high deacon, with twelve men, to instruct the Gaeidhel (for to the comarb of Peter belongs the instruction of Europe), in the same way as Barnabas went from Peter to instruct the Romans, etc. When Palladius arrived in the territory of Leinster—*i.e.*, at Inbher-Dea—Nathi, son of Garchu, opposed him, and expelled him. And Palladius baptized a few there, and founded three churches—viz., Cill-fine (in which he left his books, and the casket with the relics of Paul and Peter, and the tablet in which he used to write), and Tech-na-Roman, and Doinhnach-Airte, in which Silvester and Solonius are. On turning back afterwards, sickness seized him in the country of the Cruithne, and he died of it.' (Comarb is an Irish word which means successor and inheritor of the spiritual authority).

The pillar stone with a carved face

The dip on top of the mound at Killeen Cormac

Of all the sites in this book, this is probably the vaguest, yet no other site has been linked to Palladius, and he certainly had a role in very early stages of Christianity in Ireland.

Prosper of Aquitaine tells us that in 429 Palladius was the deacon who persuaded Pope Cellestine to send Bishop Germanus of Auxerre to Britain to combat the teachings of Pelagius. Perhaps the Pope was concerned that the Irish Christians, without a bishop sent from Rome would follow Pelagius' teachings.

Whether this was the site of a church founded by Palladius or not, it is certainly a very ancient site. The presence of seven ogham stones show that it was an important early Christian site, where people wanted to be buried close to the spiritual centre. (Only some of the stones are still in place: one is now part of the wall, and one is in the National Museum of Ireland, if you want to look at them on the Ogham in 3D site, they are Colbinstown I – VII).

So, this may or may not have been where Palladius stood, but here you can touch the work of 5th and 6th century Christians in the memorials they have left and remember those first seeds of the Faith in Ireland.

Further Reading:

(Stokes 1887)

(S. A. Green 2011)

Ogham in 3D https://ogham.celt.dias.ie

Ardmore – St Declan

On a hill over the village of Ardmore, halfway between Waterford and Cork, with a commanding view of the sea, is the site of the religious community founded by St Declan in the 5th century. St Declan is one of four saints who are known as the pre-patrician saints of Munster. Pre-patrician means that they lived and worked there before Patrick brought Christianity to the north of Ireland. The others are St Ailbe, St Ciaran and St Ibar. Munster's claim to have it's own bishops before Patrick

Ogham stone at Killeen Cormac

came was important in the 8th to 12th century tussles with Armagh, as that diocese sought to be the senior diocese of Ireland, arguing that the bishop of Armagh was Patrick's successor and so should be the Archbishop of Ireland.

The *Life of Declan* was written in the 12C and so may not give us much accurate information about him. However, the finding of an ogham stone in the 8th century St Declan's oratory shows that this is an ancient site. (The stone now stands in a niche in the 12th century cathedral near the oratory)

The Round tower at Ardmore

If the *Life of Declan* is to be believed Declan's parents were of the Deisi, his father being part of the ruling family of the Deisi Muman, a tribe which settled in both South East Ireland and in South Wales. A visiting priest called Colman baptised Declan, and as a boy he was fostered by his uncle, as was the Irish custom. He was taught to read, write and pray by local holy man, and then went to Wales to study more about the Christian faith. He returned with a group of followers to found his first religious community, at Ardmore. When challenged on why he chose a fairly low hill for his settlement, he replied 'Don't call it a low hill but a high place'. High Place in Irish is Ard More, hence the name of the settlement

Ogham stone in the ruined Cathedral

Christianity in Ireland in the 4th to the 7th Centuries

From his base at Ardmore, Declan took Christianity to the Deisi of South East Ireland, travelling as far as Cashel, where the King of Muman rejected his teaching but permitted him to teach others. In his later years he found life in the community too noisy for contemplation of God, and so went to Declan's Desert, a mile from Ardmore, where there is still a well named for him. When he died, he was buried at the Ardmore community site, and in time the Oratory was erected over his grave.

While the details of Declan's life from the Life of St Declan may not be correct, it is clear he founded a community here, and was buried here. His community survived the ups and downs of life in Ireland including Viking invasions, and in the 12C built the round tower, part bell tower, part secure storage, part watch tower. The Cathedral was built in the same century for Declan's episcopal successor seven centuries later.

Declan's oratory built in the 8th century

Further reading

Elizabeth Rees (2013) Celtic Saints of Ireland pp63-67

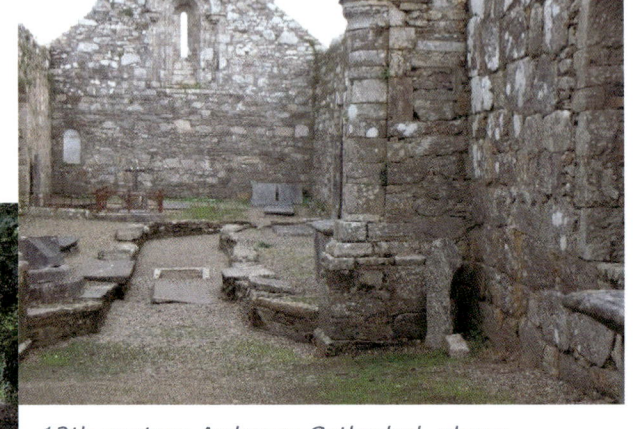

12th century Ardmore Cathedral, above

St Declan's well, left

West face of Declan's Cathedral Ardmore, below

From Nazareth to Northumbria

Emly, St Ailbe

While Declan may not have managed to convert the then King of Muman in Cashel, in time the foundation of St Ailbe at Imleach (now called Emly) became the seat of the bishop of the Muman. St Ailbe's name is anglicised as St Elvis.

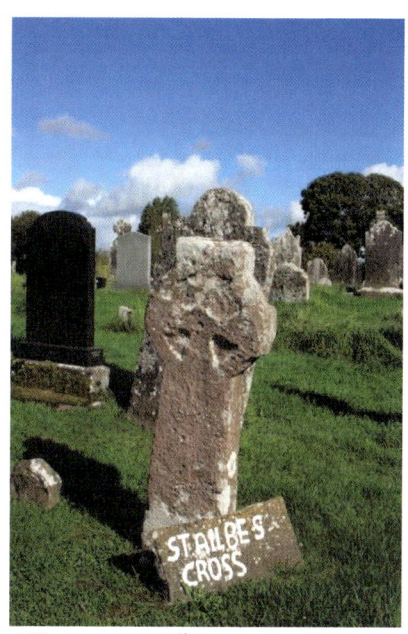

Unusually for Ireland the sites related to Ailbe are to be found in the grounds of the Roman Catholic Church in Emly. Most sites, if they are not abandoned or used only as burial grounds have a Church of Ireland building still in use on the site. This is because the state church in Ireland was related to the Church of England – the Church of Ireland was the Irish part of the Church of England that broke with the bishop of Rome in the 16th century. It sees itself as both Catholic – part of the international church which can trace it roots back to the beginning of Christianity in Ireland - and Protestant and Reformed, since it rejected the authority of the Pope, bishop of Rome, over the church. Instead the church in each land would be self-governing, under their Christian king. This was after all Christendom, where everyone was a Christian, in the mould of the later Roman Emperors who called councils of the church. In Ireland many resisted this, since the English Protestants were dominating them and they rejected an English King as their legitimate ruler, and so continued Roman Catholic practise in secret, until eventually the Roman Church was emancipated in 1829.

Ailbe's cross 9th century

St Ailbe was another of the Pre-patrician saints of Munster, but little is known about him. He is mentioned in the 8th century 'Voyage of St Brendan', and then in the Vita Tripartita of Patrick written in the 9th century. He is regarded as the first Bishop of Munster and later its patron saint.

A Life of St Ailbe is in the 14th century collection Vitae Sanctorum Hiberniae (Lives of Irish Saints) and may have been written as early as the 7th century based on the language used, but it is hard to be sure. It contains much that is fantastical, such as Ailbe being raised by a wolf. However other ideas are more believable – that Ailbe was baptised by St Palladius, which fits with Ailbe being an early bishop in the south of Ireland. The legendary tale suggests that in time the wolf left Ailbe in the forest where he was found by a British (Welsh) couple, who found that they were then unable to go home until they decided to take him with them.

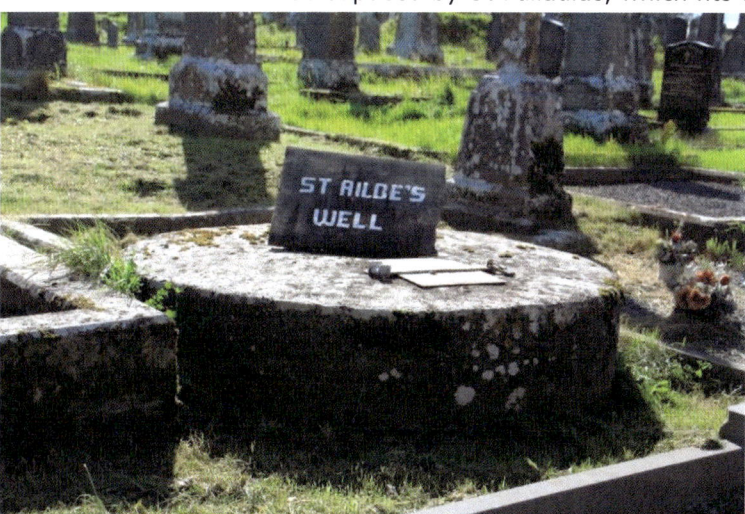

This link with Wales is also found in the 11th century Life of David which says that St Ailbe (St Elvis) baptised David and educated him, before returning to Ireland as a missionary.

Such a link to Wales is quite likely – Wales clearly had good links to southern Ireland as attested by the oghams of Wales.

Back in the churchyard of St Ailbe's church in Emly there is little ancient to show Ailbe was here – the well has a modern surround, but likely would date back to before Ailbe himself. St Ailbe's cross is said to mark where he is buried. It was probably carved in the 9th century, but may replace an older grave marker. But this churchyard is where St Ailbe had his foundation in Munster, this ground he walked when he played his part in bringing the Christian faith to Ireland.

Christianity in Ireland in the 4th to the 7th Centuries

Seir Keiran, St Ciaran of Saigir

In the depths of county Offaly is another ancient site. Today it is called Seir Keiran, but when Ciaran had it as his hermitage it was called Saighir. As with Ailbe, it is hard to be sure how seriously to take the Life of Ciaran which is found as part of the Vita Sanctorium Hiberniae in different versions in several medieval manuscripts. But he is also mentioned in the Annals of Innisfallen: '352 AD St Ciaran, Bishop of Saigher and patron saint of the people of Ossoraidhe (Ossory), was born on the island called Cape Cleere, a promontory of Corca Laidhe in the County Cork'

'402 AD Ciaran and Declan, two bishops, came from Rome to preach the gospel in Ireland. Ciaran after having preached the Gospel in Inis Cleere, and all over Corca Laidhe, founded a Bishop's See at Saighier in Ossory, and Declan also another Bishop's See at Ardmore in Decies'

If the basics of his life are to be accepted, Ciaran was born to Christian parents, his father being a nobleman of the rulers of Osraige, a sub-kingdom on the border between Muman and Laiglin (Munster and Leinster), his mother a local girl of the Cork region, hence his birth in Cork but his ministry in Ossory. As a young man he went to Tours to study in St Martin's community and Rome to be educated further and be ordained. When he returned to Ireland; he came not to evangelise but to find space to pray. So, he came to Saigir and lived a simple life there, but people came to visit him and stayed. Thus he accidently founded a religious community, and was accepted as the first bishop of Ossory (being the name of the modern Diocese, which derives from the ancient kingdom of Osraige). The kings of Osraige were buried at the spiritual centre of their kingdom – Seir Kieran.

The stories of the 'Life' may not be historical, but they do give a flavour of who people thought St Ciaran was. So we hear that when he chose Saighir, he first tamed a wild boar whose territory it was. So, this boar was his first disciple and helped him gather the wood he would need for his church. Boars occur quite often in the lives of the Irish saints – perhaps this is because the boar was an ancient symbol of authority.

Today the remains of a round tower and a 12C monastic church mark the site where Ciaran's community lived and prayed for the people of Ossory.

Remains of the round tower at Sier Kieran

The last of the Pre-patrician saints of Ireland is St Ibar of Begerin Ireland, now part of Wexford. Even less is known about him than the others, since he does not have a medieval 'Life' at all, and so what we do know is pieced together from annals and mentions of him in other 'Lives', particularly that of St Abban who was thought to be his nephew. The 'Annals of the Four Masters' tells of his noble birth. He, like Ciaran, went to Tours to study there, having heard of Christianity from people of Armorica (now Brittany). When he returned, he first set up a community on the Aran Islands in Galway Bay, but later moved to Geshille in County Offaly and finally to Begerin, which was then an island in Wexford Bay. Here he built his oratory and cell, and others started to join him. The chronicles put his death in 500AD.

Further Reading

(Rees 2013) Ciaran of Saigir, pp67-71

(O'Halloran 1916)

The Ends of the Earth - Skellig Michael

Image © Jerzy Strzelecki used under CC BY-SA 3.0

I didn't get to Skellig Michael, so I've had to rely on other people's pictures and videos, and a trip to the Skellig Experience visitor centre on Valentia Island to get a sense of what this far outpost of Christendom was like. You can also see Skellig Michael on the Star Wars films *The Force Awakens* and *The Last Jedi* as the place where Luke Skywalker has gone to live, to get away from it all.

Beehive cells on Skellig Michael Image © Towel401 - Own work, CC BY-SA 4.0

Skellig Michael is the larger of two rocks which stick up out of the Atlantic Ocean 8 miles off the far south west of Ireland. To go by the videos and pictures it is always sunny and calm out there, but that is of course misleading – you can only cross the sea to the Skelligs when it is indeed sunny and calm. These islands are home to gannets, shearwaters, storm petrels and puffins, among other seabirds.

In the centre of the island is a small valley called Christ's Saddle. The steps from the landing points on the north and the south meet here. Another landing point made by the first inhabitants is to the

Christianity in Ireland in the 4th to the 7th Centuries

east of the island. Up another set of steps on the taller peak of the mountain is a terraced shelf where the monks of the 6th century chose to come and live and contemplate God.

They built two small chapels, or oratories, and six beehive like cells These were a common form of hut in Kerry in the Iron Age and into the Early Medieval period. They could be built with the rocks that were to hand, and by making sure some rocks stuck in a bit or out a bit at the right height a ceiling, possibly an upper floor and thatch could be added to the hut. The huts may have slept two, so at most 12 monks lived this isolated, austere existence.

The diet for the monks included fish and the eggs of the seabirds and any vegetables they could manage to grow in the thin soil on the island. They may also have traded fish and sea birds' eggs for flour and vegetables. In winter food would have been tight, and the storms would have made living out here challenging. With no trees to provide firewood it could be a very cold, wet wait for the storms to abate.

Here, Christianity had truly reached the ends of the earth.

Caherlehillan

In the far south west of Ireland is the Iveragh Peninsular of County Kerry. The stunning Ring of Kerry route goes round the coast of the peninsular, and each summer many people come here as the jumping off point for Skellig Michael and the famous beehive cells of its early medieval monastery. To get across you need a calm day – it was blowing a gale and raining the two days I was in the area so instead I visited Caherlehillan.

Early Christian cross on Skellig Michael Image © by Ecmc23 - Own work, CC BY-SA 4.0

This was the site of the University of Cork's training digs from 1992 to 2004 and is on a small terrace looking over the Fertha River, and when it is not tipping with rain or foggy you can see down to Valentia Harbour.

What remains of the site today is a rectangular area surrounded by stone slabs with two standing pillars with crosses on them. It sits within an enclosure which is about 30m in diameter but has been partly lost to the 19th century road and is cut through by field boundaries in places. At the top of the hill is a stone fort or cathair.

Once excavated radiocarbon dating and the relative positions of features to each other showed that a wooden church was built with an enclosing bank in the mid-5th to early 6th centuries. Pottery found at the same level was also dated to mid-5th to early 6th centuries (it is called type Bii and comes from the north-east Mediterranean). The church was small – only 3.8 m by 2m, and had graves aligned with it. Inside the church there was a post hole about a third of the way from the east end – this may have been the base of a wooden altar which stood on a single post. Such altars were being used in the Marseilles region in the 5th and 6th century, and so this may show a link, however indirect, with the church in the south of France of that time.

Inscribed stones at Caherlehillan

A drain was found leading from the east end of the southern wall out for about 5 meters. This probably came from a piscina, the basin used to wash the vessels after communion.

Alongside the church were 18 graves, mainly to the south and east of the building. One of these was carefully lined with stones which had been worked especially for the purpose. In later years a structure was built over this grave, as a shrine to the memory of the person here. Since it is one of the earliest graves, it is probably that of the person who founded this small community. We know nothing else about him or her since the bones have not survived in the peaty soil.

The two cross pillars were erected next to this shrine. The taller one has a simple cross with scroll like ends to each arm of the cross. It was carved in the 6th or 7th century. The shorter stone has a more complex design.

In the centre is a Maltese cross in a disc on a handle. This shape is called a flabellum, and it was a liturgical fan used in the early eastern church. Above this is a bird which has been interpreted as a simplified form of a peacock. This was a symbol of immortality to the Greeks and so readily adopted into Christian symbolism.

The taller stone bears a simple cross

Stone with the outline of a flabellum (liturgical fan) with a peacock above it

In the excavations, two more fragments of slabs with the flabellum and peacock were found. Whoever carved these was happy to use the symbolism of the eastern Mediterranean for the Christians of this far western European site.

Here we have evidence that the Christianity that took the journey from Judea, to Turkey, on through Gaul and to Britain, arrived in Ireland with a sense of continuity with its eastern origin.

Further Reading:

(Sheehan 2009)

The Dingle Peninsular

All around the coast of Ireland are islands where small groups of monks could live an isolated austere life. They sought a place where they could get control of their desires, hence commitment to celibacy, poverty and obedience. By taking these vows they turned their backs on seeking power or pleasure through earthly means so they could focus on giving their lives to God.

Not all crossed the sea to find seclusion. On the Dingle Peninsular are the remains of several of the early medieval settlements whose members were committed to living out their faith at the ends of the earth.

Reask Monastic site

As a result of excavations in the 1970s the layout of the small religious community at Reask can be seen today.

Around the community was a curving containing wall, and into this were built half a dozen beehive huts. There was also a stone-built oratory, with a graveyard. Shards of late Roman amphorae, large vessels used to transport wine, dating from the 6th century were found during the excavation.

Christianity in Ireland in the 4th to the 7th Centuries

A view across the monastic site at Reask

An idea of what the beehive cells would have looked like can be gained from the huts which are still standing at the Iron Age site of Fahan, 8 miles away on the south of the peninsular.

Fahan beehive huts

About ten carved slabs were found on the site, most simple crosses but two are pillars still in the enclosure.

The thinner one has a simple cross and letters which have been read as DNS for dominus. The more elaborate carving is of a Greek cross, with a handle. This could, like the stone at Caherlehillan, be a flabellum, or liturgical fan, from the eastern Mediterranean.

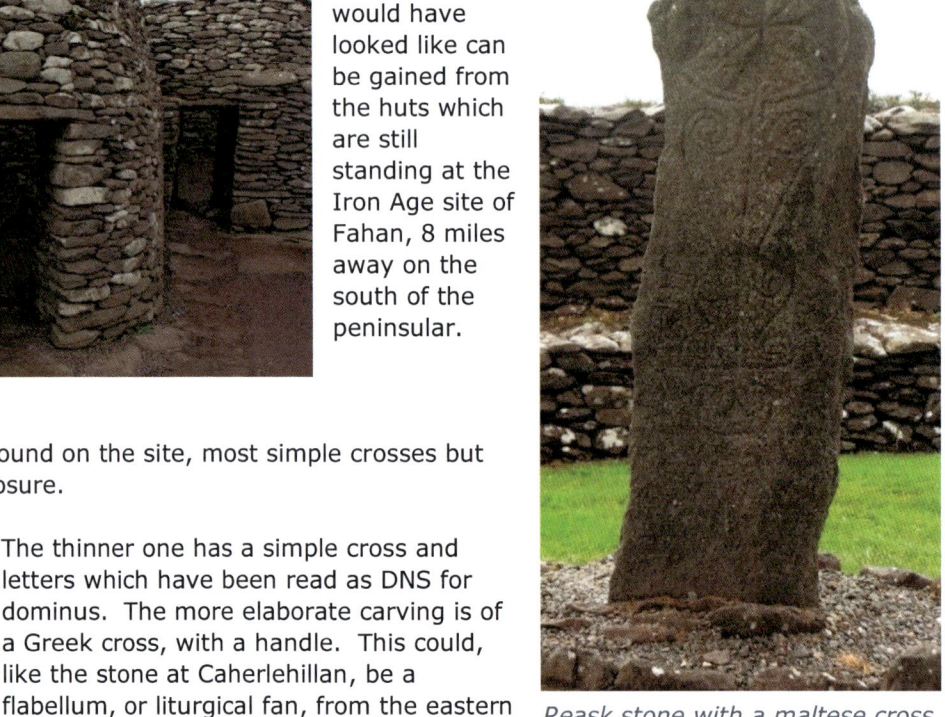

Reask stone with a maltese cross

Simple cross marked stone at Reask

The Oratory at the Reask monastic site

86

Gallarus Oratory

The Gallerus Oratory

Carved stone at Gallerus

To see an oratory as it would have been in the early medieval period a visit to Gallarus is needed. The oratory here stands in splendid isolation, with no sign of huts for a community. It is still watertight, and the inside measures about 4.8 m by 3m. There is debate about its age. It could date to the 7th or 8th centuries or to the 18th century or any time in between. It may have been plastered inside, but today it is plain inside as out.

Near the oratory stands a carved stone, with an equal armed cross in a ring and the inscription 'COLUM MAC DINET', which is probably from the 7th or 8th century, showing that it is an ancient site, even if the oratory may be younger.

Inside the oratory

Christianity in Ireland in the 4th to the 7th Centuries

Kilmalkedar

Lacking the top layer of stones, the St Brendan's oratory at Kilmalkedar is open to the elements now. As at Gallarus there is no sign of other buildings today, and this oratory's purpose may not have been to serve a local community but to be a place for prayer for pilgrims coming along 'the Saint's Road' from Ventry Bay 7 miles to the south, to Mount Brandon 7 miles north east of the oratory. Near end of this road is an ogham stone with a cross. At Kilcolman near Ventry is a squat stone

Kilmalkedar oratory

with oghams reading 'Colman the pilgrim'. In the saddle on Mount Brandon, at Arraglen where pilgrim routes meet before going to the top is a pillar stone, with a similar cross and oghams reading 'of the priest Rónán son of Comgán'. Mount Brandon is one of the ancient holy mountains of Ireland and was probably used for festivals in honour of the God Lug, before the festival was Christianised and dedicated to Brendan the Navigator.

Colman stone at Kilcolman

Mount Brandon from the East

Arraglen ogham pillar ©kevin higgins / Ogham Stone / CC BY-SA 2.0

Most people who visit Kilmalkedar go to see the 12th century church just fields away from the oratory but miss the older church altogether. This site is also ancient, with several ogham stones and ancient crosses. The church is dedicated to St Maolcethair, a local saint and probably the founder of the early Christian site in the 6th or 7th century.

Kilmalkedar church from the oratory

From Nazareth to Northumbria

The presence of so many ancient carved stones show that it was significant to those who lived in the area. The ogham stone in the graveyard in front of the church is unusual since it has a hole through the top. Inside the church is another ogham stone and a stone caved with a cross, and with the letters of the Latin alphabet in the side, dating to the 6th century. Outside, as well as the ogham with a hole, are several stone crosses, including a small one in the shape of a tau, lacking the upper part of the cross. This ma have been deliberate as the tau cross in one of the early forms of the cross. In about 200 Clement of Alexandria wrote 'They say, then, that the character representing 300 is, as to shape, the type of the Lord's sign.' The Stromata (Book VI) ch 11. In Greek tau was used to represent 300. There is also a very large plain stone cross.

The ogham stone with the hole

The Alphabet stone inside Kilmalkedar Church

Inside the ruined church at Kilmalkedar

The large cross at Kilmalkedar

The tau cross

89

Christianity in Ireland in the 4th to the 7th Centuries

Temple Manachan Ballymoreagh

Set today in farmland, on a man-made terrace near the top of a hill, is another early church. This is Temple Managhan, also called Temple Geal and Temple Mancháin

The views from this Early Christian site are deliberate – to the east can be seen Mount Brandon and to the west the Skelligs. The people who built this oratory wanted to be spiritually in touch with holy places even if they also desired solitude.

Today, the place is very solitary

Inside the oratory

apart from the dog who greets you and seems to want to act as your guide to the oratory. In front of the oratory is a pillar with oghams and a cross. Traditionally, it was thought to mark the grave of Manachan who founded the church, but the oghams read QENILOCI MAQI MAQI-AINIA MUC[OI-, so the grave is of Qeniloci, about whom we know nothing other than he died in the 5th or 6th century.

The inscribed stone at Temple Manachan

90

From Nazareth to Northumbria

Kilfountain cross slab

The field in which the Kilfountain cross is set must be the muddiest in the Dingle peninsular.
The claggy red soil sticks to your boots, but the beauty of the cross slab makes the cleaning the boots worth it. The pillar is at the remains of an oratory and is inscribed with the name Fintan, the founding saint of this small church. The oghams on the pillar read EQODDI. The cross is in a Greek style and a has a stylised chi rho. As at Caherlehillan the Greek cross in a circle appears to have a stylised handle and so may be a flabellum, the fan used in the early eastern church in services.

Christianity in Ireland in the 4th to the 7th Centuries

Saul, Downpatrick, Slane and Armagh -Patrick

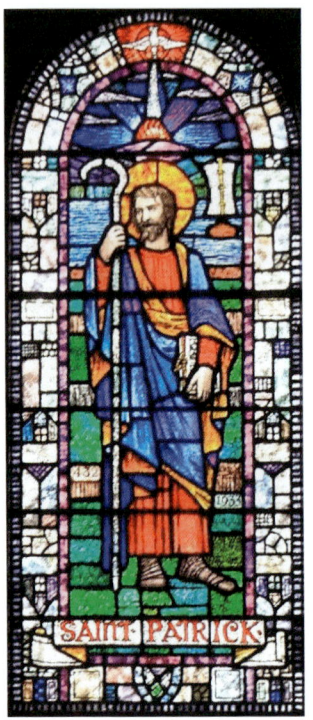

In Patrick, history, tradition and archaeology meet beautifully. For Patrick wrote of his own life in his 'Confessio', and what he wrote has come down to us. We also have a letter, the 'Letter to the soldiers of Coroticus'. There are also later Lives, with all their wonderful tales, which may or may not be true, but do show the impact Patricius, as he terms himself in his Latin writing, had on Ireland.

Patrick was born in Britain. In his 'Confessio' he says:

My name is Patrick. I am a sinner, a simple country person, and the least of all believers. I am looked down upon by many.
My father was Calpornius. He was a deacon; his father was Potitus, a priest, who lived at Bannavem Taburniae.
His home was near there, and that is where I was taken prisoner.
I was about sixteen at the time.'

Unfortunately, we don't know where Bannavem Taburniae was, some say Devon, others Wales, others Cumbria, others even South-West Scotland. Nor can we be sure when Patrick was born.

St Patrick Window, Saul Church

The Annals of Ulster were composed in the mid-6th century and give a date for the arrival of Patrick in Ireland of 432AD, but this may be earlier than it really was to deal with the fact that Palladius had come in 431AD, and so to make the latter's part in the conversion of Ireland tiny compared with Patrick's. The Annals then tell us that the elder Patrick died in 457AD (probably Palladius, who was also given the name of Patrick by the Irish- since the name means father of the people), and that some record that Patrick died in 461/2 AD. The trouble is they also record in 492/3 the death of "Patrick, the arch-apostle of the Scoti", on 17 March, at the age of 120, '60 years after he came to Ireland to baptise the Scoti'.

If Patrick really was 120 when he died, he was born in 373 AD, but that seems unlikely. Probably he was born in the early years of the 5th century.

What we do know, for Patrick tells us himself, is that he was captured by the Irish and taken to Ireland as a slave. At this point he gave the faith of his father and grandfather a go and found consolation in God. He tended sheep and prayed, and after 6 years had a dream in which God said '"You have fasted well. Very soon you will return to your native country." Again, after a short while, I heard a someone saying to me:

The current church at Saul built 1933

"Look – your ship is ready." It was not nearby, but a good two hundred miles away. I had never been to the place, nor did I know anyone there. So, I ran away then, and left the man with whom I had been for six years. It was in the strength of God that I went – God who turned the direction of my life to good; I feared nothing while I was on the journey to that ship.'

Eventually Patrick made it home to his family, and set about studying Christianity, probably going to Northern Gaul to study, and was ordained. He then had a dream of the Irish calling to him "We appeal to you, holy servant boy, to come and walk among us."

From Nazareth to Northumbria

So, he went to Ireland and began his mission there. His work began in the North East, and his first church was at Saul. Tradition says that when he landed in the area the local chieftain Dichu gave him a barn for shelter. The Irish for barn is 'sabhall', which is anglicized to 'Saul'. Patrick used the barn as his base for preaching, and after his death here an abbey was built here. Cross slabs from this abbey are held in the Downpatrick Museum. The Vikings burnt the abbey down, but it was re-founded in the 12th century, only to be dissolved at the reformation.

As well as having the remains from Saul, Downpatrick has its own part in Patrick's story. For here Patrick is reputed to be buried, and Down Cathedral was later built on the spot. The site of Patrick's grave is not known for sure, but for centuries people focused on a point at the top of the hill. In the 1900's a large slab was placed as much to protect the site from pilgrims taking handfuls of earth away as to mark it.

Grave slabs from the original religious settlement at Saul now in the museum at Downpatrick

Other places in Ireland lay claim to Patrick too. Armagh Cathedral (Church of Ireland) is built on the hilltop in Armagh which is the site of Patrick's first stone church. According to the 7th century accounts by Muirchu preserved in the 9th century Book of Armagh, Patrick asked the local wealthy man Daire for the hilltop site but was instead given a lower site. After some time one of Daire's horses was set to graze close to the new community, which disturbed it. The groom refused to move it, and the next day it was dead. Daire on hearing of this, set out to kill the Christians, but himself became ill. His servants asked for Patrick to give them something to heal him, so having first sprinkled the horse with holy water which revived it, he sent holy water in a bronze bowl to be sprinkled over Daire. Daire recovered, and now

Patrick's grave slab, in the churchyard of Downpatrick Cathedral

was willing to give Patrick the site he first asked for. So, on the high place of Ard Macha, the stone church was built.

Another site associated with Patrick is the Hill of Slane. Muirchu tells in a story clearly meant to echo that of Daniel, that the High King was celebrating a pagan festival, and had decreed that anyone who lit a fire that night before it was lit at the High King's palace at Tara was to be killed. It being Easter Eve, Patrick lit the fire on the Hill of Slane which can be seen clearly from Tara. When men were sent to kill Patrick, he called on God who sent darkness and an earthquake to confuse those who were attacking him, so they killed each other. Eventually the King decided it as better to believe Patrick than to die.

View from the Hill of Slane

Patrick sent his followers to found churches and religious communities and these formed a federation bearing Patrick's name. One follower was Patrick's nephew Mel, whose settlement at Ardagh, Co Longford, was said to have been founded by Patrick in 454 at Ardagh, and he installed Mel as bishop there. The current remains are 8/9th century, and excavation has shown that there was a wooden church there before.

Christianity in Ireland in the 4th to the 7th Centuries

Remains of the century cathedral of St Mel at Ardagh, Co Longford

Further Reading

Hennessy ((trans) 1887)

(Rees 2013)

St Patrick 'Confessio'

Muirchu's Life of Patrick both at https://www.confessio.ie/

Kildare, St Brigid

Having the same name as a Celtic goddess has led some people to question whether there ever was a nun called Brigid. However, someone founded the religious communities which claim her, and Brigid is a good a name for this woman as any other.

St Brigid's well, Kildare

Modern statue of Brigid at St Brigid's well Kildare

Brigid was born in Faughart, County Louth and in 470 AD she founded a religious community for women and men at Kildare. The site of the community is now the church of Ireland cathedral of Kildare.

In the grounds is the 'fire temple', the site of the original oratory of the community, where for centuries a fire was kept burning in Brigid's honour.

From Nazareth to Northumbria

The goddess Brigid was associated with fire, fertility and spring. Cormac's Glossary, written in the 10th century by Christian monks, says that Brigid was "the goddess whom poets adored" and that she had two sisters: Brigid the healer and Brigid the smith. This suggests she may have been a triple deity. The presence of triple deities in pre-Christian Celtic religion may have helped the acceptance of Christianity. Brigid the goddess was particularly invoked at the festival of Imbolc, held on the 1st February, which celebrated the start of Spring and the beginning of lambing. St Brigid's day is 1st February, so it is likely that the woman named for the goddess has attracted the pre-Christian commemorations.

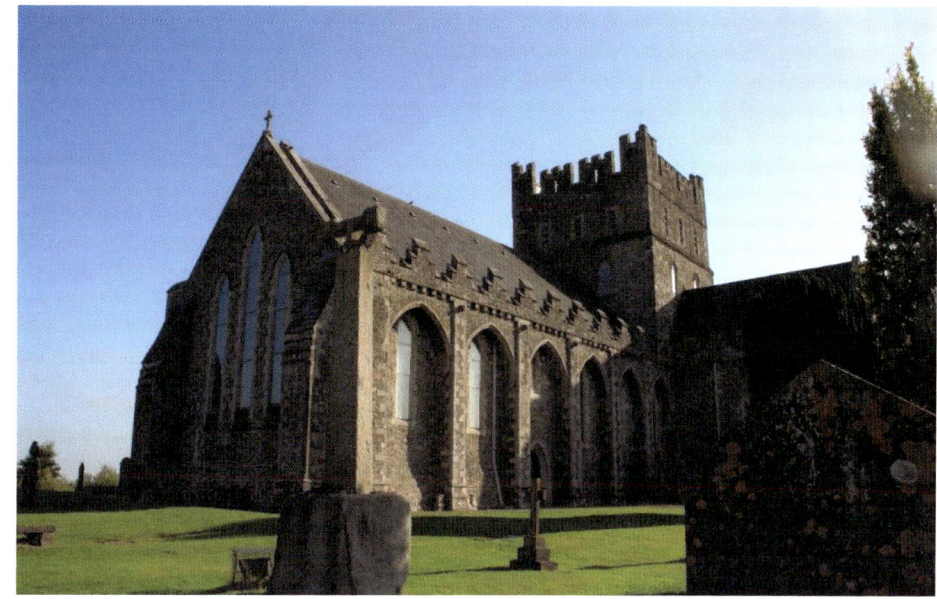

St Brigid's Cathedral Kildare

In the 7th century a member of the Kildare community, Cogiotos, wrote a Life of Brigid. It was followed by another by an unknown author, and a third attributed to Coelan, both also in the 7th century. The three accounts conflict in important aspects so we are left unclear about much of her life. They also have plenty of stories which today seem unlikely.

The accounts do agree that Brigid was the daughter of Brocca, a Christian Pict slave who had been baptized by Saint Patrick. They name her father as Dubhthach, a chieftain of Leinster. Dubhthach sold Brocca to a druid when his wife insisted that he get rid of her since she was pregnant. Brigid returned to Dubhthach at 10 years old as a servant.

The Lives are full of tales of Brigid's generosity – with food or possessions of her father since she had none of her own. In two of the Lives, Dubhthach was so annoyed with her that he took her in a chariot to the King of Leinster to sell her. While Dubhthach was talking to the king, Brigid gave away his jewelled sword to a beggar to barter it for food to feed his family. The king recognized her holiness and convinced Dubhthach to grant his daughter her freedom. She took her religious vows in about 468 A.D. from either St Mel, the nephew of Patrick or St Mac Caill at Croghan.

Kildare (Cill Dara, 'church of the oak') was founded in 480 and Brigid was its abbess. It was a community of women and men later seen as a twin house with a convent and a monastery. It was founded on the site of a shrine to the goddess Brigid where the devotes of the goddess tended an eternal flame. The church took on the tradition, in time, but the fire was now in honour of the Christian Trinity. Brigid invited Conleth (Conláed), a hermit from Old Connell near

Walls marking the site of the 'fire temple' in Brigid's community in Kildare

Christianity in Ireland in the 4th to the 7th Centuries

Newbridge, to help her in Kildare. She gave canonical jurisdiction to Conleth, and he was consecrated Bishop of Kildare, and the abbey was governed over the subsequent centuries by an abbess and a bishop. The Abbess of Kildare was regarded as superior general of the monasteries in Ireland and accorded the honour due to a bishop.

In the 9th century 'Bethu Brigte' Brigid's consecration as a bishop is described. "The bishop being intoxicated with the grace of God there did not recognize what he was reciting from his book, for he consecrated Brigit with the orders of a Bishop. This virgin alone in Ireland, said Mel, will hold the Episcopal ordination. While she was being consecrated a fiery column ascended from her head". This tale was continued in Lives written between the 11th and the 15th centuries, perhaps to explain the way the abbess of Kildare was honoured.

Kildare round tower

Clonard, St Finnian

The Danes did a good job of destroying the monastic site at Clonard in Meath, when they came in the 8th and 9th centuries. The Norse carried on the tradition of burning Clonard, and then the Normans, having first rebuilt it, abandoned it in favour of Trim in 1202. But in its day the community of St Finnian at Clonard was one of the foremost schools of Irish Christianity.

Finnian was probably born in New Ross, Laiglin, now Leinster, and baptised as a child. He went to Tours, and the Latin life of St Cadoc the wise says that Finnian accompanied him when he returned from Ireland to Wales. So Finnian studied under Cadoc at Llancarfan, not far from Barry and Llantwit Major in Glamorgan.

His 'Life' is contained in the *Codex Salmanticensis,* an 8th or 9th century collection of the lives of saints from the Irish midlands. This suggests that Finnian stayed in Wales for 30 years before returning to Ireland. He may have founded the monastery on Skellig Michael, and then stayed at Kildare for a time before being led by an angel to Cluain Eraird (anglicised to Clonard) on the River Boyne. Here in 520 A.D. he started work on his chapel.

The site was central in Ireland, on the main East-West road and so easily accessed. While at first Finnian may have lived the life of an austere hermit, he was also willing to teach those who came to him, and so a community developed. Many of those who would found other religious communities in Ireland studied first at Clonard, including those who became known as the twelve apostles of Ireland:

19th-century church of the Church of Ireland at the ancient monastic site of St. Finian, Clonard, County Meath, Ireland photograph by Andreas F. Borchert, Creative Commons Attribution-Share Alike 3.0

From Nazareth to Northumbria

Saint Finnian of Clonard himself; Saint Ciarán of Clonmacnoise; Saint Brendan of Birr, County Offaly Saint Brendan of Clonfert (the Navigator); Saint Columba of Terryglass; Saint Columba of Iona; Saint Mobhí of Glasnevin; Saint Ruadháin of Lorrha; Saint Senan of Iniscathay (Scattery Island); Saint Ninnidh the Saintly of Lough Erne; Saint Laisrén mac Nad Froích, the son of Nadfraech, he was the brother of Aengus, the first Christian king of Munster; Saint Canice of Aghaboe in County Laois.

When they left his community to go and found their own they are described as going with a crozier or a book and so it is likely that Clonard had a scriptorium and workshops.

The Penitential of Finnian may have been written by Finnian of Clonard. He believes that sinful thoughts and actions can be cured by penance – which is seen in abstaining from wine and meat for a set period of time depending on the sin. For example:

'If a cleric is wrathful or envious or backbiting, gloomy or greedy, great and capital sins are these; they slay the soul and cast it down to the depth of hell. But there is penance for them, until they are plucked forth and eradicated from our own hearts' *The Penitential of St Finnian* 29 (in Medieval Handbook of Penance, John T McNeill and Helena M Gamer, 1938)

Detail of a stained glass window in a series depicting the life of St. Finian in the Church of St. Finian at Clonard: Saint Finian and followers building Clonard.

Finnian died of plague in 549. His biographer says he was 140 years old, but 65 to 70 is more likely.

Ardfert, St Brendan the Navigator

The ruined cathedral at Ardfert in Kerry is a 12th century building on a much older site. It became the cathedral of the newly named Diocese of Ardfert in 1117. Previously the diocese for the Ciarraige (the people of Kerry) was at Ratass near Tralee. The remains of the 10th century church at Ratass still stand in the burial ground there with a 6th century ogham stone, as evidence of the earliest Christian community there.

Ardfert also has an ogham stone, now in the small museum at the site. There are also other early Christian grave slabs in the museum. Ardfert Cathedral is dedicated to St Brendan, who was born nearby in 484 and is known as one of the twelve apostles of Ireland. We first hear of Brendan in Adamnan's life of St Columba, written at the end of the 7th century, but few details are given there of his life. He is called a seafarer in the 9th century 'Martyrology of Tallaght', but details of the legends of his life are only found in the 'Life of Brendan' which exists in several Latin and Irish versions, written in the 9th century, and in the 'Voyage of St Brendan the Abbot', possibly written as early as the 8th century. While historically unreliable, they give some good tales about this seagoing pilgrim.

Ogham stone at Ratass

According to the legends Brendan was baptised by St Erc at Tubrid. Although his parents planned to name him Mobhi, this was changed at his christening to Broen-finn' or 'fair-drop'.

His early education was under St Ita, known as the 'Brigid of Munster'. She moved to the area that became known as Killeedy and founded a religious community of both men and women there.

Ratass Church

Christianity in Ireland in the 4th to the 7th Centuries

Nothing remains of this community now but the name Killeedy, with the local school named for the saint.

Later Brendan was tutored by St Finnian and is numbered among the twelve apostles of Ireland who were all students of Finnian of Clonnard. He was ordained by St Erc at the age of 26.

The school in Killeedy is named for St Ita who founded the original Cill Ite for which the villages is named

He is best known for his legendary voyages. These included on to the Aran Islands where he founded a religious community, and then to Hinba Island off Argyll in Scotland where he met St Columba, and then he sailed on to Wales and Brittany. Back in Ireland he founded communities at Ardfert and at Shanakeel at the foot of Mount Brandon sometime between 512 and 530 A.D.

Ardfert Cathedral

Brendan also founded a community in Clonfert in Galway, which grew to about 3000 monks and from here he supposedly set off for a seven-year voyage in search of the Land of the Blessed. His adventures are recounted in the 'Voyage of Brendan the Abbot', and much of what is written is allegorical, but it is possible that the historical figure was also an explorer although we have no evidence of Brendan landing anywhere beyond Ireland and Britain. At the end of the book the monastic steward tells Brendan that the Promised Land is to be found back at home.

The story became popular throughout Europe and was translated into Dutch, German, French and Italian. Brendan died about 577 at Clonfert in Galway where he had founded a community. The 12th century cathedral there has an impressive doorway

Ardfert Ogham Stone

Clonfert cathedral doorway

Glendalough, St Kevin

The name Glendalough comes from the Irish Gleann-da-loch, meaning 'Glen of the two lakes', and it is a beautiful place, with tree covered hillsides sloping down to the two lakes, about 25 miles south of Dublin in the Wicklow Mountains.

Here Kevin founded his monastery, deliberately close to the pass running south through the Wicklow Mountains, yet away from current centres of population – accessible yet secluded.

Six Lives of Kevin have survived, three in Irish and three in Latin, although all were written over 300 years after Kevin's

The lower lake at Glendalough

An early cross on a mound near the lower lake at Glendalough

Poulanass waterfall

death. The earliest was penned in the tenth or eleventh century by a monk of Glendalough. From them we know that Kevin was born in the early sixth century to a noble family of Leinster who had lost the kingship. His parents Coemlog and Coemell named their son Coemhghein which means 'fair born' and has been anglicised to Kevin.

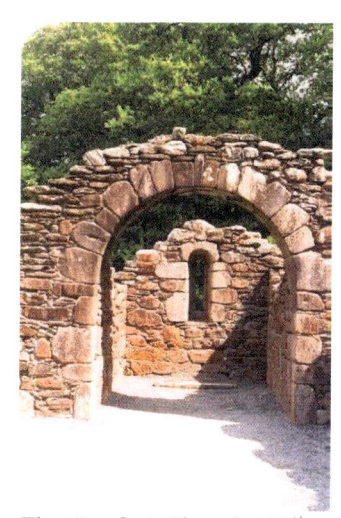

Little is known of Kevin's early life, if legends such as that of a white cow appearing morning and evening at his parent's house to ensure that the saintly boy had milk are discounted as later additions.

The Reefert Church, 11th century

However, we do know that Kevin was ordained by a bishop called Lugidus, who sent him off to found a new church somewhere. Once a community had been formed, Kevin moved it to Glendalough and founded his monastery in the lower part of the valley. Once it had settled, he then withdrew to the upper valley, where he built himself a hermitage and a small oratory and retreated there much of the time. This area became known as Kevin's Desert.

Today the area close to the upper lake has several ancient stone crosses and the remains of the Reefert Church. This was used by later monks who chose a more solitary existence in part of the valley. Nearby the Poulanass river forms a waterfall down the steep valley side as it flows into the upper lake.

The Cathedral

The monastery that Kevin founded flourished; people were drawn by Kevin's reputation as a teacher and a holy man. It would have developed many buildings for workshops, writing and copying books, and a guesthouse for those staying with the community as well as farm buildings an infirmary and several churches.

When he knew he was nearing death in about 618, Kevin returned to the monastery for his last days. He died there and was buried to the east of the

Kevin's kitchen, a 10 to 12C church

Ruins of an ancient Church near the lower lake at Glendalough

Christianity in Ireland in the 4th to the 7th Centuries

lower lake, probably where St Mary's Church now stands.

Today, the remains of the monastic city at Glendalough contain five churches, and a plain but impressive cross, called Kevin's Cross, They are protected by a round tower, and the tenth century gateway into the monastery still survives, and marked the beginning of the sanctuary. Within the grounds of the monastery someone fleeing would be protected from those who sought them.

The best preserved of the churches is St Kevin's Church, which is a 12th century structure. The much larger abbey or cathedral church was started in the 10th century and finished in the 13th. Kevin's community continued for many centuries surviving being burnt 19 times, the first being in 770 AD. Under the Normans it was given to Augustinian Canons, and finally closed in the 16th century.

Clonmacnoise

Kevin's cross, Glendalough

Not far from Athlone on the banks of the River Shannon is the ancient monastic site of Clonmacnoise. Here is 544 A.D. Ciaran founded a community, in a location at the point where a major East West route crossed the River Shannon. This was to be an accessible community, serving the people, rather than a retreat from society.

Ciaran is reckoned as one of the twelve apostles of Ireland. He is sometimes called 'Ciaran the younger' to distinguish him from Ciaran of Saighir, who was active in the 5th century.

Clonmacnoise round tower

Born in around 516 in County Roscommon, Ciaran's father was a carpenter and Ciaran himself worked as a cattle herd as a young boy. He studied at Clonard under St Finian, and then went to Inishmore to study under Enda of Aran. He became a teacher in his own right and Columba said of him 'He was a lamp, blazing with the light of wisdom'. When he was ordained by Enda, he was advised to go to found his own community in the centre of Ireland.

Ciaran and eight fellow monks set to work on his new site, with the blessing of the local king Diarmait mac Cerbaill. Ciaran and Diarmait are depicted on the east face of the Cross of the Scriptures at Clonmacnoise driving a stake into the ground to start the building work at Clonmacnoise.

The Scripture Cross of Clonmacnoise (10th century)

Replica of the Cross of the Scriptures, where the original once stood

100

From Nazareth to Northumbria

Dairmait subsequently became the High King of Ireland, the last to be invested with pre-Christian rituals. His sons were given Christian names, and so Diarmait could well be the first Christian High King of Ireland.

Within seven months of founding the community Ciaran was dead. The Yellow Plague, which was a pandemic affecting the whole of Europe at the time, killing between a third and a half of the population, was no respecter of age or sanctity, and caused Ciaran's death. Ciaran was buried in a chapel in the centre of the community he had founded.

Ciaran's chapel

However, his community continued and thrived, becoming in time one of the great centres of learning in Ireland. It survived the plundering of the Vikings, and the coming of the Normans, only to be dissolved in 1552. The monastic site is still much visited today.

Durrow, Kells, Iona and Tiree – St Columba

Colm Cille, or Columba as he is known in English was born in Donegal and baptised at Temple-Douglas in 521 A.D. His father, Fedlimid was a great-grandson of the famous Irish king Niall of the nine hostages. Colm Cille means Church Dove, and may have been Columba's baptismal name, or may be a name he adopted later. If so, his original name was probably Crimthann or 'fox', which may have been more suited to the son of a ruling family.

We know about Columba from the Life which was written by one of his successors as Abbot of Iona, Adomnan, who wrote in the 7th century, about 100 years after Columba's death. While it may well contain some embellishment, since its purpose was to convince the church of Columba's sanctity, it is likely to be trustworthy in the basic framework of his life.

The remains of Movilla Abbey, Newtownards, 12th century buildings

Columba started his education at Movilla, which is now in Newtownards in Northern Ireland, at the northern tip of Strangford Lough. The abbot was Finnian of Movilla who had studied at Ninian's community in Whithorn in Galloway. In Movilla Columba was ordained as a deacon.

After some years he moved south to Leinster where he studied under an otherwise unknown bard Gemman. He then moved to Clonard on the banks of the River Boyne border of Leinster and Meath. Clonard was founded by Finnian of Clonard in 520 AD. Finnian had travelled to Tours in France and to Llancarfan in Wales and so brought insights into Irish Christianity from Gaul and Wales. During the sixth century many of those who would be most significant in the church in Ireland studied at Finnian's foundation, including Brendan of Clonfert, Ciaran of Saghir and Ciaran of Clonmacnoise.

Columba also spent time with St Mobhi at Glasnevin, today in the outskirts of Dublin, but in 544 A.D. St Mobhi died, probably as part of the pandemic called the Justinian Plague that spread across Europe from 541 A.D. It was caused by the same microbe that would bring the Black Death to late medieval Europe, *Yersinia pestis*, and killed about a third of the population of Europe.

Christianity in Ireland in the 4th to the 7th Centuries

The community dispersed and Columba went back to Ulster, and began to found his own communities, including those at Derry, (Londonderry to some); Durrow, County Offaly; Kells, County Meath; and Swords in Fingal just north of Dublin. These were all to be significant foundations, which flowered in the subsequent centuries. The Book of Kells which is in Trinity College Dublin was probably written and illustrated at Kells about 800 A.D. It is a collection of all four gospels, whose illustrations make it a great work of art as well as a way of passing on Jesus words.

Book of Kells, Folio 292r, Incipit to John. In principio erat verbum. 'In the Begining was the word'

Durrow in County Offaly was where Columba was based from its foundation in around 553 A.D. to his move to Scotland a decade later. Here or in Iona, or possibly in a Northumbrian community, the Book of Durrow was painted. This was over a century before the Book of Kells was made, and is dated to between 650 and 700 A.D.

A tradition links such a book to Columba leaving Ireland. The story goes that, while he was at Movilla, Columba copied out a psalter intending it for his own use. In 560 A.D. St Finnian of Movilla disputed his right to keep it. The High King Diarmait mac Cerbaill decided in favour of Finnian arguing that just as a calf belongs with the cow so also a new book belonged with the original.

In 561 A.D. there was a great battle at Cúl Dreimhne (Cooladrumman in County Sligo), where many men died, and the tradition sees Columba's quarrel as a key factor in the battle. Columba being upset by the High King's ruling stirred up dissension in the Ui Neill clan of Ulster and they contested the rule of the High King in the battle. A different tradition gives the reason for Columba's anger as being due to the High King violating the right of sanctuary in the Columban communities, by entering, removing and killing a man under Columba's protection. In the Annals of Tighernach for the year 559, we find that Curnan son of Aed, son of Eochaid Tirmcharna by Diarmait mac Cerbaill died, while Curnan was 'ar comairce Coluim chilli - under Colum Cille's protection'.

Either way, Columba was involved in the battle and many died. Although he was spared punishment by a synod of churchmen, he felt uneasy about what he had done, and so on the advice of a holy hermit, Molaise, he chose to leave Ireland and become a travelling missionary. So, in 563 he set off with 12 companions for the land that would become Scotland. He probably landed on the Kintyre peninsular, and then moved further north along the West Coast of Scotland. According to legend this was because he could still see Ireland, although it may be because Conall mac Comgaill, King of Dál Riata, which was a region of Scotland that had been settled by people from Ireland, offered him Iona as a base.

Here he founded his community, and it became a centre of learning and one of the few places of literacy among the Dál Riata. Columba became a diplomat, helping Conall mac Comgaill in his dealings with the Picts, and used the opportunities to teach them about Christ. Many stories relate to this period, including an encounter with a mythical monster that some take to be the Loch Ness monster, in 565.

High cross and round tower at Kells

From Nazareth to Northumbria

So, in the Life of Columba written by Adomnan, his successor the 9th abbot at Iona we read:

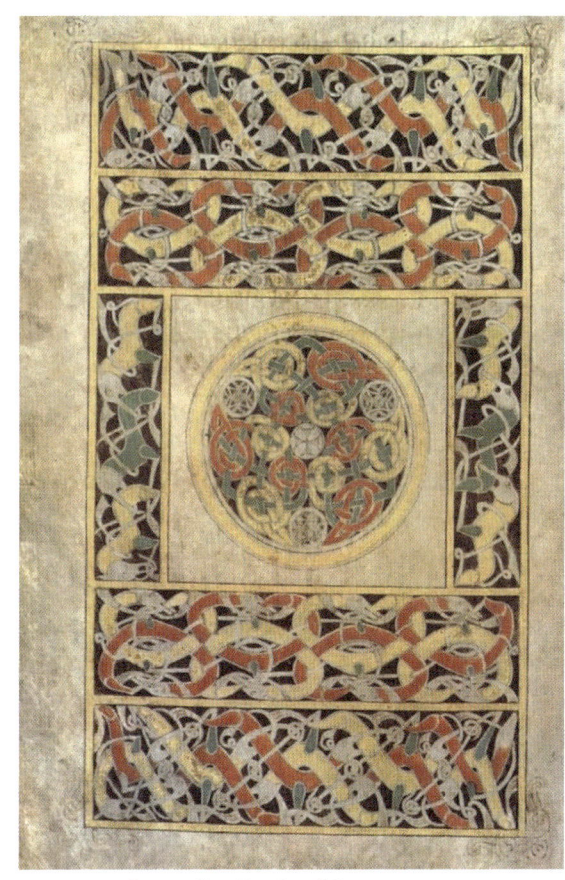

'On another occasion also, when the blessed man was living for some days in the province of the Picts, he was obliged to cross the river Nesa (the Ness); and when he reached the bank of the river, he saw some of the inhabitants burying an unfortunate man, who, according to the account of those who were burying him, was a short time before seized, as he was swimming, and bitten most severely by a monster that lived in the water; his wretched body was, though too late, taken out with a hook, by those who came to his assistance in a boat. The blessed man, on hearing this, was so far from being dismayed, that he directed one of his companions to swim over and row across the coble that was moored at the farther bank. And Lugne Mocumin hearing the command of the excellent man, obeyed without the least delay, taking off all his clothes, except his tunic, and leaping into the water. But the monster, which, so far from being satiated, was only roused for more prey, was lying at the bottom of the stream, and when it felt the water disturbed above by the man swimming, suddenly rushed out, and, giving an awful roar, darted after him, with its mouth wide open, as the man swam in the middle of the stream. Then the blessed man observing this, raised his holy hand, while all the rest, brethren as well as strangers, were stupefied with terror, and, invoking the name of God, formed the saving sign of the cross in the air, and commanded the ferocious monster, saying, "Thou shalt go no further, nor touch the man; go back with all speed." Then at the voice of the saint, the monster was terrified, and fled more quickly than if it had been pulled back with ropes, though it had just got so near to Lugne, as he swam, that there was not more than the length of a spear-staff between the man and the beast. Then the brethren seeing that the monster had gone back, and that their comrade Lugne returned to them in the boat safe and sound, were struck with admiration, and gave glory to God in the blessed man. And even the barbarous heathens, who were present, were forced by the greatness of this miracle, which they themselves had seen, to magnify the God of the Christians.'

Carpet page from the Book of Durrow

By Meister des Book of Durrow - The York Project (2002) 10.000 Meisterwerke der Malerei (DVD-ROM), CC license from Wikipedia

Cross marked stone at the site of St Patrick's chapel on Tiree

St Patrick's chapel Tiree. What can be seen is a later chapel, which aligned East West, built over foundations of the earlier chapel which was aligned towards Iona

Christianity in Ireland in the 4th to the 7th Centuries

Columba founded churches in the Hebrides including on Tiree. A geophysical survey of the chapel of St Patrick on Tiree in 2004 by Revd Dr Timothy Astin of the Department of Archaeology in the University of Reading showed that the original chapel on this site faced toward Iona rather than to the East. Columba also travelled inland in Scotland, including to Inverness where he impressed the King Bridei, King of Fortriu, the northern kingdom of the Picts.

While St Columba remained based in Iona for the rest of his life, he returned to Ireland to attend church synods there. In 574/5 A.D., during his return for the Synod of Drum Ceat, he founded the monastery of Drumcliff in Cairbre, now County Sligo, near to the battlefield at Cúl Dreimhne where so many had died.

Columba died in 597 A.D. and was buried on Iona, although his relics were moved by the monks when they left the island under pressure from the Vikings in 794 A.D.. They may now be buried with those of Patrick and Bridget at Downpatrick. He left behind a thriving federation of church communities.

St John's cross c800 A.D. in the Infirmary Museum, Iona Abbey

Nendrum Monastic Site

The most complete remains of an early monastic site in the north of Ireland is at Nendrum, which was founded in the 5th century. From the air the outline of the three enclosures can be seen.

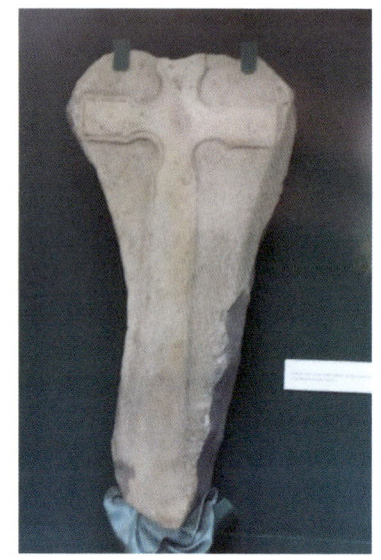

The plan on one of the information boards shows what each of the areas was used for. The foundations of the church, the huts where the monks lived and the school where the young ones studied are all visible. This was a small community compared to Clonard which must have covered a very much larger site to accommodate 3000 students.

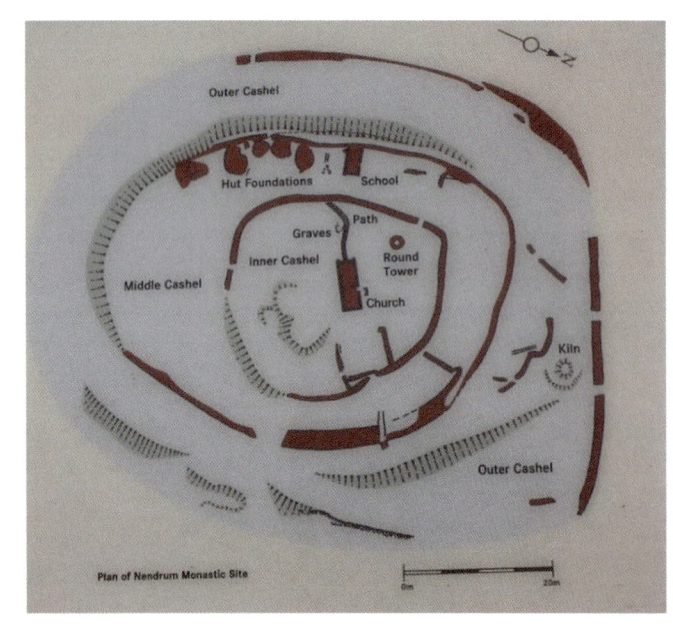

Church at Nendrum

Grave slab with the Nendrum cross

There are remains of a tidal mill in the lough and a small museum at the site holds several 7th and 8th century carved grave slabs with the distinctive 'Nendrum cross'. Crosses of this form have been found in several places in County Down. With the indents it looks like a precursor to the later Celtic cross form.

Plan of the Nendrum site from one of the information boards

Nendrum early monastic site from the air. Photo: Davidcorkill / CC BY-SA (https://creativecommons.org/licenses/by-sa/4.0)

Is the Celtic church Johannine?

At the end of our tour of the places in Israel which John mentioned, we saw three aspects of the Johannine strand of Christianity. They were the physical and the spiritual coming together, the importance of water and the value of learning. If these are present then it is consistent with the historical suggestion from Bede that the Irish church, at least, saw John as it's lead apostle.

1. **Valuing the physical and the spiritual together**.

The west of Britain and in Ireland have plenty of physical remains of the earliest Christianity that came to these lands. We can identify over 200 churches in Ireland that were founded before 700 A.D. in many places from the buildings that marked the site as holy for many centuries. A map of Early Medieval Churches in the Atlas of the Irish Rural Landscape (ed: Kevin Whelan, F. H. A. Aalen, Matthew Stout), shows the whole country had eccesiastical sites.

Nurney cross head, possibly 6C, but note the roundness of the head, this may be the beginning of the ring cross

The early christian stones of Cornwall, Wales and Scotland also show the importance of marking places as holy. While some are grave markers, others such as the Peter Stone at Whithorn and the simple crosses of Ireland are placemarkers. Over the centuries from 700 to 1000 A.D. these developed into the dramatic High Crosses.

2. **Water.**

Several of the sites mentioned have holy wells, such as St Non's well near St David's, Brigid's well near Kildare, St Ailbe's well at Emly. There are many more such wells which have not been mentioned in this book so far, since often they have recent surrounds, but they are clearly connected to the holy place. The website https://ihwcbc.omeka.net/, has pictures of the many such wells in Ireland.

Christianity in Ireland in the 4th to the 7th Centuries

The well chapel is a unique feature of the celtic church. In The Lost Saints of Britain (2005, p61) Ian Thompson describes these 'They were rather like overgrown well houses, being built directly over a spring or its outfall, and contained an open channel which allowed the water to flow either lengthwise through the building or transversely across it, in the latter case usually beneath the altar fron north to south...Seven definite well chapels survive: three of them, at Callington and st Clether(Cornwall) and Rhos-on-Sea Denbighshire rebuilt at the end of the 19th century....The other four survive as mere ruins: Madron(Cornwall), Capel Erbach and Capel Begewdin (Carmarthenshire) and Ffynnon Fair, near St Asaph, though in all cases the water still flows through them.'

3. Learning.

While many of the early medieval Christian sites were home to very few, some clearly grew into significant communities, with later writers calling them sites of learning. Llantwit Major, the community of St Illtyd was where St Samson of Dol was educated according to his 7th century 'Life' as were Paul Aurelian and Gildas who moved from Scotland for his education here before settling in Brittany. At its peak there were about 2000 students in the community. Irish communities such as that of Brigid at Kildare, Finnian of Cloanard and Columba's foundations of Kells and Durrow also were the universities of their day. The beautiful Kells and Durrow books were probably the later product of their scriptoriums.

Clether Well Chapel Cornwall Rob Purvis / St Clether Holy Well / CC BY-SA 2.0

A link with the Johannine tradition is consistent with what we know of the early church in Wales, Cornwall and Ireland, and because Christianity came to these area from Roman Britain, can also be used to give us insight into the British Church in the area that would become England, if we can find evidence that it survived the century after the Roman Empire ceased to govern Britain.

Chi Rho folio from the Book of Kells, which kept at the library of Trinity College Dublin

6. British Christianity in 'Anglo Saxon' Areas of Eastern Britain

There is much evidence of Christianity in Ireland, and the West and North of Britain during the 5th and 6th centuries. But in the East of Britain during this time immigrants from the continent were arriving – just as they had over many millennia before. These are known to us today as the Angles, the Saxons and the Jutes, and the picture we learnt from schoolbooks inspired by Victorian historians was of the Britons fleeing west before them.

This would have left the countryside empty for these warlike people to settle in and to develop their own farms, bringing with them their own religion. They had no knowledge of Christianity until Augustine was sent by Pope Gregory in 597 A.D. However, the evidence of archaeology over the last 50 years has questioned this understanding.

While certainly there were immigrants from the continent, and in time families which viewed the lands of Saxony as their ancestral home came to dominate the populations, the evidence for a wipe out or expulsion of the native population is thin.

Francis Pryor in his book 'Britain AD' (2005, Harper Perennial) marshals some of the evidence that the population in Roman times continued into the early Saxon times. The Welland Valley where he excavated has signs that the Roman roads run across previous landscape features, but the Roman landscape was respected by post Roman and early medieval occupiers. He also comments on work by Oliver Rackman in Essex in 1986 which analysed the pollen found in the soil in excavated sites. By ensuring the soil was dated by finds he could see if there was a regrowth of woods which would be expected to happen if the people farming the area had been driven out. He didn't find any evidence of such woodland, although he did find that the land was less used for growing cereal after the end of the Roman period and agriculture shifted to the less intensive keeping of livestock.

"The point that arises from this is obvious, but needs making, nonetheless. This diversity of land use shows an extraordinary degree of adaptation to contrasting landscapes and soil conditions, at precisely the time when Anglo-Saxon settlers are supposed to have been colonising the landscape. I believe it would have been impossible for large numbers of migrants to have adapted so fast and so thoroughly to such diverse conditions; if there actually were any incomers, they must have been few in number, and have settled within existing communities. It is also worth stating that secondary woodland will start to develop very rapidly once a farmed landscape ceases to be maintained - the process has already started in parts of upland Britain where sheep-farming is no longer possible. Within one- or two-years hawthorn and sloe bushes appear, followed swiftly by birch. Close on the heels of the birch trees come the true forest trees, oak and ash. If the process is rapid today, it would have been very much more so in the Early Saxon period, when introduced species such as grey squirrels, Muntjac deer and rabbits were not around to nip off growing shoots or ringbark young trees. Once an arable field had been abandoned, scrub would have colonised it in about five years; secondary birch (or alder in wet areas) woodland would soon grow up through the briars and bushes. The field would have become an almost impenetrable thicket within a decade. The absence of such scrub and woodland regeneration is very significant for what it tells us about the East Anglian landscape in the early fifth century. "

Pryor, Francis. Britain AD: A Quest for Arthur, England and the Anglo-Saxons. HarperCollins Publishers. Kindle Edition. Location 3355 (Pryor 2005)

The book 'Fields of Britannia' by Stephen Rippon, Chris Smart and Ben Pears (OUP 2015) is subtitled 'Continuity and Change in the Sub-Roman and Early Medieval Landscape'. (Rippon, Smart and Pears 2015) In the 'Fields of Britannia' project they have shown that, broadly speaking, the South East saw a gradual evolution from the Roman period all the way through to the Norman Conquest, without any major changes in how the landscape looked.

Catherine Hills in 'Origins of the English' (Hills 2003) considers the genetic evidence as well as the archaeology. She suggests that the Anglo-Saxon settlement about which the contemporary sources tell us little, may well have been like the Viking settlement which took place over the period from about 800 to 1066, but led to some areas with little Scandinavian settlement and some with more.

Just so the Anglo-Saxon settlement took time, but probably was mainly about the establishment of a Germanic elite slowly taking control over eastern Britain, with much of the population staying the same. But

British Christianity in the 'Anglo Saxon' areas of eastern Britain

the previous population was not homogenous – it was varied before the Romans came and stayed varied over the centuries.

The evidence that the population was varied before the Romans came is given by Tacitus. In 'Agricola' he describes the three peoples of the British Isles.

"Who were the original inhabitants of Britain, whether they were indigenous or foreign, is, as usual among barbarians, little known. Their physical characteristics are various and from these conclusions may be drawn. The red hair and large limbs of the inhabitants of Caledonia point clearly to a German origin. The dark complexion of the Silures, their usually curly hair, and the fact that Spain is the opposite shore to them, are an evidence that Iberians of a former date crossed over and occupied these parts. Those who are nearest to the Gauls are also like them, either from the permanent influence of original descent, or, because in countries which run out so far to meet each other, climate has produced similar physical qualities. But a general survey inclines me to believe that the Gauls established themselves in an island so near to them." (chapter 11, in translation, Cornelius Tacitus, The Life of Cnæus Julius Agricola, Alfred John Church, William Jackson Brodribb, Ed)

Fifty years earlier Julius Caesar wrote of the population of the British Isles in these terms: "The interior portion of Britain is inhabited by those of whom they say that it is handed down by tradition that they were born in the island itself: the maritime portion by those who had passed over from the country of the Belgae for the purpose of plunder and making war; almost all of whom are called by the names of those states from which being sprung they went thither, and having waged war, continued there and began to cultivate the lands."

(Caesar's Gallic Wars book 5 chapter 12)

So, the coming of the Angles and Saxons in the 5th and 6th centuries was nothing new – they had been coming and settling for hundreds of years. Stephen Oppenheimer in 'The Origins of the British' (Robinson, 2006) uses the result of gene tracing to show that the largest part of the Y chromosome genes of modern British men came with people before the advent of farming and so well before the coming of the Celts, which developed as a people in the middle of the first millennium before Christ. The proportion varies across the country from about 81% of the Welsh to about 68% of the English. The genetic differences across the country go back to this very distant past when settlers came after the Ice Age, some from the Basque country, others from Northern Europe. Subsequent migrations added to these differences. It is possible that the language in the east of England before the Romans came was different from that spoken in the west, which may explain the lack of Celtic names in the east.

This would fit with the distribution of tribal groups before the Romans came. A map of the southern tribes shows the Belgae mentioned by Caesar.

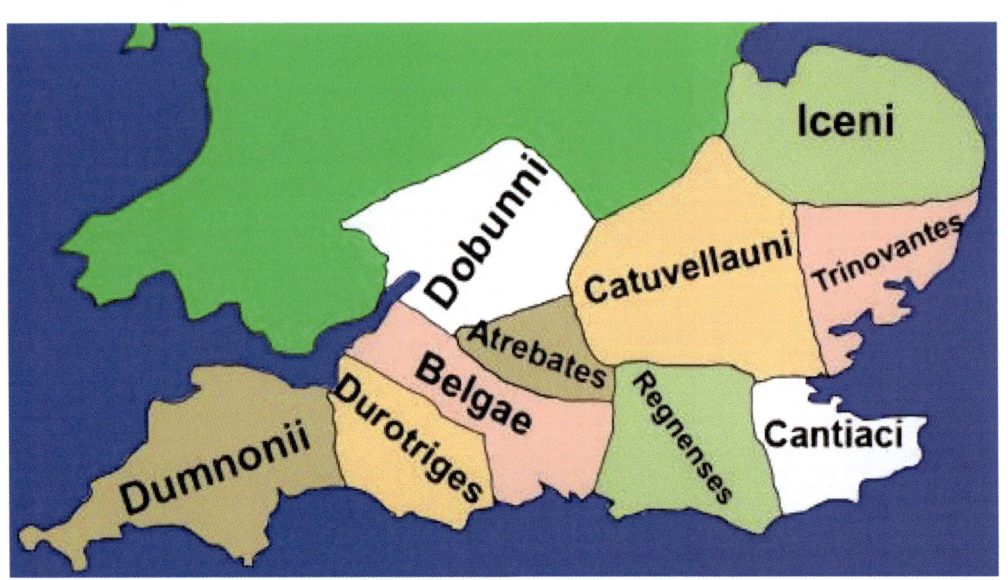

At the same time the Belgae are a tribe on the mainland of Europe, in the area where Belgium is today.

Another tribe which appears on both sides of the channel before the Romans are the Parisii, who are a tribe of East Yorkshire, just north of the Humber, and the region around modern Paris, which is how the city got its name.

Pre Roman Tribes of Southern Britain, 100 – 1 BC, Nicholas W. Beeson University of Michigan nwbeeson@umich.edu file from Wikimedia.

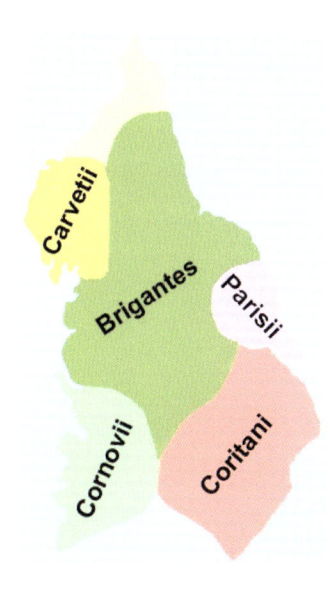

From Nazareth to Northumbria

A map of pre-Roman monuments also shows differences from the West to the East.

There are very few stone circles or standing stones on the east of the country compared to the west. To see this for yourself look at the website megalithic.co.uk where the map on the front page in 2020 shows the locations of this type of ancient monument.

This might be in part due to geography – a stone which will survive down the ages needs to be one which doesn't decay under weathering, but we know from Stonehenge that the stones were moved long distances, so this is not the whole answer.

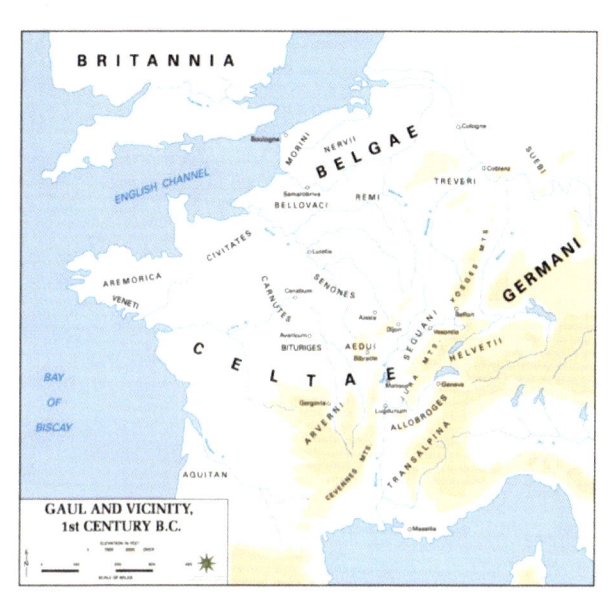

Creative Commons Attribution-Share Alike 3.0 Unported England Celtic tribes - North and Midlands.png

The Department of History, United States Military Academy / Public domain

In summary, the culture of different parts of the British Isles has varied from place to place back into the mists of time. The coming of the settlers known as Anglo-Saxons had an impact on this, but not as large an impact as was once thought.

Stephan Schiffels and Duncan Sayer in 'Investigating Anglo Saxon migration history with ancient and modern DNA' in 'Migration and Integration from Pre-History to the Middle Ages' (2017, Halle) looked at two studies of the genetics of people buried in England from cemeteries dated to the Iron Age, the Roman period, and early and middle 'Anglo Saxon' periods. They found in one early Saxon cemetery at Oakington that the four bodies had different genetic make ups, one very similar to the Iron Age burials from Linton and Hinxton, one very similar to the middle Saxon bodies at Hinxton and two somewhere between. By comparing the genetic variations in the samples to the modern English genetic samples, they concluded the current population of England owe less than 40% of its DNA to those who crossed the channel from the Netherlands and beyond. Those who came in the 5th and 6th century in places mixed well with the local population, and in others lived apart from them, but in both situations the material culture they brought with them was evident in the graveyards.

If it true that the incomers settled alongside the Romano-British, what evidence do we have of the continued presence of Christianity in the East of the country. In the far west in Wales and Cornwall we have inscribed stones, but very few of these have been found in the East. This is probably because they were never part of the culture in this part of the country. But there is evidence for the survival of Christianity here, not on the surface in the form of monuments, but underground. In the graves of the east of England we find evidence of Christianity.

Wasperton, Warwickshire

A very clear example of the continuity of a village from Romano-British to Anglo-Saxon is at Wasperton in Warwickshire. Ahead of gravel extraction, excavations were undertaken between 1980 and 1985. 200 inhumation and 26 cremations were uncovered. Prof Martin Carver and his team used radio carbon dating, assessed the arrangement of the graves and where they cut across other graves to work out a sequence of the burials. It showed that the cemetery had been in continued use from the 4th to the 7th century. The analysis of the excavation can be read at https://archaeologydataservice.ac.uk/archives/view/wasperton_eh_2008/overview.cfm.

'The alignments of graves, studied in these local groups, combined with a number that had intercut, provided a coarse framework for the sequence which was both independent of the objects and included all the graves. The exercise showed that while a few of the unfurnished graves were contemporary with the Roman group, a sizable contingent (39) could be attributed to the 5th century, and the remainder belonged with the Anglo-Saxon burials where they constituted some 44%. The 5th century contingent was notable for a sub-group, all

British Christianity in the 'Anglo Saxon' areas of eastern Britain

W-E, which contained a high proportion of coffins, planks or stone inclusions such have been noted in post-Roman cemeteries in western Britain. This sub-group was also spatially separated, in the south-eastern half of the enclosure.' (Martin Carver, 2009, from the Archaeology Data Service website)

In the later 5th century the culture of goods in many of the graves changed to be like those in East Anglia and the upper Thames, and in the 6th century the cultural links became more to those of Wessex and the rest of the Thames region.

Oakington, Cambridgeshire

In Nature, on 19 January 2016 Schiffels et al published their article 'Iron Age and Anglo-Saxon genomes from East England reveal British migration history'. It can be read online at https://www.nature.com/articles/ncomms10408.

'Here, we present whole-genome sequences from 10 individuals excavated close to Cambridge in the East of

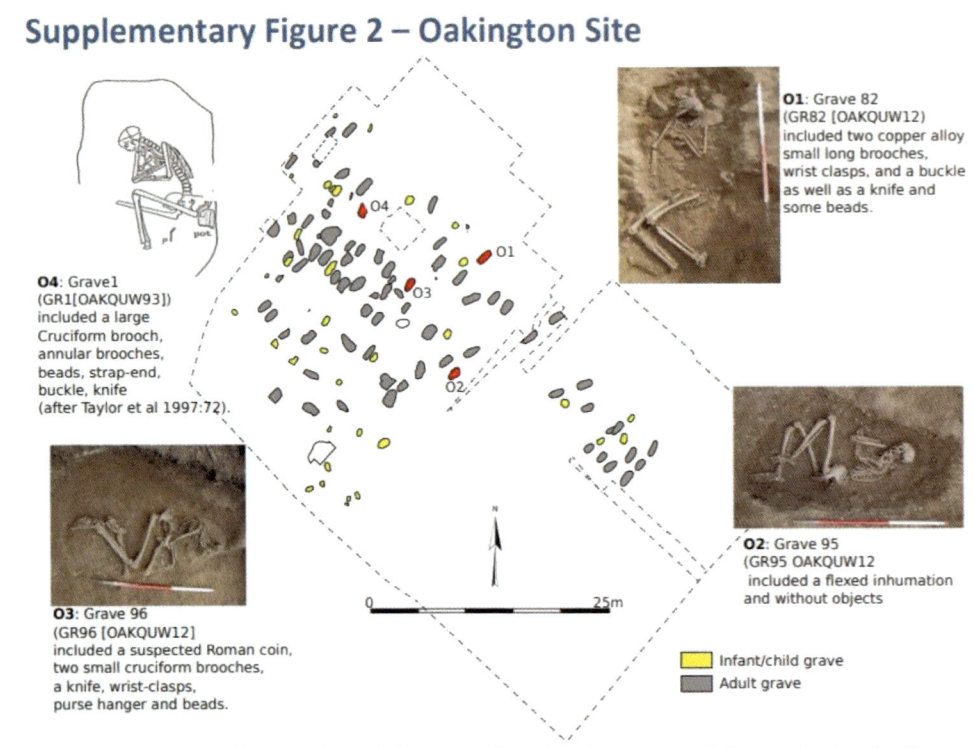

Supplementary Figure 2 – Oakington Site

O1: Grave 82 (GR82 [OAKQUW12]) included two copper alloy small long brooches, wrist clasps, and a buckle as well as a knife and some beads.

O4: Grave1 (GR1[OAKQUW93]) included a large Cruciform brooch, annular brooches, beads, strap-end, buckle, knife (after Taylor et al 1997:72).

O2: Grave 95 (GR95 OAKQUW12) included a flexed inhumation and without objects

O3: Grave 96 (GR96 [OAKQUW12] included a suspected Roman coin, two small cruciform brooches, a knife, wrist-clasps, purse hanger and beads.

Infant/child grave
Adult grave

Supplementary Figure 2: Oakington Site. A schematic of the early Anglo-Saxon cemetery in Oakington, with graves colored in grey (adult individuals), yellow (infant individuals) and red (the adult individuals used in this study).

Figure from Schiffels et al, reproduced under a Creative Commons Attribution 4.0 International License

England, ranging from the late Iron Age to the middle Anglo-Saxon period. By analysing shared rare variants with hundreds of modern samples from Britain and Europe, we estimate that on average the contemporary East English population derives 38% of its ancestry from Anglo-Saxon migrations.'

The early Anglo-Saxon samples were taken from the teeth of 4 bodies found in the Anglo-Saxon cemetery at Oakington in Cambridgeshire. The burial style was culturally Anglo-Saxon, the bodies were all buried flexed and with grave goods which had Anglo-Saxon links. But the genes showed that the people were as related to the Iron Age samples taken from Hinxton in Cambridgeshire as they were to the later Anglo-Saxon bodies from Hinxton. This was a group who were all using Anglo-Saxon items and Anglo-Saxon burial customs but were genetically a mix.

From Nazareth to Northumbria

Mucking, Essex

On the Essex bank of the Thames Estuary just east of Tilbury is the small village of Mucking. Between 1965 and 1978 an area which was soon to be a gravel pit was excavated and evidence of settlement in the area from the Stone Ages to the Middle Ages was found. The excavations were supervised by Margaret Jones, assisted by her husband Tom who took the pictures. The data they found was analysed over subsequent years and finally published in a series of volumes between 1993 and 2015. The excavations showed that there had been a village in the Roman period which had dwindled in size in the 4th century and then been revived in the 5th century. In the third volume, 'The Mucking Anglo-Saxon cemeteries' (Sue Hirst, Dido Clark, 2010, English Heritage), two cemeteries which were in use at the same time were described.

Cemetery II was much larger than cemetery I and had a mix of inhumations and cremation urns. The inhumations were at various orientations with no clear pattern. Meanwhile in cemetery I there was a very different picture. Nearly every grave was oriented west to east, with the head at the west end of the grave. This is exactly the same pattern in late Roman cemeteries, where Christianity was the state religion.

The simplest explanation is that there were two groups of people living near each other who had different ways of dealing with their dead, the smaller one using Christian rites, the larger one using other rites.

From these three locations there is evidence of new people and new ways of doing things coming alongside the original British populations. There were some who intermarried and adopted the immigrant's ways of doing things, while others maintained their traditions – perhaps with some of the newcomers adopting the ways of those who were already living in the East of Britain.

In some places there are people who chose to bury their dead in the same West East pattern as the Romano-British graveyards have when the population became Christians.

So, we have multi-culturalism in the 5th and 6th centuries in Eastern England. To see more evidence of the continuity of Christianity in this period we need to look at artefacts found in some graves, one type in particular is the 'Celtic' hanging bowl.

Scunthorpe and Hanging bowls

In the Old Vicarage of Frodingham Church, in Scunthorpe is the North Lincolnshire Museum. Its exhibits include fossils from the Frodingham Ironstone that enabled steelmaking in the area, an old ironworker's cottage rebuilt as part of the museum and upstairs the finds from excavations at the nearby Anglo-Saxon cemetery at Cleatham.

Among these is a Celtic hanging bowl. It is not easy to photograph, being in a Perspex case in a dimly lit room, so I've used a Celtic hanging bowl from Lincoln Museum for illustration. But the North Lincolnshire Museum was where I first saw such a bowl and began to wonder why it was found in an Anglo-Saxon cemetery.

It isn't a one off. 'The Corpus of Late Celtic Hanging Bowls' by Rupert Bruce Mitford posthumously published by OUP in 2005, contains details of 142 hanging bowl finds known at that date in Britain and Ireland. These bowls vary in size from 135 to 460 mm diameter (5 – 18 in), and all have usually three or occasionally four hooks mounted at equal intervals around the rim of the bowl. These are often attached with a decorated plate, a further decorated plate is found inside in the middle of the base of the bowl and often another on the outside of the middle of the base. A hanging bowl find could be a complete bowl, but may be only one decorated plate, known as an escutcheon, that looks like it was originally part of such a bowl.

These bowls can definitely be classed as Celtic. The escutcheons are decorated with designs which come straight out of the Celtic pattern book. But looking at a map of where such bowls have been found shows an interesting picture.

Found in Anglo-Saxon cremation cemetery at Loveden Hill, now in the Collection Lincoln

British Christianity in the 'Anglo Saxon' areas of eastern Britain

While a few have been found in Ireland and Scotland, none have come to light in Wales and Cornwall, areas which were clearly Celtic in the 5th to the 7th century. Instead, the vast majority of the bowls or escutcheons (117 in 2005) were found in England – many in the south and east, 16 in Lincolnshire alone – the areas more associated with the Anglo Saxons than with the Celts.

Beyond the UK, 29 have been found in Scandinavian graves – the vast majority in Norway. These, and most of the Irish examples, have been dated to the 8th to the 10th centuries. The earliest forms have been called 'A' bowls, and come from the 5th and 6th centuries, with some very early ones even being as early as the 4th century, and seem to be a development of a Romano-British style of bowl. 47 bowls or escutcheons of this type had been found by 2005. The next group, called type 'B', have been dated to the 7th and 8th centuries, and types C, D and E to the 8th to 10th centuries, with the latter two types being only found in Ireland, Scandinavia, Holland and Germany.

The distribution of the earliest, type 'A' bowls shows that they had nothing to do with Ireland, and it is thought that they developed from Romano-British precursors.

Locations of hanging bowl finds in Britain and Ireland

Before we look at how they might have got there, it is worth thinking about what they were used for. There is no agreement among people who have studied these bowls.

Bruce-Mitford rightly points out that, when thinking about what the bowls were for, we need to remember that they were designed to be hung, that they were made over a period of over 500 years so the purpose for which they were made was an ongoing one, and that they come in a range of sizes from those that could be held in the hand to those that are almost as large as cauldrons. They are designed to rest on a flat surface, since they have a flat bottom, then to be hung.

Henry who first developed the grouping of the bowls in the 1930s suggested they were used as lamps – but none has been found with any oil residue. Bruce-Mitford suggests they were used for serving drinks from – but unless this was water there is little point in having a decoration within the bowl. Dr Aldoph Mahr suggested in 1947 that they were holy water stoops.

Locations of the earliest, type 'A' bowl finds

Although few were found in churches, since many were found reused as containers for cremation ashes or as grave goods in burials, this does not mean they were intended only for domestic use.

Indeed, some of the earliest have a cross design on the escutcheons. Some have bird shaped escutcheons; others have triple spiral or wave decorations. All these are Christian symbolism.

From Nazareth to Northumbria

The three finds from Faversham in Kent illustrate these aspects well. Faversham (1) was three hanging escutcheons each with a cross between two dolphins and has been dated to the fifth century. Faversham (2) has escutcheons with a more stylised cruciform shape and is 6th century. Faversham (3), is just a base escutcheon and one escutcheon for a hanging point, the base is decorated with running waves, the hanging escutcheon is possibly a bird like shape. All three are kept by the British Museum.

Faversham (2) 6th century

In the hanging bowls that have been dated to the 5th to 7th century (Bruce-Mitford calls these type A), 16% have some sort of trinitarian symbol, another 40% have a water type decoration – running waves or running spirals, 20% have a cross, and 10% have a fish, dolphin or bird, which are also Christian symbols. Since some have more than one of these decorative types, in total 80% of the bowls have a Christian motif as decoration.

Another point to consider is that most of the bowls have three hooks for hanging. This

Faversham (3) base escutcheon, and (right) hook escutcheon

Hanging Bowl found in the Sutton Hoo ship burial, with clear cross decorations, 6th century, on display in the British Museum

The inner escutcheon extends up into a model fish

would make them stable while hanging but would enable them to be tipped to pour the water out.

When this happened, the inner design would be visible. One of the bowls found at Sutton Hoo had been repaired in such a way as the inner design was favoured over the outer design – showing that seeing inside the bowl was thought to be as important, if not more so, than the outer design.

So, we have bowls of various sizes, some with clear Christian symbols on them, designed to hold and pour out water. The most likely use for them is to hold the water for baptism, which was poured from the bowl over

British Christianity in the 'Anglo Saxon' areas of ea

the head of the person being baptised. We have seen in the Roman period the 'fonts' were designed for the baptism candidate to stand in while water was poured over them. These are the bowls that were used for such pouring in the 5th to 7th centuries.

When considering the hanging bowls which were found in Norway, Egil Mikkelsen, in his book 'Looting or Missioning' (Oxbow Books, 2019), says that twenty of the twenty six Norwegian bowls have bird shaped escutcheons, with some having a whitish coating. Mikkelsen sees these as doves and so accepts that they were used in baptism.

Found in Ingham by a metal detectorist, dates from second half of the seventh century. On display in the Collection, Lincoln

If the bowls at the beginning of the series and at the end are clearly Christian and likely used for baptism, probably many, if not all, of those in between were too.

So, we have what is probably a Christian bowl, used for baptism in 'Anglo Saxon' graves. Clearly there is some form of contact between the Romano-British Christians and the Anglo-Saxon settlers. Mikkelsen suggests that the late bowls in Norway were evidence of Christian missions to the country. Might the Celtic hanging bowls also be evidence of Christian activity in the areas where the Anglo Saxons were settling?

As we have seen from some of the cemetery evidence Anglo-Saxons and British often lived in the same areas, so it is likely some of the bowls were used by the continuing Christian population, but some might have been used by some of the newcomers as they adopted Christianity. After all, when people put an item in a grave it is clearly something of value to them. Why would those who believed in the Saxon pantheon of gods choose to be buried with a bowl with Christian symbols?

6th century Lincoln

During Roman times Christianity was established in Lincoln, and a church was built at St Paul in the Bail.

When the Victorian church was demolished and the site excavated, there were layers of material above the Roman period church.

Dr Caitlin Green published 'Britons and Anglo Saxons in Lincolnshire 400-650' in 2012 (published by the History of Lincolnshire Committee). In it she discusses the excavations at St Paul in the Bail, and the finding of a second larger church with an apse, made out of timber, over the Roman church foundations. This can be dated to about 440 A.D. (within a possible range from the late 4th century to the early 6th century). It was demolished and the site used as a graveyard, with the earliest graves dating to just before the end of the 6th century and cutting the wall line of the timber church, implying that it had been demolished by then. So, the Roman church was followed by a sub-Roman church which continued to be used until not long before Augustine reached these shores. The cemetery an open area until the 10th century when a small stone church was built over one of the graves.

St Paul in the Bail Hanging bowl, Lincoln Cathedral Treasury

Close up of one of the escutcheons on the St Paul in the Bail hanging bowl

A 7th century hanging bowl was found in this grave and can be seen in the Treasury of Lincoln Cathedral. This is the only object in any of the graves, and clearly was buried with an important Christian person, since it is over this grave that the late Saxon church was built. The bowl has escutcheons in the shape of birds and as with the other hanging bowls may well have been used in baptism.

Other evidence that Lincoln remained a British city and probably Christian comes from the distribution of cremation burials in Lincolnshire, shown as deeper blue circles on the map of Lincolnshire. As Caitlin Green noticed, they are all some way from Lincoln itself, which probably means that the people who chose to cremate their dead were kept from settling in the city and its surrounding area.

The name of Lincoln and the Anglo-Saxon kingdom of Lindsey also form part of the evidence.

Lincoln comes from a running together of the Roman name Lindum Colonia. When the Romans conquered this area in 48 A.D. they probably built a simple fort by the River Witham and then replaced it in 60 A.D. with a fort on the escarpment, looking down over the area on the River Witham now called Brayford Pool. The fort was made a colonia, a settlement for retired legionaries in the 80s A.D.

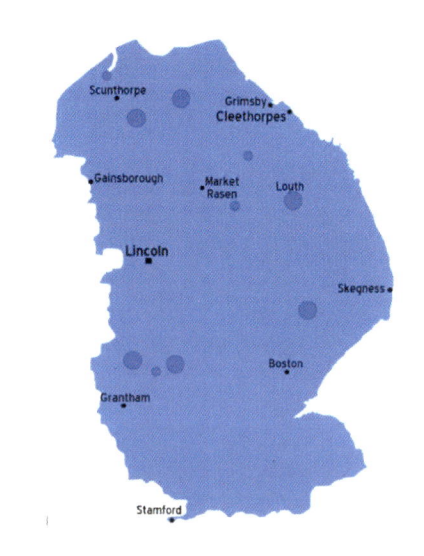

Locations of Anglo-Saxon cremation cemeteries in Lincolnshire showing how they are all over 20 miles from Lincoln

The name Lindum may come from the Brythonic for lake 'Lynn' and the word for dark 'Dun'. (Brythonic is the language that may have been spoken in parts of the British Isles before the Romans came, a relative to Welsh and Gaelic). So, the Roman fort was named for the nearby settlement of Lynndun or Lindon, and that name persisted in the sub-Roman era, to come down to us today as Lincoln.

The Linsissi, a name which eventually was spelt as Lindsey, were the people who lived in the region of Lindon.

Lincoln is not the only place in the country where there is evidence of the British kingdom surviving well into the Anglo-Saxon period. In 'Cultural Transition in the Chilterns and Essex Region, 350 AD to 650 AD' (University of Hertfordshire Press, 2006) John T. Baker looks at how the influence of Germanic culture grew in the 7th century across Hertfordshire, Middlesex and Essex and some parts of adjacent counties. He gives evidence that there are areas where a British way of life persisted while Germanic culture was spreading through the rest of the region.

The evidence John Baker uses includes probable pre-English elements to some placenames, and the absence of Germanic settlements within 15km of St Albans in the 5th and 6th centuries. Germanic artifacts are not evenly spread through the Chilterns and Essex region he studied but are found in clusters such as between Rainham and Mucking and around Shoeburyness in Essex. In these areas there is little evidence of high-status Romano-British occupation, so these were the easiest areas for settlement by migrants. In some areas there are Germanic artifacts in what had been Roman settlements, such as Harlow, where the nearest Cremation cemetery is some distance away. This looks as if the British were adopting the new objects available to buy, in the same way that they go to IKEA today!

Prittlewell

In the 19th century the south end of the village of Prittlewell in Essex was expanded by building many more houses. In time, the whole town was known as Southend, and the original name of Prittlewell is only used for an area in the north of the modern town. But it is Prittlewell which has the ancient church, with a Saxon archway.

British Christianity in the 'Anglo Saxon' areas of eastern Britain

A Roman period house was found in Priory Park and the building of a road and the coming of the railway in the 1920s and 1930s uncovered a Roman era burial ground.

In 2003 a 7th century chamber tomb was uncovered, previously undisturbed, beneath a mound close to the park, by archaeologists from the Museum of London Archaeology (MOLA), as part of preparing the area for road widening scheme, which in the end never happened.

The furnishings of the tomb were of such high quality that the person buried must have been of some status and may have been part of the royal family of the East Saxons. Over 100 objects were found in the tomb which at 4 m² is the largest ever found in England. The objects went on display in Southend Museum in May 2019.

Items from the grave on display in Southend-on-Sea Museum

The objects included the metal decorated ends of drinking horns. No bones of the body remained, since the soil was sandy and acidic, but some of the horn where it met the decorated metal did survive. The MOLA team sampled this material and dated it using the radiocarbon technique to between 575 and 606 A.D., with a most likely date around 580 A.D. This was surprising since the body had been buried with gold crosses over the eyes.

A gold belt buckle

This is a clearly a rich person who is also a Christian in an area ruled by Anglo Saxons in the 6th century. Indeed, among the grave goods was a well-preserved hanging bowl, with equal armed crosses on the escutcheons.

Prittlewell hanging bowl

To cope with the person having grave goods which were thought to show that the person was not a Christian and yet having gold crosses on their eyes it was suggested that they were put in the coffin by Christians and then into the chambered tomb by pagans, but in the end, it is easier to accept that we have

Decorated metal ends of drinking horns

to abandon the idea that Christians are never buried with grave goods. Rather, grave goods are a sign of the status of the person, not of their religion.

The crosses which were over the eyes of the body

From Nazareth to Northumbria

Clearly in the late 6th century there was a high-status man who was openly a Christian, buried with gold crosses and his hanging bowl, as well as many other riches.

East Kent and Canterbury

East Kent is one of the areas which is believed to have been settled first by those who came from the north of Europe in the 5th century. Again, it is to Kent that Augustine came in 597 A.D. and according to Bede had an impressive track record in converting the population to Christianity. But is there evidence that some at least were already Christians?

Andrew Richardson in 'The Anglo-Saxon Cemeteries of Kent' (2005, BAR) brought together data from all the cemeteries from the 5th to the 8th century that had been found and excavated. When looking at the orientation of the graves which had been recorded by degrees, rather than just by noting that they were west-east or north-south, he found that 96% were orientated in the range NW-SE to SW-NE, with only 2% N-S or S-N.

When he looked at the dates of the graves, he found that while as expected the orientations of the later graves were more consistently broadly W-E, as expected from an area which was mainly Christian from the 7th century onwards, in the 5th and 6th century out of 279 graves, 257 were in the range NW-SE to SW-NE, that is 92%. He concluded that the orientation of the grave is not an indicator of the religion of the person buried, some other factor must be leading to this broadly W-E orientation.

But looking across the channel to where the Jutes came from would help to settle this. For if the burial of bodies on a W-E orientation is common in 4th and 5th century in North West Germany and Denmark, then this is a custom that has been brought with the settlers. If not, then they have developed it on coming into Kent.

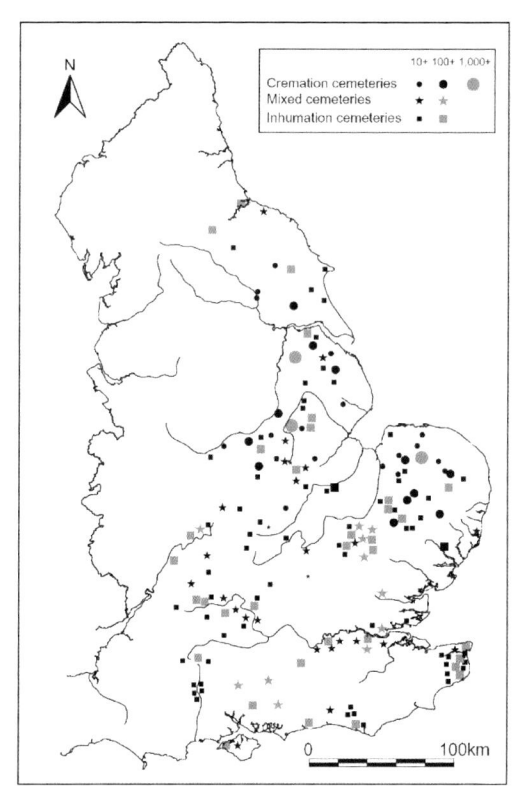

Locations of 5th and 6th century cemeteries

In his 'Early Medieval Cemeteries: An Introduction to Burial Archaeology in the Post-Roman West' 1995 Guy Halsall (available to read on academia.edu) describes the mortuary practices in different regions of western Europe in the early medieval period. In North West Germany he describes the main rite as cremation. Where bodies were buried, they were usually laid N-S. In Scandinavia cremation and inhumation were both practiced, burial with goods was rare, but unfortunately Guy Halsall does not comment on the orientation, but for north western France and the lower Rhineland he mentions that N-S is the most common orientation.

In Kent cremation is very rare – a handful of instances compared with the dominant burial of bodies, so somehow the settlers have forgotten that they cremate their dead, or bury them N-S, but immediately adopted the Roman-British burial style of W-E.

So, if in their homelands N-S burial, or cremation, was most common, why did the settlers adopt W-E on settling in Kent? Unless there were not actually that many settlers and what we see in Kent is a population descended from the Romano-British, retaining their Christian burial practices.

Looking at place name evidence we come back to Eccles, a village in Kent with a name meaning church in Latin. The name of the county itself is curious, for it goes back to the pre-Roman tribe of the Cantiaci who were described by Julius Caesar in 51 B.C., who felt that they were the most civilised of the British tribes. The name Cant may be derived from the Brythonic 'cant' meaning rim – it may be related etymologically to Cantabria in Spain, a coast region with many place names with Celtic roots. Canterbury derives is name from being the fortified town ('burg' in Old English) of the people of Kent, the Cantware.

Darenth, Dartford

Before we look at the evidence in Canterbury itself, the Darenth Bowl is worth commenting on.

British Christianity in the 'Anglo Saxon' areas of eastern Britain

In 1978, an excavation by the Dartford District Archaeology Group found two Early Medieval graves. Both had grave goods and in one the Darenth Bowl was uncovered. It had been placed in the grave upside down above the left shoulder. It is now in the museum at Dartford.

In the centre of the bowl is a decorated area, with a 'Chi-Rho' monogram. This is surrounded by vine leaf scroll and a continuous abbreviated Latin inscription. Two different translations have been made depending on where you start and what might be added to the abbreviation. So it could be DEIURIUITAINTETUIASRUUIN 'Justly (eternal) life and the way (are found) in your Saint Rufinus' or VITAINTERUIASRUUINDEIURI 'O King Invincible Eternal Life is in You and the Way of Salvation and Redemption the Very Truth of the Word of God'. The bowl has been dated to about 450 A.D.

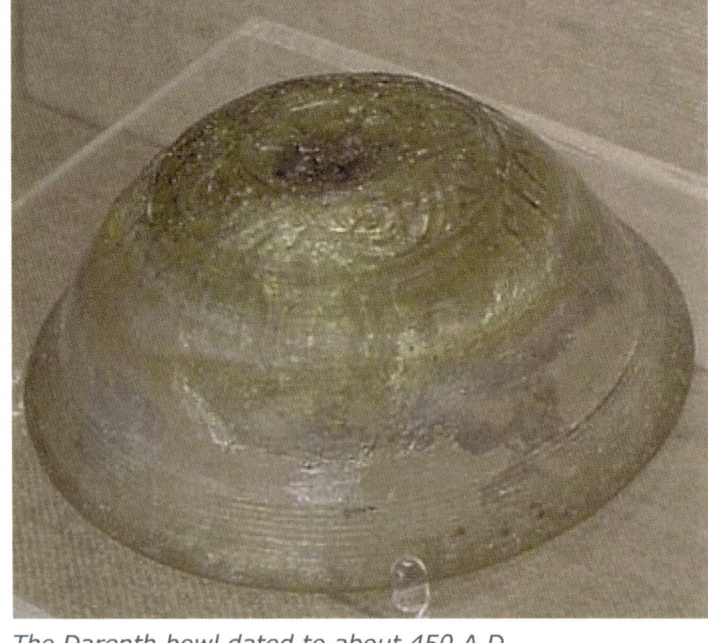

The Darenth bowl dated to about 450 A.D.

The design on the Darenth Bowl

The main argument that the grave must be that of a 'pagan' despite the presence of a Christian artefact is that it has grave goods in it. Early in English archaeology the assumption was made that if a grave has grave goods the person buried was not a Christian, so it was easy to see which were Anglo-Saxon graves. But it could equally be possible that people started to bury their dead with grave goods in the 5th century because of other reasons than being settlers with a different religion. Indeed, we know that the Prittlewell burial was of a Christian and that had plenty of grave goods. And if we look across the channel to France, Guy Halsall, in his book of essays 'Cemeteries and Society in Merovingian Gaul: Selected Studies in History and Archaeology, 1992-2009' (2010, Brill, available to download from academia.edu), wrote 'Bailey K. Young had made most of the important critical points in dismantling the connections between paganism and burial with grave-goods, or unfurnished inhumation and Christianity' (p6).

Canterbury

Canterbury was the capital of the pre-Roman kingdom of the Cantiaci. For the Romans it was a significant town on Watling Street, where road from Dover, Richborough, Reculver and Lympne met. Under the Romans it was rebuilt and called Durovernum Cantiacorum.

Evidence for Christianity in sub-Roman Canterbury includes the two silver spoons found in the Longmarket area of the city in 1962. These are kept with the rest of the horde in the Canterbury Roman Museum. As you can see, they have swan shaped handles and a chi-rho on them. These were buried in the early 5th century, since they accompany coins dating to 407-411 A.D.

Swan spoons with chi rho 5th century

From Nazareth to Northumbria

Excavations have shown that occupation of Canterbury continued into the 5th century – Christopher Snyder in 'Age of Tyrants: Britain and the Britons' (1998, Penn State Press, pp148-149) brings together some of the evidence including reuse of the public buildings with renewal in timber rather than stone. Some 5th century buildings were erected over the Roman roads – so the town wasn't as busy as it had been, but it was still occupied in this century. A visigothic copy of a gold coin, which probably came from southern Gaul and was made in about 480 A.D. was dropped into the soil over a Roman courtyard in the Marlowes area of the town. Nearby four phases of 5th century material were found in a Roman stone building.

In the sixth century we have evidence of the existence of churches in Canterbury. This comes in written form from Bede himself.

"There was on the east side of the city a church dedicated to the honour of St. Martin, built whilst the Romans were still in the island, wherein the queen, who, as has been said before, was a Christian, used to pray. In this they first began to meet, to sing, to pray, to say mass, to preach, and to baptize, till the king, being converted to the faith, allowed them to preach openly, and build or repair churches in all places." (Ecclesiastical History of the English Nation, BOOK I CHAPTER XXVI)

Roman walls in St Martin's Canterbury

St Martins is still a parish church in Canterbury. It has complete sections of Roman wall and contains other reused Roman building material in its walls. Canterbury History and Archaeology Society suggests that 'The church is thought to have been a Roman mortuary chapel before AD400, as the area has produced many Roman burial sites and the Roman road into Canterbury from the Roman port of Richborough passed close by.' (http://www.canterbury-archaeology.org.uk/stmartin/4590809556)

As well as the evidence of the Roman stonework, we have evidence of the presence of Queen Bertha's chaplain Bishop Liudhard having been in this area for a medal was found in a grave in the churchyard in 1844 with his name in the inscription. The Liudhard medalet is now part of the collection at the World Museum in Liverpool. It was originally a coin that was probably struck between 578 and 589 A.D. and then made into a necklace. Liudhard died in the late 590s so anyone wanting to align themselves with him would have been a Christian before Augustine came to Canterbury.

The Liudhard medalet

St Martin's Canterbury

British Christianity in the 'Anglo Saxon' areas of eastern Britain

But St Martin's wasn't the only church standing in Canterbury at the time Augustine came, Bede tells us that the king allowed them to build or repair churches in all places.

Building stone was a sought-after commodity in the 6th century, and would not be left in place to be a church that could be repaired, if the church had not been in very recent use.

Northumbria

We have seen that in Kent and in Essex there is evidence of the migrants living alongside the already settled population in the period from 400 to 600, and that the settled population continued to bury their dead, with the grave broadly west east with head at the west end. This at the very least indicates a continuity of burial custom from the Roman period, when this form of burial developed in the 3rd and 4th centuries as Christianity spread.

In East Anglia there is also evidence of the British continuing to live alongside the immigrants. In her paper 'Continuity within change: Two sites in the borders of the former Iceni territory in East Anglia' (ACE Conference Brussels: The very beginning of Europe? Early-Medieval Migration and Colonisation (2012), pp109-122) Penelope Walton Rogers uses the results of examining the imprints left behind by fabric in graves to show that the styles of fabric used in Romano-Britain persist in some graves in the area of the pre Roman tribe of the Iceni in the 5th and 6th centuries alongside graves which have more typical Anglo Saxon fabric imprints.

In Lincolnshire the migrants settled mainly on the coast, leaving the area around Lincoln to the descendants of the Romano-British, until they eventually inter-married and the Angles took over the leadership.

If we look north of the Humber, we see a similar pattern.

In Fox, B. 'The P-Celtic Place-Names of North-East England and South-East Scotland', A Journal of Early Medieval Northwestern Europe Issue 10 (May 2007) online at https://www.heroicage.org/issues/10/fox.html

Map by Mike Christie at English Wikipedia CC

Bethany Fox brings together all the place names of the area which was Northumbria in the 7th century – which reaches north to the Firth of Forth and south to the Humber. Her work includes an interactive map at https://www.heroicage.org/issues/10/placenames/frames.htm which plots all the possibly Celtic names and the clearly English names (the places ending in -ingham and -ham).

She concludes:

"The most obvious interpretation of the evidence in this study is, however, a synthesis of mass-migration and elite-takeover models. Large-scale Anglian cultural influence, and therefore implicitly settlement, seems likely in the river valleys. Following this, an Anglian power base would have been established, which would enable the political domination of the uplands without further wholesale resettlement of Anglians. This synthesis would help to explain the distribution patterns seen in this study. Either way, the combined distributions of place-names in the interactive map may be considered to provide a snapshot of the advance of Anglian cultural influence in the North. It suggests that the most likely model for this advance is first spreading along the river valleys of the major rivers of the Tyne, Tees, Alne and Tweed, and over the plain of the East coast. It seems plausible that p-Celtic speech survived for longer in the upland areas of the Pennines, Cheviots, Moorfoots and Lammermuirs, surviving perhaps longest of all in the area to the north of these latter two upland areas, where archaeological evidence supports the idea of an independent British kingdom surviving for a time after the Anglicisation of the population further south. In the past, scholars have tended to posit a 'fan-shaped' model for the spread of Anglian cultural and linguistic dominance in the North, whereby influence spreads outwards from a single point (for a classic example, see Higham 1986, 254). However, the distribution maps in this study would seem to suggest a more diffuse model, whereby influence travels mainly

From Nazareth to Northumbria

by water, along the coast and up major river valleys. This mirrors developments in southern England." (Fox 2007)

So, it seems the settlement of the Angles, Saxons and Jutes was not a wipe-out of the Romano-British, but a settlement alongside them. Settling along the coast and the larger rivers they grew in strength and organisation. The British, after the Romans left, probably returned to their previous smaller units of government, and as the Anglo-Saxons formed their kingdoms, they incorporated these. Some British kingdoms survived alongside the Saxon ones for longer - https://www.historyfiles.co.uk/FeaturesBritain/BritishMapAD450-700.htm gives a good idea of the development of the Saxon kingdoms.

Vindolanda

Evidence of the continuation of Christianity in Northumbria from the Roman period into he 7th century is found at Vindolanda Fort just south of Hadrian's Wall on the Stanegate Roman road.

The site has been subject to extensive excavation since the 1930s. In the 1970s the Vindolanda Trust bought the site and each summer has held an excavation. They found that there were 9 different versions of the fort,

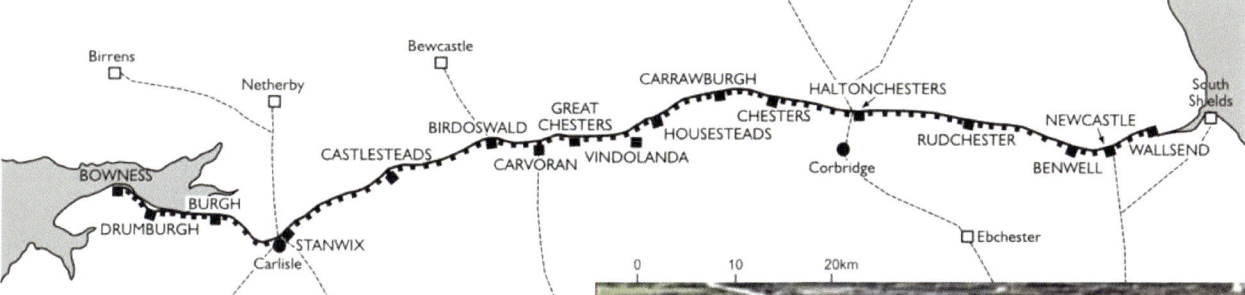

Map of Hadrian's wall showing the forts

the first 5 of turf and timber were built, demolished and capped with clay before the new fort was built over the top. These forts were built by different units of the army between 85 A.D. and 122A.D. Between Hadrian's Wall being built and the end of the Roman occupation 4 stone forts occupied different parts of the site at different times.

The excavations of the fort and the associated 'Vicus' or civilian village that grew up alongside it show that the area was occupied after the Roman command of Britain was lost. Indeed it stayed occupied into the 9th Century.

4th/5th century church at Vindolanda

In the late 4th century a church was built in the courtyard of the commanders house in the fort. It was dated from the evidence of the latest coins underneath it being from 370 A.D. and is interpreted as a church because of the shape of the building with an apse.

Other evidence for Christianity at the site includes a metal strap end with decoration of a bishop holding a crook, a stone with a chi rho and a 5th to 6th

Map of the location of the 5th/6th C churches at Vindolanda. Picture © Vindolanda Trust, used with permission

British Christianity in the 'Anglo Saxon' areas of eastern Britain

century tombstone with the inscription BRIGOMAGLOS IACIT. As we saw in South Wales the words HIC IACIT are a sign of a Christian.

Subsequent excavations have revealed two later churches, from the 5th and 6th centuries.

In 2020 the Vindolanda Trust announced that they had found the remains of a Christian cup or chalice in the remains of a 6th century church. 'Buried amongst a rubble filled building, now known to be the remains of a 6th century Christian church, were 14 fragmentary remains of an incredibly rare lead Christian cup or chalice. Although in very poor condition due to its

Fragments of the 'chalice'. Picture ©Vindolanda Trust, used with permission

proximity to the surface of the ground, each fragment of the vessel was found to be covered by lightly etched symbols, each representing different forms of Christian iconography from the time. The combination of so many of these etchings and the context of the discovery makes this artefact one of the most important of its type to come from early Christianity in Western Europe. It is the only surviving partial chalice from this period in Britain and the first such artefact to come from a fort on Hadrian's Wall.

The marks appear to have been added, both to the outside and the inside of this cup, by the same hand or artist and although they are now difficult to see with the naked eye, with the aid of specialist photography, the symbols have been carefully recorded and work has started on a new journey of discovery to unlock their meanings. The etchings include some well-known symbols from the early church including ships, crosses and chi-rho, fish, a whale, a happy bishop, angels, members of a congregation, letters in Latin, Greek and potentially Ogam.' https://www.vindolanda.com/news/unique-christian-artefact-uncovered-at-vindolanda

Yeavering - Ad Gefrin

As Diera and Bernicia were being united by Aethelfrith in 604 A.D. Elmet, Rheged and Goddodin were continuing Romano-British kingdoms. But it is now clear that many who were ruled by Anglo-Saxon kings were the descendants of those who had been living in the land since before the Romans came.

What we read in Bede (book II, chapter IX), about how Northumbrian kings came to Christianity may be true for the kings themselves, but is not the whole story for the people whom they ruled. Indeed, it may be that Edwin, whose conversion Bede describes at the preaching of Paulinus, who had been sent North by the Roman Christianity mission in Kent in the late 620s, was already well acquainted with Christianity. According to Reginald of Durham and Geoffrey of Monmouth, he was an exile in Christian Gwynedd while

Slate which marks the suggested site of Ad Gefrin at Yeavering

Aethelfrith was uniting Northumbria, In 625 A.D. he married Athelburg, the daughter of Bertha, the Moravian wife of Aethelberht of Kent, on condition that he convert to Christianity.

From Nazareth to Northumbria

Bede writes of the advice of a counsellor as they were sitting in the Great Hall at Edwin's royal township of Ad Gefrin. 'The present life man, O king, seems to me, in comparison with that time which is unknown to us, like to the swift flight of a sparrow through the room wherein you sit at supper in winter amid your officers and ministers, with a good fire in the midst whilst the storms of rain and snow prevail abroad; the sparrow, I say, flying in at one door and immediately out another, whilst he is within is safe from the wintry but after a short space of fair weather he immediately vanishes out of your sight into the dark winter from which he has emerged. So, this life of man appears for a short space but of what went before or what is to follow we are ignorant. If, therefore, this new doctrine contains something more certain, it seems justly to deserve to be followed.' (Bede EH Book II, chapter XIII).

Yeavering in northern Northumbria is a large Anglo-Saxon site that was identified by Brian Hope-Taylor as Ad Gefrin.

(Hope-Taylor 1977)

If this advice did indeed seal Edwin's conversion it came at the end of a long process, with many other influences along the way.

Since the area is one with many British place names Hope-Taylor suggested the Anglian kings deliberately had this as an inland stronghold to subdue the locals.

Bamburgh

Another major stronghold of the Northumbrian rulers was at Bebbanburh, today called Bamburgh. Prior to the Angles settling in the area there was a hill fort on the site called Din Guarie. Eventually after passing between the Britons and the Angles three times, the fort finally came permanently under Anglo-Saxon control in 590 A.D..

Nick Higham (An English empire: Bede and the early Anglo-Saxon kings' (Manchester University Press ND, 1995) suggests that it was the capital of the Godonnin, whose kingdom Bernicia was founded in 420 A.D. and was conquered by Ida the Angle, who took the castle in 547 A.D. His son Hussa lost the castle briefly in 590 but won it back the same year. His successor Aethelfrith renamed it Bebbanburh, after his then queen Bebba.

Bamburgh Castle from the sea, the core of the current castle is Norman.

By Sabrebd – own work licensed for reuse https://en.wikipedia.org/wiki/sv:Creative_Commons

Aethelfrith married his second wife Acha of Deira in 604 A.D. to seal the unification of the two kingdoms, while her brother Edwin went into exile in East Anglia, which implies that Aethelfrith used force to depose him and make the union of the kingdoms. Acha's son Oswald was born in about 604 and Oswiu in about 612A.D..

British Christianity in the 'Anglo Saxon' areas of eastern Britain

To recover his throne in Deira, Edwin eventually persuaded the king of East Anglia to attack Aethelfrith in 616 A.D. In the battle Aethelfrith died and his sons Eanfrith, Oswald, and Oswiu went into exile. Oswald and Oswiu chose to go to the Irish Dal Riata, who had a kingdom in what is now the South East of Scotland, for sanctuary. This is curious since his father Aethelfrith had defeated their king and killed many of them in 603. Bede believes that Oswald and Oswiu learned their Christianity while in exile. Certainly, they were much influenced by their time there, and Iona, the monastery of Columba in Dal Raita territory, was where they looked to for missionaries to come to Northumbria in time.

The natural stronghold is clear in this view taken from the seaward side of the castle

In 632 A.D. Penda of Mercia made an alliance with Cadwallon of Gwynedd to challenge Edwin of Northumbria's dominance. They met at the battle of Hatfield in 632 or 633 A.D. Edwin died, as did his son Oswith, while his other son Eanfrith was captured by Penda and killed sometime later. On his death Northumbria was split again, with Bernicia going to Aethelfrith's son Eanfrith and Deira to Edwin's cousin Osric.

Eanfrith may have been part of the alliance with Penda and Cadwallon, but was soon in dispute with him, and was killed by Cadwallon in 634 A.D.. Bede tells us that Eanfrith renounced his Christianity on becoming king.

Heavenfield

His half-brother Oswald mustered an army and attacked Cadwallon at Heavenfield. Today like at Yeavering there is little to see, but according to Bede for Northumbria this is a vital site.

'The place is shown to this day, and held in much veneration, where Oswald, being about to engage, erected the sign of the holy cross, and on his knees prayed to God that he would assist his worshipers in their great distress. It is further reported, that the cross being made in haste, and the hole dug in which it was to be fixed, the king himself, full of faith, laid hold of it and held it with both his hands, till it was set fast by throwing in the earth and this done, raising his voice, he cried to his army, "Let us all kneel, and jointly beseech the true and living God Almighty, in his mercy, to defend us from the haughty and fierce enemy; for He knows that we have undertaken a just war for the safety of our nation." All did as

The current St Oswald's church at Heavenfield

he had commanded, and accordingly advancing towards the enemy with the first dawn of day, they obtained the victory, as their faith deserved. In that place of prayer very many miraculous cures are known to have been performed, as a token and memorial of the king's faith; for even to this day, many are wont to cut off small chips from the wood of the holy cross, which being put into water, men or cattle drinking thereof, or sprinkled with that water, are immediately restored to health.

Heavenfield today

'The place in the English tongue is called Heavenfield, or the Heavenly Field, which name it formerly received as a presage of what was afterwards to happen, denoting, that there the heavenly trophy would be erected, the heavenly victory begun, and heavenly miracles be wrought to this day. The same place is near the wall with which the Romans formerly enclosed the island from sea to sea, to restrain the fury of the barbarous nations, as has been said before. Hither also the brothers of the church of Hagulstad, which is not far from thence, repair yearly on the day before that on which King Oswald was afterwards slain, to watch there for the health of his soul, and having sung many psalms, to offer for him in the morning the sacrifice of the holy oblation. And since that good custom has spread, they have lately built and consecrated a church there, which has attached additional sanctity and honour to that place: and this with good reason; for it appears that there was no sign of the Christian faith, no church, no altar erected throughout all the nations of the Bernicians, before that new commander of the army, prompted by the devotion of his faith, set up the cross as he was going to give battle to his barbarous enemy.'
Bede EH (Book III chapter II)

This is surprising since Bede himself tells of Edwin's conversion, and the evidence of the continuity of settlement from Romano-British days, through the Celtic kingdom of Bernicia, is also strong in the place names. Still, there is no doubt that Oswald acquired the reputation of a saint and soon outshone Edwin as a Christian Anglian king.

Bede tells us that Oswald sent to the 'Scots' (that is the Irish in Dal Raita) for a bishop and Corman came to him. However, Bede tells us he was too harsh so Aidan was sent instead.

Lindisfarne

Aidan had been a monk at Iona from an early age and was consecrated a bishop for Northumbria. He founded his priory/cathedral on Lindisfarne, the island just off the Northumbrian coast not far south of Bamburgh.

Information board at Heavenfield

The name Lindisfarne is itself interesting, since while it is of uncertain origin it may mean 'island of the people of Lindsey', Lindsey being the British and then Anglo-Saxon Kingdom in Lincolnshire.

Aidan was a gentler character, and his mission was well received by the people of Northumbria. Many churches and monasteries were founded, which served as schools as well.

British Christianity in the 'Anglo Saxon' areas of eastern Britain

Bede describes Aidan: "He was one to traverse both town and country on foot, never on horseback, unless compelled by some urgent necessity; and wherever in his way he saw any, either rich or poor, he invited them, if infidels, to embrace the mystery of the faith or if they were believers, to strengthen them in the faith, and to stir them up by words and actions to alms and good works. ... This [the reading of scriptures and psalms, and meditation upon holy truths] was the daily employment of himself and all that were with him, wheresoever they went; and if it happened, which was but seldom, that he was invited to eat with the king, he went with one or two clerks, and having taken a small repast, made haste to be gone with them, either to read or write. At that time, many religious men and women, stirred up by his example, adopted the custom of fasting on Wednesdays and Fridays, till the ninth hour, throughout the year, except during the fifty days after Easter. He never gave money to the powerful men of the world, but only meat, if he happened to entertain them; and, on the contrary, whatsoever gifts of money he received from the rich, he either distributed them, as has been said, to the use of the poor, or bestowed them in ransoming such as had been wrongfully sold for slaves. Moreover, he afterwards made many of those he had ransomed his disciples, and after having taught and instructed them, advanced them to the order of priesthood." (Bede EH Book III Chapter V)

Lindisfarne Castle on the natural stronghold on the island

The Norman Priory on Lindisfarne – the site of the one Aidan founded is probably under the houses of the village

The church in Bamburgh is named for Aidan and claims to have a roof beam which had been part of the wooden church of Aidan's day -indeed it is claimed to be the one Aidan leant against as he died.

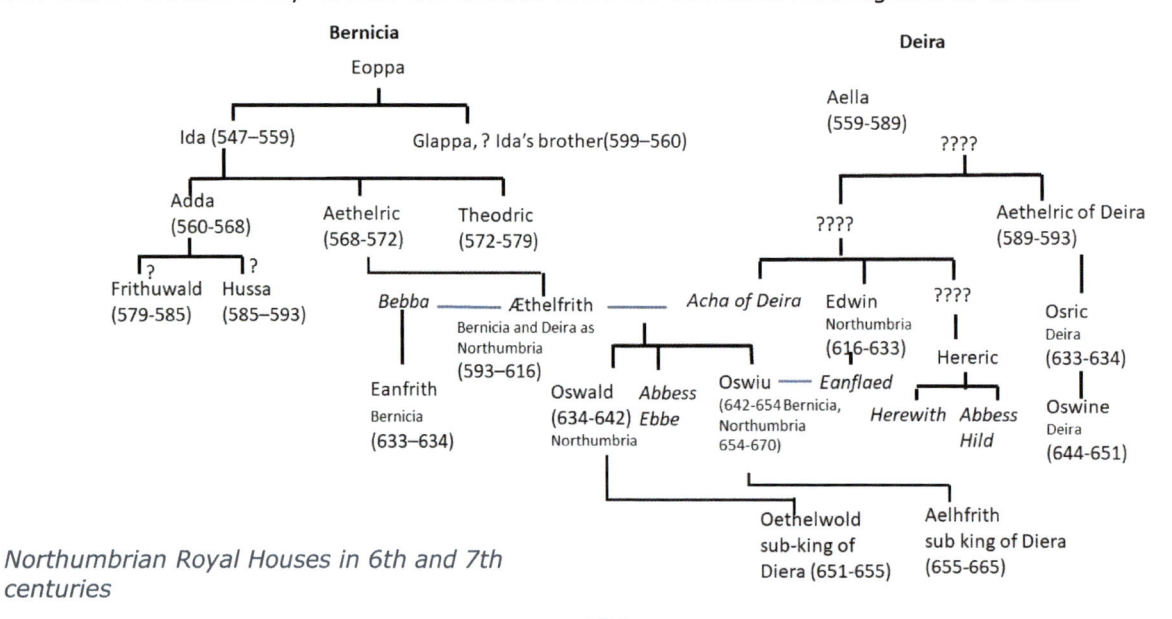

Northumbrian Royal Houses in 6th and 7th centuries

Bernicia

Eoppa
- Ida (547–559)
  - Adda (560-568)
    - Frithuwald (579-585) ?
    - Hussa (585–593) ?
  - Aethelric (568-572)
  - Theodric (572-579)
- Glappa, ? Ida's brother (599–560)

Bebba — Æthelfrith — Acha of Deira
Bernicia and Deira as Northumbria (593–616)

Eanfrith Bernicia (633–634)

Oswald (634–642) / *Abbess Ebbe* Northumbria

Oswiu — Eanflaed (642-654 Bernicia, Northumbria 654-670)

Deira

Aella (559-589)
- ????
  - ????
  - Aethelric of Deira (589-593)
    - Edwin Northumbria (616-633)
    - ????
      - Hereric
        - *Herewith* *Abbess Hild*
    - Osric Deira (633-634)
    - Oswine Deira (644-651)

Oethelwold sub-king of Diera (651-655)

Aelhfrith sub king of Diera (655-665)

126

From Nazareth to Northumbria

Whitby (Streonshalh)

Today Whitby is known for its scampi and the Dracula story told by Bram Stoker. But before Whitby in the bay was named by the Danish settlers (the -by ending is a typical Scandinavian place name marker) on the cliff tops was an abbey named Streonshalh. On the site, or near it, today are the impressive remains of the 13th century Benedictine monastery built on what is now the cliff tops. The Early Medieval Abbey was probably mostly in an area which has now succumbed to the sea.

This earlier abbey was founded in 657 A.D. by King Oswiu, who appointed his cousin Hild the first Abbess. She had been the abbess at Hartlepool, the successor to Hieu who founded that abbey in 640 A.D. and was the first early medieval abbess to lead a double house, of both monks and nuns.

The 13th century Whitby Abbey

Escutcheons and a roundel from at least 5 different hanging bowls were found when the remaining early medieval area of the Abbey site was excavated in the 1920s and are held in the British Museum collection.

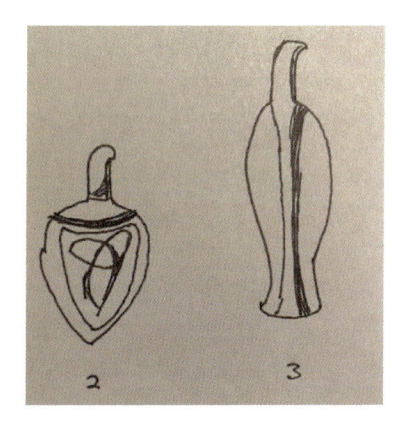

Sketches of some of the escutcheons and the roundel found at Whitby Abbey

Hild led a similar double house at Streonshalh, and it is here that Oswiu summoned a council of the church in his kingdom in 664 A.D. The problem Oswiu had was that while he followed the British church as he had learnt it in his youth among the Dal Raita in its timing of Easter, his wife, Edwin's daughter, who had spent her exile in Kent, followed the Roman practices brought with Augustine's mission. The British Church saw no reason to change how Easter was calculated just because the Bishop of Rome backed a new calculation, but the Roman Christians in Britain naturally went with the current Roman way. This was a very practical difference – the Queen might be celebrating Easter while the King was still observing Lent.

Another major point of disagreement was how monks should show in their hair cut that they were monks. The British church, following a style that originated in the Eastern Church, had its monks shave their head from a line from ear to ear forward, with the hair at the back of the head kept fairly long, while the Roman practice for the tonsure was to shave the top of the head, and to have shorter hair. It is hard to find a picture of the 'Celtic' tonsure now, but a sculpture in Sompting Church in Sussex shows a bishop with what looks like this form of tonsure.

Today this seems a strange thing to be bothered about but, like the dating of Easter, it was really about who had the right to decide, was it the Pope, or did the British church have the authority to have its own local

British Christianity in the 'Anglo Saxon' areas of eastern Britain

traditions, even when the Pope was seeking to assert his authority in such matters. Bede tells us of the debate:

"King Oswy first observed, that it behooved those who served one God to observe the same rule of life; and as they all expected the same kingdom in heaven, so they ought not to differ in the celebration of the Divine mysteries; but rather to inquire which was the truest tradition, that the same might be followed by all; he then commanded his bishop, Colman, first to declare what the custom was which he observed, and whence it derived its origin. Then Colman said, "The Easter which I keep, I received from my elders, who sent me bishop hither; all our forefathers, men beloved of God, are known to have kept it after the same manner; and that the same may not seem to any contemptible or worthy to be rejected, it is the same which St. John the Evangelist, the disciple beloved of our Lord, with all the churches over which he presided, is recorded to have observed."…..

Early medieval carving, Sompting Church, East Sussex

Then Wilfrid, being ordered by the king to speak, delivered himself thus :- "The Easter which we observe, we saw celebrated by all at Rome, where the blessed apostles, Peter and Paul, lived, taught, suffered, and were buried; we saw the same done in Italy and in France, when we travelled through those countries for pilgrimage and prayer. We found the same practiced in Africa, Asia, Egypt, Greece, and all the world, wherever the church of Christ is spread abroad, through several nations and tongues, at one and the same time; except only these and their accomplices in obstinacy, I mean the Picts and the Britons, who foolishly, in these two remote islands of the world, and only in part even of them, oppose all the rest of the universe...

"But as for you and your companions, you certainly sin, if, having heard the decrees of the Apostolic See, and of the universal church, and that the same is confirmed by holy writ, you refuse to follow them; for, though your fathers were holy, do you think that their small number, in a corner of the remotest island, is to be preferred before the universal church of Christ throughout the world? And if that Columba of yours (and, I may say, ours also, if he was Christ's servant), was a holy man and powerful in miracles, yet could he be preferred before the most blessed prince of the apostles, to whom our Lord said, 'Thou art Peter, and upon this rock I will build my church, and the gates of hell shall not prevail against it, and to thee I will give the keys of the kingdom of heaven?'"

When Wilfrid had spoken thus, the king said, "Is it true, Colman, that these words were spoken to Peter by our Lord?" He answered, "It is true, O king " Then says he, "Can you show any such power given to your Columba?" Colman answered, "None." Then added the king, "Do you both agree that these words were principally directed to Peter, and that the keys of heaven were given to him by our Lord?" They both answered, "We do." Then the king concluded, "And I also say unto you, that he is the door-keeper, whom I will not contradict, but will, as far as I know and am able, in all things obey his decrees, lest, when I come to the gates of the kingdom of heaven, there should be none to open them, he being my adversary who is proved to have the keys." The king having said this, all present, both great and small, gave their assent, and renouncing the more imperfect institution…" (Bede EH Book3 XXV)

So Oswiu sided with the Roman party over the matter of Easter. Colman and his followers left Northumbria for Iona, while Wilfred became the bishop of Northumbria and moved the see from Lindisfarne to York. But this does not mean that the customs of the British church faded immediately. Oswiu had influence on other kings in the British Isles but was not able to direct their churches. The movement to accept the Roman way in areas beyond Northumbria was one of slow persuasion.

From Nazareth to Northumbria

7. Where did the British Church go?

We have seen that there is a fair amount of evidence that the British continued to live where they had lived across the area that would become England after the coming of the Anglo-Saxons. Those in the East may have already spoken a form of English, but those to the west of the country almost certainly spoke Brythonic, a language that would evolve into Welsh and Cornish. The majority were buried in the late Roman way, showing they retained a Christian orientation of burial, even if some started to be buried with items to show what they had been in life. Such items do not tell us that they were now pagans – even the Bishops of Rome at this period were sometimes buried with items. We know for sure that Cuthbert was buried with a gospel in his coffin.

In 664 A.D, the Northumbrian royal family opted to follow the customs of Rome, which were already being followed by those in Kent. But why did all memory of the majority of the founders of church in the East of the country get lost? In Wales, Cornwall and some areas of Devon and the Welsh Marches churches are still named for the 5th or 6th century person who founded them. In England there are almost no such dedications. Yet surely the British still met in churches when the Saxons came, and would remember their saints. So why did they forget them?

The answer is to be found in the Archbishop of Canterbury's attitude to the British Christians. We saw from Bede's account of the coming of Augustine and his meeting with some British bishops that he viewed himself and the version of Christianity he brought with him as superior to theirs.

This continued to be the view of the Archbishops of Canterbury. Since the Pope, the Bishop of Rome, had decided that the timing of Easter was to be calculated in a particular way, the churches of the West were expected to fall into line with him. This was all part of the growing sense of those around the Pope that he was a bulwark of orthodoxy while the Eastern Church dallied with heresy. The major church councils were all held in what is now Turkey, in the continuing Roman Empire, known as the Byzantine Empire.

The Orthodox Church in Kadikoy, Istanbul

This view was based both on the understanding of the Pope as the successor of Peter, and the experience of these church councils. An example of this is how the Pope dealt with the Council of Chalcedon in 451 A.D. This was the fourth of the 'Ecumenical Councils' and was called by the Emperor Marceon. (An ecumenical council is one which had representatives of the whole church present – although there were often very few from the Western parts of the church at them). When the issue of Jesus's natures was reopened by the teaching of Eutyches in 444, as part of trying to resolve the issue the Bishop of Constantinople sent an account of Eutyches teaching to Pope Leo I. Leo's reply was delayed and was not read at the Council of Ephesus in 449, and that council sided with Eutyche's teaching. When Leo heard this he declared the Council a synod of robbers. A fresh council was called at Chalcedon – now a suburb of Istanbul on the Asian side called Kadikoy.

At this council the Emperor Theodosius insisted on Leo's views being read – Leo was not there in person but represented by legates. When his letter, now called 'Leo's Tome' was read the council was reported to have agreed 'This is the faith of the fathers, this is the faith of the Apostles. So, we all believe, thus the orthodox believe. ...Peter has spoken thus through Leo. So taught the Apostles. Piously and truly did Leo teach, so taught Cyril. Everlasting be the memory of Cyril. Leo and Cyril taught the same thing,..This is the true faith...This is the faith of the fathers. Why were not these things read at Ephesus?' From the 'Extracts from the Acts, Session II.

This confirmed the sense in the Bishops of Rome that they were the embodiment of orthodoxy. Eventually this led to the schism of 1054 between the Bishops of Rome and Constantinople, which means we today have

Where did the British Church go?

the Roman Catholic Church and the Eastern Orthodox Churches, since the Eastern churches recognised the Pope to have a primacy of honour, but not one which meant he could dictate to the whole church on doctrine. Indeed, at Chalcedon among the Canons passed was Canon 28:

'The bishop of New Rome shall enjoy the same honour as the bishop of Old Rome, on account of the removal of the Empire. For this reason the [metropolitans] of Pontus, of Asia, and of Thrace, as well as the Barbarian bishops shall be ordained by the bishop of Constantinople.'

This gave the Bishop of Constantinople primacy in much of the church and an equal honour (the New Rome is Constantinople) – the Popes refused to accept this canon.

The Popes felt they could dictate doctrine across the whole church, and so certainly in the West. So when the British churches refused to accept the Roman decision on the dating of Easter and on tonsures, this was elevated to a matter of doctrine in the minds of the Romanisers. For them, it was part of the doctrine of the church that the Pope could determine such things, while for the British church such matters were not up for debate – they were part of the Christianity as they had accepted it.

As the Anglo-Saxon kings consolidated their control over the area that would become England so they backed the authority of the Archbishop of Canterbury, in church matters, who was following the Roman traditions.

By the end of the century, the Archbishop of Canterbury was Theodore of Tarsus – a Greek serving the church in the far West. He was asked his views on various matters, including how long people needed to do penance for various offenses. These are collected in the 'Penitential of Theodore'. He covers drunkenness and a variety of sexual matters at great length. Towards the end comes his attitude to the British and Irish churches:

'Of the Communion of the Irish and Britons who are not Catholic in respect to Easter and the Tonsure

1. Those who have been ordained by Irish or British bishops who are not Catholic with respect to Easter and the tonsure are not united to the Church, but they shall be confirmed again by a Catholic bishop with the imposition of hands.

2. Likewise also the churches that have been consecrated by these bishops are to be sprinkled with holy water and confirmed by some collect.

3. Further, we have not the liberty to give them, when they request it, the chrism or the eucharist, unless they previously confessed their willingness to be with us in the unity of the Church. And likewise a person from among these nations, or anyone who doubts his baptism, shall be baptized.'

p206-207 in John T. Neill and Helena M. Gamer, Medieval Handbooks of Penance (1938)

Theodore made it clear – the British and Irish were not proper Christians since they were not part of the unity of the Church. However great their holy people may have been, they couldn't be seen a proper saints – and so their churches needed new dedications – ideally to a universally accepted saint – so the apostles and Mary were mostly used.

Such men as Aidan, Boisil who taught Cuthbert in his youth, and Cedd, younger brother of Chad all died as part of the British church, before the Synod of Whitby, and their cults as saints were suppressed. The English church failed to suppress the cult of Oswald who had died fighting a pagan army and so was seen to be a martyr. But otherwise the Celtic saints of the east of Britain are lost to history as their church was taken over by the Anglo-Saxons who accepted the Roman ways.

Photo by Dave Hitchborne / Interior of St Oswald, Crowle / CC BY-SA 2.0. A 9th or 10th century cross shaft, which shows the antiquity of worship at this site.

But did the British Church disappear altogether in England? In some ways it did, but perhaps the sense of the British Church as an autonomous entity went underground, to re-emerge in the 16th century when the English church rejected the authority of Rome.

Bibliography and Further Reading

(trans), Hennessy W. M. 1887. *Annals of Ulster.*

Baker, John T. 2006. *Cultural Transition in the Chilterns and Essex Region.* University of Hertfordhire Press.

Bede. 2003. *Ecclesiastical History of the English People.* Penguin Classics.

Brown, P.D.C. 1971. "The Church at Richborough." *Britannia* 225-231.

Bruce-Mitford, Robert. 2005. *The Corpus of Late Celtic Hanging Bowls.* OUP.

Carver, Martin. 2019. *Formative Britain: An Archaeology of Britain Fifth to Eleventh Century AD.* Routledge.

Charles Munier, ed. 1963. *Concilia Galliae a314 - a506 Corpus Christianorum Series Latina Vol 1.* Vatican City: Typographi Brepols Editores Pontificii.

Dark, Ken. 2000. *Britain and the End of the Roman Empire.* Tempus.

Dark, Ken. 2021. "Stones of the saints? Inscribed stones, monasticism and the evangelisation of western and northern Britain in the fifth and sixth centuries." *The Journal of Ecclesiastical History* 72 (2): 239-258.

Davies, Oliver. 1996. *Celtic Christianity in Early Medieval Wales.* Cardiff: University of Wales Press.

Edwards, Nancy. 2007. *A Corpus of Early Medieval Inscribed Stones and Stone Sculpture in Wales. Volume II: South West Wales.* University of Wales Press.

Edwards, Nancy. 2001. "Early-Medieval Inscribed Stones and Stone Sculpture in Wales: Context and Function,." *Medieval Archaeology* 15 -39.

Fox, Bethany. 2007. "The P-Celtic Placenames of North East England and Sout East Scotland." *A Journal of Early Medieval Northwestern Europe.*

Gerrard, James. 2010. "Cathedral or Granary, the Roman Coins from Colchester House, City of London." *London and Middlesex Archaeological Society Transactions* 81-88.

Green, Caitlin. 2012. *Britons and Anglo Saxons in Lincolnshiren 400 - 650.* History of Lincolnshire Committee.

Green, Sharon A. 2011. "Killeen Cormac, Colbinstown an ecclesiatical site on th eKildare-Wicklow border." *Co Kildare Online Electronic History Journal.*

Halsall, Guy. 2010. *Cemeteries and Society in Merovingian Gaul: Selected Studies in History and Archaeology 1992 -2009.* Brill.

Halsall, Guy. 1995. "Early Medieval Cemeteries: An Introduction to Burial Archaeology in hte Post Roman West." Cruithne Press.

Higham, Nick. n.d. *An English Empire: Bede and the early Anglo-Saxon kings.* 1995: Manchester Univerity Press.

Hills, Catherine. 2003. *Origins of the English.* Duckworth.

Hirst, Sue, and Dido Clark. 2010. *Mucking Anglo Saxon Cemeteries Volume 3.* English Heritage.

Holbrook, N., and A. Thomas. 2005. "An Early Medieval Monastic Cemetery at Llandough, Glamorgan Excavations in 1995." *Medieval Archaeology.*

Bibliography and Further Reading

Hope-Taylor, Brian. 1977. *Yeavering: An Anglo-British centre of early Northumbria.* London: Her Majesty's Stationary.

Hurst, Sue, and Christopher Scull Scull. 2019. *The Anglo Saxon Princely Burial at Southend-on-Sea.* Museum of London Archaeology.

Hylson-Smith, Kenneth. 1999. *Christianity in England from Roman Times to the Reformation: Vol 1 From Roman Times to 1066.* SCM Press.

Knight, Jeremy. 2005. "From Villa to Monastery: Llandough in Context." *Medieval Archaeology.*

Leach, P, and A. Woodward. 1993. *The Uley Shrines: Excavation of a ritual complex on West Hill, Uley, Gloucestershire 1977-9.* English Heritage.

Mikkelsen, Egil. 2019. *Looting or Missioning.* Oxbow Books.

Nash-Williams, V.E. 1950. *The Early Christian Monuments of Wales.* Cardiff: University of Wales.

Neill, John T., and Helena M. Gamer. n.d. *Medieval Handbooks of Penance.* 1938: Columba.

O'Connor, Jerome Murphy. 1980. *The Holy Land, An Oxford Archaeology Guide from Earliest Times to 1700.* Oxford: OUP.

O'Halloran, W. 1916. *Early Irish History and Antiquities and the West of Cork.*

Openheimer, Stephen. 2012. *Origins of the British: the New Prehistory of Britain: A Genetic Detective Story.* Robinson.

Petts, David. 2003. *Christianity in Roman Britain.* Tempus.

Pryor, Francis. 2005. *Britain AD: A Quest for Arthur, Engand and the Anglo-Saxons.* Harper Collins.

Redknapp, Mark, and John M. Lewis. 2007. *A Corpus of Early Medieval Inscribed Stones and Stone Sculpture in Wales: Glamorgan, Brecknockshire; Radnorshire...* Univeristy of Wales Press.

Rees, Elizabeth. 2013. *Celtic Saints of Ireland.* The History Press.

Richardson, Andrew. 2005. *The Anglo Saxon Cemeteries of Kent.* BAR.

Rippon, Stephen, Chris Smart, and Ben Pears. 2015. *Fields of Britannia.* OUP.

Schiffels, Stephan, and Duncan Sayer. 2017. "Investigating Anglo Saxon migration history with ancinet and modern DNA." In *Migration and Integration from Pre-History to the Middle Ages*, 255-266. Halle.

Schiffels, W. Haak, P. Llamas, B. Pajaanen, and Poposcue E. 2016. "Iron Age and Anglo Saxon genomes from East England reveals British migration history." *Nature Communications.*

Sheehan, John. 2009. "A Peacock's Tale: excavations at Caherlehillan, Iveragh Ireland." In *The Archaeology of the Early Medieval Celtic Churches*, by Nancy Edwards, 191-206. Leeds: Society for Medieval Archaeology.

Snyder, Christopher. 1998. *Age of Tyrants: Britain and the Britons.* Penn State Press.

Sykes, Stephen. 2007. *Blood of the Isles.* Corgi.

Thomas, Charles. 1981. *Christianity in Roman Britain to AD500.* Harper Collins.

Thomas, Charles. 1991. "The Early Christian Inscriptions of Southern Scotland." *Scottish Archaeological Journal* 17 (1): 1-10.

Thomson, Ian. 2005. *The Lost Saints of Britain: Rediscovering our Celtic Roots.* Bluestone Books.

Whelan, Kevin, F.H.A. Aale, and Matthew Stout. 2010. *Atlas of the Irish Rural Landscape.* Cork University Press.

Willams, Nancy, Mark Redknap, and John M. Lewis. 2007. *A Corpus of Early Medieval Inscribed Stones and Stone Sculpture in Wales.* 3 vols. Cardiff: University of Wales.

Index

Ad Gefrin. *See* Yeavering
Aidan, 125, 126, 130
Ailbe, 79, 81, 82, 105
Ardagh, 93
Ardfert, 97, 98
Ardmore, 79, 80, 82
Bamburgh, 123, 125, 126
Bede, 2, 51, 52, 75, 105, 117, 119, 120, 122, 123, 124, 125, 126, 128, 129
Bethany, 3, 23, 24, 25
Bethesda, 12
Bethphage, 23, 26
Bethsaida, 4, 5, 6
Brendan, 81, 88, 97, 98, 101
Brigid, 77, 94, 95, 96, 97, 105, 106
Caerleon, 49, 50
Caherlehillan, 84, 86, 91
Caldey Island, 74
Cana, 6, 10, 11, 37
Canterbury, 60, 62, 70, 71, 117, 118, 119, 120, 129, 130
Capernaum, 6, 10, 11, 15
Carmarthen, 65
Catherine Hills, 107
Celtic hanging bowl, 111
Chedworth, 60
Christopher Snyder, 119
Church of the Holy Sepulchre, 32, 34, 36
Ciaran, 79, 82, 100, 101
Ciaran the younger, 100
Cirencester, 47, 48, 58
Cleatham, 111
Clonard, 96, 97, 100, 101, 104
Clonfert, 97, 98, 101
Clonmacnoise, 97, 100, 101
Clydau, 72
Colchester, 57, 58
Darenth, 117, 118
David, 12, 17, 18, 20, 22, 23, 27, 68, 70, 71, 73, 81, 105
Declan, 79, 80, 81, 82
Dingle, 85, 91

Downpatrick, 92, 93, 104
Duncan Sayer, 109
Durrow, 101, 102, 106
Ecclesiastical History, 42, 51, 75, 119
Elvis. *See* Ailbe
Emly, 81, 105
Ephesus, 41, 42, 45, 46, 129
Finnian, 96, 97, 98, 101, 102
Francis Pryor, 107
Gallarus, 87, 88
Gihon Spring, 17, 21
Gildas, 50, 52, 65, 68, 70, 106
Glendalough, 98, 99, 100
Hinton St Mary, 59
Illtyd, 68, 69, 74, 106
Iona, 97, 101, 102, 103, 104, 124, 125, 128
Kells, 101, 102, 106
Kevin, 62, 98, 99, 100, 105
Kildare, 78, 94, 95, 96, 105, 106
Kileen Cormac, 78
Kilmalkedar, 88
Kirkmadrine, 75
Lincoln, 54, 58, 59, 111, 114, 115, 120
Lindisfarne, 125, 128
Llandawke, 71
Llandissilio, 72
Llandough, 65, 66, 69
Llangammarch Wells, 74
Llantwit Major, 68, 96, 106
Llanychaer, 73
London, 54, 56, 58, 116
Loughor, 71
Lullingstone, 56, 58, 59
Lyons, 45, 47
Margam, 66, 67, 68
Marthry, 73
Mel, 93, 95, 96
Mount Brandon, 88, 90, 98
Mount of Olives, 7, 25, 26, 29
Mucking, 111, 115
Nazareth, 2, 3, 4, 6
Oakington, 109, 110

ogham, 67, 71, 73, 77, 78, 79, 88, 89, 97
Patrick, 63, 78, 79, 81, 92, 93, 94, 95, 104
Paul Aurelian, 70, 106
Pool of Siloam, 17, 20, 21
Prittlewell, 115, 118
Qasr al Yahud, 3, 4
Ratass, 97
Reask, 85
Richborough, 50, 62, 118, 119
Samaritan, 8, 9, 10, 12, 14
Samson, 68, 69, 70, 74, 106
Saul, 92, 93
Scunthorpe, 111
Sea of Galilee, 4, 5, 13, 15, 38
Seir Keiran, 82
Silchester, 52, 53, 58
Skellig Michael, 83, 84, 96
Slane, 92, 93
Smyrna, 42, 44, 45, 46
Sompting, 127
St Albans, 51, 115
St Davids, 70
St Dogmael's, 73
Stephan Schiffels, 109
Stephen Rippon, 107
Streonshalh, 2, 127
Sychar, 8, 12, 40
Taghba, 13
Temple, 7, 8, 10, 12, 17, 18, 20, 22, 23, 26, 29, 30, 32, 40, 101
Temple Manachan, 90
Tiree, 101, 104
Traprain Law, 63
Uley, 60, 64
Via Dolorosa, 30, 31, 32
Vindolanda, 121, 122
Vortiporius, 65
Wasperton, 109
Water Newton, 55, 58
Whitby, 1, 2, 127, 130
Whithorn, 75, 101, 105
Yeavering, 122, 124

Printed in Great Britain
by Amazon